Praise for
The Entrepreneurial Mindset Advantage

"With a 30-year career in technology at companies like Google, Accenture, and Charles Schwab, as well as founding a startup, I've seen how technological change has rapidly accelerated. AI's impact is just the start; technologies like quantum, neuromorphic, and biological computing are coming. *The Entrepreneurial Mindset Advantage* is a timely guide to navigating this era of rapid innovation and unlocking human potential in organizations."

—Jaime Casap, former Chief Education Evangelist, Google

"In a field crowded with how-to advice for entrepreneurs, it is difficult for any author to stand out. But Gary Schoeniger more than passes this test. In his fascinating *The Entrepreneurial Mindset Advantage*, Schoeniger gets inside the heads of successful entrepreneurs, and fortunately for any reader, especially would-be entrepreneurs, he provides tons of useful advice. This is one of those books you pick up and won't put down."

—Robert Litan, former Vice President of Research, Kauffman Foundation

"Gary Schoeniger's new book is an important contribution to the literature on entrepreneurship. He clearly defines an entrepreneurial mindset as the development of dispositions that everyone can benefit from in a rapidly changing world. Parents and teachers have a vital role to play in nurturing these dispositions to enable all kids to be more future-ready."

—Tony Wagner, EdD, Author, *Learning by Heart*, and Senior Research Fellow, Learning Policy Institute

"Gary brings clarity and precision to our understanding of the entrepreneurial mindset, its underlying causes as well as its capacity for unlocking human potential. This book equips all of us—especially those of us who focus on building entrepreneurial ecosystems—with powerful tools for cultivating entrepreneurial mindsets in ourselves and others."

—Jonathan Ortmans, President, Global Entrepreneurship Network

"All people wish to flourish, but too many believe that external circumstances will prevent them from ever achieving their dreams. *The Entrepreneurial Mindset Advantage* reveals that a decisive choice is always open to us: to use an entrepreneurial perspective to reframe barriers and problems as opportunities to help others in a manner that also empowers us. Read this book and join the ranks of visionary leaders who said yes when life seemed to be saying no."

—Matthew T. Lee, PhD, Professor, Baylor University, and Director, Flourishing Network at the Human Flourishing Program at Harvard University

"*The Entrepreneurial Mindset Advantage* reframes conventional thinking about economic development priorities. For too long, we've elevated larger-than-life entrepreneurs as the gold standard, while ignoring the mindset and methods of everyday entrepreneurs. Finally, there is a how-to manual for communities and practitioners for unleashing everyone's hidden entrepreneurial potential. Schoeniger gives practical insight and evidence for investing in ourselves and others as they pursue the American Dream."

—Thom Ruhe, President and CEO, NC IDEA Foundation

"As the former president of the Ewing Marion Kauffman Foundation, I have encountered numerous works on entrepreneurship, and Gary G. Schoeniger's *The Entrepreneurial Mindset Advantage* is exceptional. This book uncovers the hidden logic that drives everyday innovators, combining extensive research with real-world stories to provide a compelling, practical guide for applying the entrepreneurial mindset in daily life. A must-read for aspiring entrepreneurs, educators, and business leaders, this book is an important contribution to the field of entrepreneurship, with the power to change lives and communities."

—Wendy Guillies, Founder, Guillies OnPoint, and retired CEO, Kauffman Foundation.

"There are books that must be written to extend the frontiers of our collective understanding, books that can only be penned by someone with a unique perspective and experience, and then there are rare books that distill a lifetime of learning into a message so powerful it transforms our worldview. *The Entrepreneurial Mindset Advantage* by Gary Schoeniger is one such book. It is the culmination of Gary's unwavering dedication to a singular cause: the profound possibilities unlocked by fully embracing an entrepreneurial mindset.

Having known Gary for more than a decade, our paths crossing on different continents in our shared mission to make the world more entrepreneurial, I can attest to the consistency and authenticity of his message. He has been a steadfast advocate for broadening the understanding and application of the entrepreneurial mindset, living out the principles of this book every day.

At a time when we face daunting challenges to our sense of personal agency in an increasingly complex world, this book is more crucial than ever. It deciphers the code at the core of our humanity—the entrepreneurial spirit. This spirit propels us into the unknown with confidence and creativity. As Gary's life and teachings demonstrate, the entrepreneurial spirit is, ultimately, the human spirit."

—Anthony Farr, CEO, Allan & Gill Gray Philanthropy Africa

"In recent years, research has revealed a great deal about the importance of entrepreneurship—most notably, that startups are disproportionately responsible for the disruptive innovation that drives gains in productivity and, therefore, economic growth, and account for virtually all net new job creation. In other words, entrepreneurship is a powerful force for value creation, but also opportunity expansion and economic and social progress. Against the backdrop of that critical reality, in *The Entrepreneurial Mindset Advantage* Gary Schoeniger explores equally important but less understood terrain: the nature, mindset, and temperament of the innovator and risk-taker, and tackles head-on the ever-intriguing and hotly debated question: Are entrepreneurs a rare phenomenon of genetic make-up, or can anyone become or learn to be entrepreneurial? The remarkable analysis and insights Schoeninger provides amounts to essential reading for not just entrepreneurs themselves but also parents, educators, scholars, policymakers, and anyone else interested in the profoundly consequential journey of entrepreneurship."

—John R. Dearie, Founder and President, Center for American Entrepreneurship

"Your journey as an entrepreneur is defined by your mindset. In *The Entrepreneurial Mindset Advantage*, Gary shares invaluable insights and practical strategies that can empower anyone looking to turn ideas into action and challenges into opportunities."

—Brian Scudamore, Founder and CEO, 1-800-GOT-JUNK?

"*The Entrepreneurial Mindset Advantage* is a must-read for anyone looking to transform their approach to business and leadership. In this book, Gary G. Schoeniger skillfully outlines the mindset and the methods that drive successful entrepreneurship, emphasizing resilience and resourcefulness as well as the importance of making a meaningful contribution to the organizations and communities we inhabit. As someone who has navigated the challenging transition from military service to founding and leading a successful company, I can attest to the power of the mindset principles discussed in these pages. This book is not just a guide, but a source of inspiration for aspiring entrepreneurs and seasoned business leaders alike."

—Dawn Halfaker, Entrepreneur, Investor, Philanthropist, and Veterans' Advocate

"In *The Entrepreneurial Mindset Advantage*, Gary Schoeniger demystifies the concept of the entrepreneurial mindset, expanding it beyond business to encompass life and daily decision-making. Drawing from his personal growth and research, Schoeniger presents the entrepreneurial mindset as a universal asset that drives change and fuels optimism, symbolized by the mantra 'Yes, You Can.' This book chronicles his ongoing journey and the impact of this mindset on himself and others."

—Clifton L. Taulbert, Pulitzer Prize–Nominated Author and Entrepreneur

"Gary Schoeniger's *The Entrepreneurial Mindset Advantage* is transformative, offering invaluable wisdom to urban entrepreneurs. Despite our different backgrounds, Gary's mentorship has been crucial in my quest to unlock the entrepreneurial potential in urban communities. He challenges us to think differently about entrepreneurship, making this book a bold blueprint for building grassroots entrepreneurial communities worldwide. Read this book and join us in reshaping the future of entrepreneurship."

—Myron Pierce, Founder, Own the Pond

"As an educator with 50 years of experience in K–12 and higher education, I can unequivocally say that entrepreneurship is often misunderstood and misrepresented. Gary's book addresses this issue by reframing our perception of entrepreneurship, recognizing it as a mindset. His insightful narrative, including the story of Ted Moore and his own journey, makes this a compelling read for educators, parents, business leaders, and aspiring entrepreneurs.

Chapter 11, "Entrepreneurship in Education," resonated deeply with me. Gary critiques our current education system and highlights the importance of entrepreneurial mindset education in unlocking the potential of disenfranchised students. He explains why current efforts fall short and provides practical ideas for fostering entrepreneurship in schools. This book is an essential resource for understanding and improving how we prepare students for a future that relies on their creative potential. Gary's work offers a road map for creating a better educational trajectory and an entrepreneurial mindset that benefits all."

—Gary R. Bertoline, PhD, Distinguished Professor, Purdue University

THE
ENTREPRENEURIAL
MINDSET
ADVANTAGE

Also by Gary G. Schoeniger

Who Owns the Ice House? Eight Life Lessons from an Unlikely Entrepreneur

THE
ENTREPRENEURIAL
MINDSET
ADVANTAGE

The **HIDDEN LOGIC** That Unleashes Human Potential

GARY G. SCHOENIGER

Matt Holt Books
An Imprint of BenBella Books, Inc.
Dallas, TX

Matt Holt is an imprint of BenBella Books, Inc.
10440 N. Central Expressway
Suite 800
Dallas, TX 75231
benbellabooks.com
Send feedback to feedback@benbellabooks.com

BenBella and *Matt Holt* are federally registered trademarks.

Printed in the United States of America
10 9 8 7 6 5 4 3 2 1

Library of Congress Control Number: 2024024372
ISBN 9781637745779 (hardcover)
ISBN 9781637745786 (electronic)

Editing by Lydia Choi
Copyediting by Scott Calamar
Proofreading by Michael Fedison and Sarah Vostok
Indexing by WordCo Indexing Services, Inc.
Text design and composition by Jordan Koluch
Cover design by Brigid Pearson
Printed by Lake Book Manufacturing

For my mother, Mary, who encouraged me to think for myself.
And for my father, Otto, who taught me to see the beauty in everyday life.
And for my granddaughter, Milena, to whom the future belongs.

Contents

PART THREE: THE ENTREPRENEURIAL SITUATION

Foreword

A s a professor of medicine, one might not expect my commentary on a book about the entrepreneurial mindset. After all, I have spent more than forty years in academia, studying the benefits of compassionate care. Nevertheless, my steadfast principle of "never a no without a yes" has empowered me to surpass the confines of a conventional career. Having served as a "spiritual entrepreneur" on the Board of the John Templeton Foundation, I recognize the transformative potential of the ideas in this book. Throughout his life, "Sir John" sought innovative thought leaders to carry forward the psychological and spiritual dimensions of entrepreneurial life. It is from this perspective that I invite you to undertake a transformative journey guided by the wisdom of Gary G. Schoeniger, a visionary whose insights transcend the boundaries of conventional thinking.

Schoeniger's work illuminates the pathway to personal fulfillment and societal progress through the lens of an entrepreneurial mindset. With unparalleled clarity and practicality, he explores how individuals from all walks of life can cultivate this mindset to embark on a journey of self-discovery, resilience, and contribution. In these pages, Schoeniger revolutionizes our understanding of work, education, and societal norms, offering invaluable insights that will resonate with readers of all ages and backgrounds. His message is a beacon of hope for those seeking purpose and direction in a world often clouded by doubt and disillusionment. This groundbreaking book is essential reading for high school students, college freshmen, business scholars, and anyone passionate about human potential and self-realization. Schoeniger's words transcend mere instruction; they inspire a profound shift in perspective, empowering readers to embrace entrepreneurship as a vehicle for personal and collective growth.

Through captivating storytelling and insightful analysis, Schoeniger demystifies the entrepreneurial journey, revealing it as a path accessible to all. He emphasizes the importance of service, resilience, and self-discovery, guiding readers toward a deeper understanding of their unique gifts and potential contributions to society. With each page, Schoeniger challenges outdated notions of work and success, inviting readers to blur the lines between professional fulfillment and personal passion. His message resonates deeply with parents, mentors, and educators, urging them to nurture the entrepreneurial spirit in future generations. As Schoeniger reminds us, the entrepreneurial mindset is not merely a skill set; it is a way of life—one that holds the key to fulfillment and resilience in an ever-evolving world. Through engaging anecdotes and practical advice, he equips readers with the tools they need to navigate the complexities of modern life with confidence and purpose. In a society marked by division and disillusionment, Schoeniger's vision offers a ray of hope—a road map to a future defined by creativity, autonomy, and collective well-being. His insights transcend ideological divides, offering a path toward unity and progress rooted in shared values of empathy, resilience, and collaboration.

In today's era, the field of positive psychology stands at the forefront of the human flourishing movement. I predict that this book will provide a concrete context for us to rededicate ourselves to our great strengths and virtues: vision, future-mindedness, diligence, hope, practical wisdom, perseverance, and, importantly, loving kindness. Were he alive today, I am confident that "Sir John" would be thrilled with the innovative brilliance underlying this book.

In conclusion, Gary G. Schoeniger's work is more than a book; it is a manifesto for societal transformation and individual empowerment. By embracing the entrepreneurial mindset, we can unlock the full potential of humanity and create a world where every individual is empowered to pursue their dreams and contribute to the common good. This book is a call to action—a prescription for healing and renewal in an age of uncertainty and division. Embrace it, and join the movement toward a brighter, more inclusive future for all.

—Dr. Stephen G. Post
Founding Director of the Center for Medical Humanities,
Compassionate Care & Bioethics at Stony Brook University

Introduction: How Do Underdogs Win?

The duty of a man is to be useful to his fellow men; if possible, to be useful to many of them; failing this, to be useful to a few; failing this, to be useful to his neighbours, and, failing them, to himself: for when he helps others, he advances the general interests of mankind.

—Seneca, "On Leisure," circa AD 62[1]

As one of eleven children raised by a single mother, Ted Moore got a rough start in life. When he was a young boy, he slept in the dining room on a folding cot he shared with his mentally disabled brother, who eventually became too much for his mother to manage and was turned over to the state. From a very early age, Ted felt obligated to contribute to his family, finding odd jobs polishing apples and sweeping floors before and after school. If he did not earn his keep, he feared his mother would send him away. The only male role models he knew were those he saw on popular television shows like *Leave It to Beaver* and *My Three Sons*.

School was also a struggle for Ted. By the time he reached high school, he was reading at a third-grade level. He made it until tenth grade before he finally dropped out. Now a teenager and barely literate, Ted realized he was on his own. Despite his circumstances, he was determined to avoid the temptations of the street. "I lived on the block where there were drug addicts and gangbanging . . . I just didn't want that way of life for myself."

Before long, he was married with children of his own and struggling to make ends meet. After drifting from job to job, he finally managed to get a union card that would enable him to earn a living wage. As an unskilled laborer on a construction crew, his responsibility was to keep the jobsite clean and well organized. He soon earned a reputation for being reliable, and it wasn't long afterward that he began to take on a leadership role. "I've always tried to be the best at whatever it was that I was doing," Ted told me. "If I'm nothin' but a broom sweeper, I'm gonna be the best broom sweeper there is."

As his confidence increased, Ted was compelled by the idea of starting a construction cleaning business of his own, yet he had very little discretionary income and was in no position to quit his job or take on debt. Nevertheless, he and his teenage daughter, Sirena, set up a makeshift office in an unused bedroom in their spare time. With little more than a used fax machine and an old desk they found in the trash they were now open for business. Their first customer was a roofing contractor who agreed to pay them a few hundred dollars to haul away shingles from a residential job. While it didn't amount to much, it was a start, and they remained determined to deliver exceptional service regardless of how small the job might be. Slowly but surely, as their reputation began to grow, the scope of their customers also began to increase. Before long they were landing five- and six-figure contracts on a regular basis, which eventually enabled them to quit their jobs and go all in. From humble beginnings, they had now built a thriving enterprise that brought both meaning and prosperity to their lives while also creating dozens of jobs in their community.[2]

We're all familiar with the stories of iconic entrepreneurs like Steve Jobs, Jeff Bezos, and Elon Musk, yet we often overlook the typical entrepreneurs like Ted Moore who start with little or nothing yet somehow manage to succeed. The question is: *How do they do it?* How do they manage to recognize opportunities that the rest of us overlook? And how do they mobilize the resources and the resilience that enables them to flourish and thrive?

To the casual observer, entrepreneurs often appear to be a rare breed endowed with unique personalities that somehow enable them to accomplish extraordinary things. On the surface, they appear to be innately driven, confident, and creative, natural-born risk-takers who somehow manage to succeed regardless of where they start. Yet when we look beneath the surface, we find a common underlying logic—*a mindset*—that drives the behavior that enables them to accomplish extraordinary things. Embracing this way of thinking can certainly benefit those who want to start a business, yet a closer look reveals a powerful framework for thinking that has become essential for individuals, organizations, and communities to adapt and thrive in today's rapidly changing world. Ultimately, studying the mindset and the methods of everyday entrepreneurs reveals how small changes can unlock human potential on a much broader scale.

My quest to understand the entrepreneurial mindset arose as a result of my own experience as an unlikely entrepreneur. As one of three boys, I was born and raised in a blue-collar suburb of Cleveland, Ohio. My father, a gifted artist, managed to eke out a living as a commercial illustrator while my mother occasionally found office work to help make ends meet. While we never considered ourselves to be poor, we certainly didn't have much.

In grade school I was a reasonably good student, well-liked by my teachers, and I found it relatively easy to fit in. Yet, as I progressed from grade school to middle school, I became increasingly alienated and disengaged. Learning, as I knew it, soon became an unpleasant experience, and as my grades began to plummet, I found it harder and harder to fit in. By the time I graduated from high school, I had neither the inclination nor the grades to pursue a four-year degree. In many ways, I felt alone and adrift. I thought there must be something wrong with me, that I was somehow inherently flawed. I was floundering to survive in a world that didn't seem to make much sense.

Not long after I graduated from high school, my parents divorced, and I was living on my own and struggling to make ends meet. Like others who find themselves in such a position, I took on whatever jobs I could find, from factory work and construction labor to food service, landscaping, and door-to-door sales. While I always tried to do my best at whatever job I could find, inside I felt aimless and began drinking as a way to fill the void. Nevertheless, an opportunity was about to emerge.

While working in a small family-owned restaurant at the age of twenty-three, I stumbled across an opportunity to start a small sandwich shop of my own. In many ways, it seemed like a dream come true. For the first time, I had a sense of direction, a clear and compelling goal, and a corresponding focus and energy that I had never felt before. With a few thousand dollars I cobbled together from family and friends, I managed to pull it off. This sandwich shop was my chance for a brighter future, and I was willing to do whatever it took to succeed.

In the beginning, I worked sixteen-hour days, six and a half days a week, doing everything I could to please every customer who came through the door. Slowly but surely, my fledgling business began to blossom. I was now earning as much as, if not more than, my schoolmates who had gone on to college and followed a more traditional path, but that early success soon went to my head. As a result, I began taking on debt in order to expand my fledgling sandwich shop into a full-scale restaurant. As a result, the business began to falter as it soon became clear that I had been blinded by my own hubris and had stopped paying attention to my customers' needs. It also became clear that my drinking was getting out of control. While I managed to stop drinking with the help of a support group, my once-thriving business was now struggling to stay afloat. I had made a series of bad decisions and, within a few short years, what was once a promising small business eventually collapsed. Now, at the age of twenty-eight, I was unemployed and deeply in debt. Without a college degree, my chance for a brighter future once again seemed out of reach. Newly sober, I was now painfully aware of my mistakes as the harsh lessons of my hubris were staring me right in the face. From where I stood, I saw no choice but to pick myself up, swallow my pride, and start anew.

With nothing more than a borrowed ladder strapped to the roof of my car, I began going door-to-door in the wealthier neighborhoods of Fairmount Boulevard in Cleveland Heights, offering to clean gutters. It was late November, the skies were cold and gray, and the trees were bare. My assumption was that clogged gutters might be a problem that I could solve and that upper-income clients might be willing to pay to have them cleaned. Never mind the fact that I am afraid of heights.

As luck would have it, I managed to find a customer on my first day. Still smarting from the painful lessons of the past, I went out of my way to make sure that my customer was satisfied with my work. As a result, one customer led to another and, seeing that I was conscientious and reliable, my customers soon began to ask me to take on other odd jobs. As a result, I began to learn everything I could about home repair, often stopping at the Lee Road library searching for answers in books and magazines. I soon began to realize that despite my negative experiences in school, I actually enjoyed learning. And the more I learned, the more my fledgling business grew. Within a few short years, what started as gutter cleaning evolved into a successful construction and remodeling business. Once again, I was back on my feet, now earning as much as, if not more than, my contemporaries. More importantly, I was now learning how to think like an entrepreneur.

My "aha" moment came in late January 1991 as I happened across an article about rising unemployment due to economic recession. The story featured a man who had lost his job and was struggling to adapt. His wife was working double shifts to help make ends meet. His unemployment benefits were running out, and they were in danger of losing their home. Then it struck me: I could now see opportunities everywhere; why couldn't he? Surely this man had some knowledge, skills, and abilities that could be useful to others. What was it that blinded him to the opportunities that were within his reach? What was it that was holding him back?

That was the moment I realized that I had learned to think differently—*not because of my personality* per se but as a result of my experience as an entrepreneur. That was the moment I realized that if I could somehow understand and articulate the entrepreneurial mindset, it could be useful to others. And not just those who might want to start a business, but anyone who might be searching for a more meaningful and prosperous life. My interest was not in the mechanics of starting a business but in the underlying beliefs and assumptions that enabled ordinary people to accomplish extraordinary things. My sense was that the entrepreneurial mindset somehow held the key to unlocking the hidden potential that lies dormant in ourselves and others.

I began by reading everything I could find about entrepreneurs that might provide insight into their underlying beliefs. At the time, most of what I found were the biographies of well-known businessmen like Henry Ford and Sam Walton, which were helpful but did not provide much insight into their underlying beliefs. Besides, I wanted to understand the mindset and the methods of common, everyday entrepreneurs: those who start with little or nothing yet manage to succeed. Frustrated by the lack of available information, I began to interview ordinary entrepreneurs in my own community in my spare time to try to get a sense of the underlying assumptions that were driving their behavior. At first they were not easy to find. After all, these were not high-profile entrepreneurs who stood out from the crowd. In fact, many did not identify as entrepreneurs. Yet, one seemed to lead to another, and the more I looked, the more I began to find. I soon realized that these garden-variety entrepreneurs were everywhere, yet they were largely ignored. Meanwhile, I continued running the construction business I had started just a few years earlier with little more than a borrowed ladder and a business card. Nearly two decades passed as I continued to run my business while spending every spare moment I could find searching for clues. Through dogged persistence and a bit of dumb luck, I stumbled into an opportunity to undertake a project at the Cisco Entrepreneur Institute in San Jose, California. Little did I know this would begin a new chapter in my life.

The team at Cisco asked me to explore existing efforts in entrepreneurship education across North America and highlight areas for improvement. It was through this experience that I saw firsthand that entrepreneurship was being portrayed in classrooms and entrepreneurial support organizations in ways that were almost entirely distinct from the mindset and the methods that I had gleaned from my interactions with everyday entrepreneurs. I found that aspiring entrepreneurs were often being encouraged to approach their fledgling startups as if they were managers of large, established companies. I also found that many entrepreneurship initiatives failed to distinguish between entrepreneurial and managerial attitudes, behaviors, and skills. It soon became clear that the entrepreneurial *mindset* was a vital component of the entrepreneurial process that was being completely overlooked. With these initial findings in hand, the team at Cisco asked me to conduct more detailed research into the actual mindset and methods of everyday entrepreneurs. I now had a budget that would allow me to expand my research and interview entrepreneurs throughout the United States. Meanwhile, the financial crisis of 2008 was in full swing, and my construction business was quickly vanishing before my very eyes. It was the moment I decided to go all in.

Once again, finding everyday entrepreneurs in other communities wasn't easy, yet one seemed to lead to another, and the more I looked, the more I managed to find, in small rural towns and big cities, in suburbs and urban communities alike. Some were side hustlers and solopreneurs, some were small business owners, and some were serial entrepreneurs. They were men and women, young and old, from teenagers to midcareer adults and retirees. They were students and stay-at-home moms; they were teachers, veterans, managers, and government employees. They were ordinary people who seemed to be doing extraordinary things, and they all had interesting stories to tell.

One such story that arose from one of these chance encounters was that of Clifton Taulbert, whose story became the inspiration for my first book, *Who Owns the Ice House? Eight Life Lessons from an Unlikely Entrepreneur*,[3] which we coauthored. It also became the inspiration for the Ice House Entrepreneurship Programs, which we developed with initial support from the Ewing Marion Kauffman Foundation.

At first, I wasn't sure what to make of the stories I was hearing, yet over time common themes began to emerge. Most everyday entrepreneurs had humble beginnings, and their paths were anything but direct. Some were driven by necessity, embracing entrepreneurship as a means of last resort, while others were driven by a desire to change the world. Many had been influenced by exposure to other entrepreneurs. They all seemed to be enthusiastic, inexperienced, and vastly unprepared for the challenges that lay ahead. Most started with simple ideas or niche opportunities that were highly uncertain and therefore unlikely to attract outside investment. Like Ted Moore, the vast majority started with limited resources: a few hundred or a few thousand dollars at best. Very few had spent much time writing business plans and conducting in-depth market research. In many ways, they seemed to be driven by impulse and flying by the seat of their pants.

In many cases, their initial ideas were flawed, and they soon discovered that the road map they had sketched out in their minds did not match the reality of the terrain. Yet somehow they managed to persist, often stumbling into adjacent opportunities that they did not initially foresee. I was also surprised to find that few had undertaken any formal training in entrepreneurship. Instead, these everyday entrepreneurs seemed to be following a logic and a process that they were unable to describe. Indeed, it seemed as if they were somehow guided by intuition or a mysterious sixth sense of which they themselves were largely unaware. In other words, they seemed to know more than they were able to explain.

While their circumstances and interests varied widely, I soon began to recognize common patterns of beliefs and behavior. This led me to explore the latest research in motivation and other behavioral sciences, which is where I began to recognize the subtle underlying cognitive, motivational, and situational factors that were causing them to think and act like entrepreneurs. I came to understand the ways in which our deeply held beliefs and taken-for-granted assumptions can either hinder or enhance our ability to adapt and thrive in the face of change. I also came to understand the ways in which other-directed (as opposed to self-directed) learning and work can inhibit the development of entrepreneurial attitudes, behaviors, and skills.

Through my journey, I came to see the entrepreneurial mindset as a framework for thinking that can empower ordinary people to accomplish extraordinary things. I came to see that, while not everyone may want to start a business, we all have both the inclination and the capability to be innovative and entrepreneurial, and that by doing so, we can empower ourselves. Now, having interviewed hundreds of these everyday entrepreneurs around the world, I have come to see humanity in a new light.

The ideas in this book represent a distillation of attitudes and beliefs, logic, and insights that I have gleaned from interviewing hundreds of entrepreneurs. They are not complex ideas obscured by abstract scientific theory. They are simple, actionable ideas that anyone can embrace. As you will see, developing an entrepreneurial mindset does not require a unique personality, exceptional intelligence, access to venture capital, or an advanced degree. Nor does it require us to quit our jobs, drop out of school, or undertake significant financial risks. By combining real-world examples of everyday entrepreneurs with research in behavioral science, this book shows us not only how to be more innovative and entrepreneurial in our own lives but also how to encourage others to do the same.

In part 1, we demystify the entrepreneurial person. Here we begin by illustrating the need to encourage and support entrepreneurial thinking at all levels of society. Drawing from first principles, we then redefine entrepreneurship in a way that anyone can embrace. From there, we explore the science of human motivation and the latent factors—both within the person and the situation—that either encourage or inhibit the development of entrepreneurial attitudes and skills. We'll also explore the mindset as a hidden mechanism that influences our behavior largely without our awareness. Lastly, we explore the origins and evolution of the managerial mindset as a dominant cultural paradigm that may now be holding us back.

In part 2, we demystify the entrepreneurial process. Using real-world examples, we examine the processes and methods that enable everyday entrepreneurs to identify, evaluate, and actualize opportunities that exist in our everyday lives. What emerges is a logical framework of thought and action that anyone can embrace regardless of their circumstances or chosen path. We conclude by encouraging you to start where you are and use what you have to undertake an entrepreneurial project of your own.

In part 3, we build on parts one and two to provide a practical framework for cultivating entrepreneurial mindsets in others. Here we introduce Entrepreneurial Discovery Learning (EDL) as a foundation for encouraging the next generation to develop the adaptive capacity that will enable them to thrive in a rapidly changing world. We introduce Entrepreneurial leadership as a new model for unlocking the entrepreneurial potential of organizations. We also explore the essential ingredients for creating vibrant, equitable, and sustainable entrepreneurial communities. What emerges is a powerful new framework for thinking, one that exposes new opportunities, optimizes engagement, and unleashes the untapped human potential that is hiding in plain sight.

By combining real-world examples of everyday entrepreneurs with research in behavioral science, this book shows us not only how to be more innovative and entrepreneurial in our own lives but also how to encourage others to do the same.

The ideas in this book offer a new theory of the entrepreneurial mindset compiled through hundreds of interviews combined with knowledge gleaned from scientific literature. While I do not claim this work to be definitive, the ideas in this book have the potential to impact millions of lives. Indeed, they have the potential to transform our society as a whole.

I have presented these ideas in hundreds of keynotes, seminars, lectures, and workshops around the world. They have influenced government, business, and academic leaders from the United Nations and the European Commission to the Vatican. Thousands of educators and business, government, and nonprofit leaders have participated in our entrepreneurial mindset workshops and training programs while tens of thousands of students have been enrolled in our entrepreneurial mindset education programs. Thus far, I have seen promising evidence that the entrepreneurial mindset is indeed the key to unleashing human potential.

The ideas in this book have encouraged entrepreneurs around the world to start and grow new businesses. They have empowered leaders to unlock the entrepreneurial potential within their organizations. They have inspired students to take ownership of their education, to persist in the face of adversity, and to become more actively engaged learners. They have reinvigorated displaced workers who are now reinventing themselves. Indeed, the ideas in this book have helped transform entire communities. *The Entrepreneurial Mindset Advantage* offers a new lens through which to see the world and ourselves, opening an untapped universe of hidden potential.

My hope is that the ideas in this book will not only empower you to recognize the opportunities that lie hidden in your day-to-day life, but that you will also feel compelled to encourage others to do the same. My hope is that you will infuse these ideas into your classrooms, organizations, and communities, and that you will use them to inspire the next generation of innovators and entrepreneurs. My hope is that you will embrace the entrepreneurial mindset advantage so as to advance the general interests of mankind.

Part One

The Entrepreneurial Person

Chapter One

The Entrepreneurial Mindset Imperative

Nothing fails like success.

—George Land[1]

Suddenly the world has changed, and the mindset that once enabled us to succeed is rapidly becoming obsolete. Job security has become an oxymoron as traditional employment is increasingly being replaced by a contingent workforce of independent, on-demand contractors rather than traditional employees. For many, ride-sharing and food delivery have replaced the high-paying, low-skilled jobs that once supported a thriving middle class. At the same time, the accelerated advancement of automation and artificial intelligence threatens to leave huge swaths of the workforce behind while millions feel trapped in low-paying jobs or unsatisfying careers. In fact, studies now show that most Americans no longer believe that hard work will lead to a better life.[2] Meanwhile, employers increasingly demand workers who possess entrepreneurial attitudes and skills.

After all, entrepreneurs are agile, resilient, and resourceful. They are self-directed, creative, and critical thinkers who can identify and solve problems, mobilize resources, and make things happen amid complexity and change. In other words, they possess the attributes a rapidly changing world now demands. The question is: Why do some people think and act this way while others do not?

Clearly, the rules for survival have changed, and the mindset that once enabled us to succeed is becoming obsolete. Yet the nature of a mindset is such that it becomes so deeply ingrained in our individual and collective consciousness that we are not aware of it, much less of the ways in which it can hinder our ability to adapt. When faced with change, we often struggle to adapt due to the deeply held beliefs, values, and assumptions that once enabled us to succeed. In fact, history is replete with examples of individuals and organizations—even entire societies—that have faded into obsolescence because they were unable to adapt in times of change. In his book *Collapse: How Societies Choose to Fail or Succeed,* author Jared Diamond describes this phenomenon in no uncertain terms: "The values to which people cling most stubbornly under inappropriate conditions are those values that were once the source of their greatest triumphs." In other words, nothing fails like success.[3]

For decades, economists have recognized entrepreneurial activity as the engine of economic growth. In fact, some would argue that entrepreneurs have become the most important players in the modern economy.[4] Yet we are just beginning to understand the broader developmental impact of entrepreneurial thinking as a means of enhancing engagement and developing resilience and the adaptive capacity of the individual. As a result of their experience, entrepreneurs develop the attitudes and skills that enable them not only to adapt and thrive amid complexity and change but also to make a greater contribution to the organizations and communities they inhabit.

Given both the economic and the developmental benefits of entrepreneurial thinking, it is not enough to develop an entrepreneurial mindset in ourselves. The broader imperative lies in our ability to inspire others to do the same. As parents, we must encourage our children to develop entrepreneurial abilities that will stimulate their innate curiosity and creativity and empower them to become self-directed lifelong learners. As educators, we are responsible for instilling in the next generation the attitudes and skills to adapt and thrive in a world we can barely comprehend. As organizational leaders, we must embrace entrepreneurial culture in order to adapt in an ever-changing globalized world. Similarly, workforce development organizations must recognize the entrepreneurial mindset as the key to enabling displaced workers to reinvent themselves. Meanwhile, small business and economic development and entrepreneurial support organizations must also acknowledge the entrepreneurial mindset as the foundation for creating vibrant and sustainable communities.

Policymakers, economists, and other big thinkers now recognize the power of entrepreneurship—not only as essential for creating new businesses and preparing the next generation of innovators and entrepreneurs but also as vital to retraining the existing workforce. For example, the World Economic Forum describes entrepreneurship education as a "societal change agent essential for developing the human capital necessary for building societies of the future." They also cite the need to "shift entrepreneurship from the perimeter to the core of the way education operates."[5] Similarly, the United Nations recognizes entrepreneurship as one of the most important drivers of job creation and economic growth, encouraging governments to adopt a systemic approach to stimulating and supporting entrepreneurial activity. Others have identified entrepreneurship as a means of alleviating poverty and reducing chronic unemployment while also providing a pathway for social mobility and economic inclusion. A 2015 paper published by the Organisation for Economic Co-operation and Development (OECD) enumerated the benefits of entrepreneurial education as not only new job creation and economic growth but also "increased societal resilience, individual growth, increased academic engagement, and improved equality."[6] As the renowned management thinker Peter Drucker once said: "What we need is an entrepreneurial society in which innovation and entrepreneurship are normal, steady, and continuous."[7]

While the need to encourage entrepreneurship at all levels of society is abundantly clear, the question remains: *How? How do we develop an entrepreneurial mindset in ourselves as well as in our children, our students, our workforce, and our communities? How do we shift entrepreneurship from the perimeter to the core of the way we think about learning and work?*

For most, the term *entrepreneur* refers to those who organize and operate a business. After all, the word *entrepreneur* arose at the dawn of the Industrial Revolution when, for the first time in history, we needed an identifier that would distinguish between those who organized and operated a business and those who worked within a business. And yet, this binary assumption—that one is either an entrepreneur or an employee—may now be holding us back. If we are to shift entrepreneurship from the perimeter to the core, we must broaden our understanding of what it means to be innovat-*ive* and entrepreneur-*ial*. We must also recognize that the attitudes and skills required to discover opportunities are almost entirely distinct from those required to exploit them. If we are to adapt and thrive in the face of change, we must recognize the importance of both.

Entrepreneurship education initiatives have exploded in recent years, from college and university programs to government and nonprofit initiatives, and reality TV. Yet the subject of entrepreneurship—*both the person and the process*—remains shrouded in popular myths and common misperceptions and is generally not well understood. As a result, many entrepreneurship education initiatives are limited in terms of efficacy and scope. For example, many programs—typically those offered by colleges and universities—are designed to emulate the venture-backed, high-growth model of entrepreneurship. Yet, for the vast majority of students, this model is either irrelevant or out of reach. After all, as Amar Bhidé finds in his book *The Origin and Evolution of New Businesses*: "Well-planned start-ups, backed by substantial venture capital are, *by far*, the exception rather than the rule." And besides, such programs often conflict with the needs of students who are singularly focused on an academic credential or a particular career path. Others are designed to embrace a plan and pitch model of entrepreneurship that does not reflect the mindset and the methods of a typical entrepreneur. In fact, research shows that the vast majority of new businesses are created by inexperienced, cash-strapped individuals who start with a few hundred or a few thousand dollars cobbled together from credit cards, savings, and friends.[8] Government-funded and nonprofit entrepreneurial-support initiatives also abound, yet many of these efforts rely on outdated managerial assumptions that are ineffective and out of touch with the needs of the typical aspiring entrepreneur. In short, there is a systemic mismatch between the way entrepreneurship is portrayed in the classroom and what a typical entrepreneur actually thinks and does.

Our ability to embrace entrepreneurship is also limited by the ways in which we define it. In many ways, we are stuck on the perimeter because of our tendency to lionize (or vilify) iconic entrepreneurs like Jeff Bezos and Elon Musk while ignoring the mindset, motivation, and methods of everyday entrepreneurs.* Our ability to embrace entrepreneurship is limited by our failure to recognize the distinction between entrepreneurial and managerial attitudes, behaviors, and skills. Regardless of the efficacy of these efforts, their scope is inherently limited because they are focused on organizing and operating a business while ignoring the broader application of the entrepreneurial mindset as an essential life skill.

We are at the dawn of a workforce revolution, one that will require everyone to be more innovative and entrepreneurial regardless of their chosen path. And yet the subject of entrepreneurship—the person, the process, as well as the underlying causes of the behavior—remain a mystery to most. While great advances have been made in our understanding of the lean startup methodology and the process for creating venture-backed

---

* The apex fallacy is the tendency to evaluate a group based solely on its top performers rather than a representative sample.

high-growth firms, the vast majority of students and workers do not have access to effective learning opportunities that will enable them to develop entrepreneurial attitudes and skills.

Meanwhile, as the world continues to change, our systems of education and organizational structures also struggle to adapt. For example, the value of entrepreneurial activity is well understood, and the evidence is abundantly clear that education plays a vital role in shaping entrepreneurial mindsets. And yet the subject of entrepreneurship—*specifically the entrepreneurial mindset*—remains largely absent from the curriculum. Instead, as the world continues to change, our schools remain tethered to industrial-era methods of teaching and learning that do not adequately equip students with the tools required to adapt and thrive amid ambiguity, dynamism, and complexity. While teachers strive to do their best, our school systems remain bound by institutional inertia, cultural norms, and incentive structures that prevent them from adapting. Rather than preparing students to function in a dynamic world, we cling to a century-old model of test-driven accountability that stifles rather than stimulates the development of entrepreneurial attitudes and skills. As a result, the vast majority of students are bored and disengaged.[9]

Evidence also suggests a growing disconnection between the higher education establishment and the society it serves. *Inside Higher Ed* found that 96 percent of chief academic officers surveyed thought they were doing a good job, while only 11 percent of business leaders "strongly agreed that graduates have the necessary skills and competencies to succeed in the workplace."[10]

The problem is compounded by the skyrocketing cost of higher education, which often leaves students lacking the requisite skills while also saddling them with enormous debt. In fact, only about half of Gen Z (those born between approximately 1997–2011) believe they will be able to afford higher education. And these challenges extend far beyond the classroom. According to numerous surveys conducted by Gallup, the Centers for Disease Control, the American Psychological Association, and others, young people are experiencing unprecedented levels of depression,[11] anxiety, and addiction, creating an ongoing mental health crisis.[12]

Organizations also struggle to adapt, as many continue to rely on top-down industrial-era assumptions, outdated management practices, and incentive structures that hinder rather than enhance an innovative and entrepreneurial culture. As author Gary Hamel points out, although organizations may rely on twenty-first-century technologies, in all likelihood, they are clinging to nineteenth-century management principles that stifle rather than stimulate entrepreneurial attitudes and skills.[13] Not surprisingly, the vast majority of workers are also disengaged. According to Gallup, a staggering 53 percent of US employees are not engaged in their work, meaning "they lack motivation and are less likely to invest discretionary effort in organizational goals or outcomes." To make matters worse, 13 percent are *actively* disengaged, meaning they are "unhappy and unproductive at work and liable to spread negativity and undermine organizational goals." That leaves only about one in three workers who are actively engaged and "psychologically committed to their jobs and likely to be making positive contributions to their organizations."[14]

Meanwhile, while the vast majority of students and workers are not engaged in learning or work, entrepreneurs are likely to be intrinsically motivated and therefore actively engaged in both. Rather than relying on others to tell them what to learn and do, they are self-directed, goal oriented, and eager to learn. They intuitively understand that, by solving problems for others, they can empower themselves. As a result, they develop the resilience and resourcefulness that enable them to succeed in spite of their limitations or the challenges they face. They are, in a nutshell, what the psychologist Mihaly Csikszentmihalyi refers to as "autotelic"—intrinsically motivated, self-driven, and optimally engaged.[15] Needless to say, there is unlimited global demand for those who possess such attitudes and skills.

While the future may seem daunting, these massive changes also present unprecedented opportunities for those who can *think* like entrepreneurs. And although the stakes have never been higher, the barriers to being entrepreneurial have never been lower in terms of access to knowledge, resources, and markets. While the future may indeed seem daunting, the good news is that opportunities abound for those who can think like entrepreneurs. And yet, the question remains: Why do some people think and act entrepreneurially while others do not? To the casual observer, entrepreneurs often appear to be a rare breed who are driven by a unique personality or enigmatic traits. Yet, when we look beneath the surface to explore the mindset and the methods of everyday entrepreneurs, a very different explanation begins to emerge.

Thus far, we have created entrepreneurs by accident rather than by design. When we consider existing efforts and the billions of dollars invested in the promotion of entrepreneurship, we must ask ourselves why there are so few people participating in the entrepreneurial process. If we are to shift entrepreneurship from the perimeter to the core, we must look beyond the iconic entrepreneurs to recognize the mindset, the motivation, and the methods of the everyday entrepreneurs. We must look beyond new venture creation to recognize the broader implications of the entrepreneurial mindset as a framework for thinking that can empower ordinary people to accomplish extraordinary things. We must also look beyond personality traits to better understand the underlying causes of entrepreneurial behavior. By doing so, a new framework for thinking begins to emerge—one that enables us not only to adapt and thrive amid complexity and change but also to make a greater contribution to the organizations and communities we inhabit.

As individuals, we must learn how to be more innovative and entrepreneurial in spite of the barriers we may face. As you will see, embracing an entrepreneurial mindset is something anyone can do, regardless of their circumstances or chosen path. It does not require big ideas, a unique personality, access to venture capital, or an advanced degree. Nor does it require us to quit our job, drop out of school, or undertake significant financial risks. It simply requires us to hone abilities that have been historically discouraged or ignored within our systems of education and managerial structures. By doing so, we not only see how small changes can make a big difference, but we also discover untapped entrepreneurial potential within ourselves.

At the same time, shifting entrepreneurship from the perimeter to the core of our institutions and organizations does not require us to tear down and build anew. It simply requires us to recognize the ways in which routinized, other-directed systems not only contribute to the lack of engagement but also hinder entrepreneurial development. If we are to normalize entrepreneurial behavior, we must recognize that entrepreneurship is not management and that the attitudes and skills required to discover new opportunities are distinct from those required to exploit them. And, in today's rapidly changing world, we must recognize that we need both.

As leaders, if we are to adapt and thrive amid complexity and change, we must recognize that the world has changed and that our thinking must also change. We must reimagine our systems of education and organizational structures in ways that optimize for learning. We must recognize the entrepreneurial mindset as a cognitive framework that can empower ordinary people to accomplish extraordinary things. We must recognize that in order to adapt and thrive, we must tap into the entrepreneurial potential of our organizations and communities. We must also recognize that, while not everyone may want to start a business, we are all driven by an innate desire to be engaged in work that matters, to identify and solve problems, and to make a difference in the world. By doing so, we not only see how small changes can make a big difference, but we also expose the untapped potential that lies dormant in our children, our students, our workforce, and our communities. If we are to adapt and thrive, it is imperative that we recognize the entrepreneurial mindset advantage as the hidden logic that unleashes human potential.

Chapter Two

Redefining Entrepreneurship

Every man thus lives by exchanging...
—Adam Smith[1]

What does it mean to be innovat-*ive* and entrepreneur-*ial*? And what is the difference between an entrepreneur and a traditional employee? After all, to exchange is human nature, so in some sense, humans have been "entrepreneuring" for as long as we've roamed the earth. The exchange of useful things is a natural tendency that can be traced back to the Paleolithic era when small bands of hunter-gatherers traded food, tools, and animal skins with each other as a means of survival. It was only relatively recently, at the dawn of the Industrial Revolution, with the emergence of mass production and the division of labor, that the need arose for a term that would distinguish those who organized and operated a business from those who performed individualized tasks within a business. Prior to that time, in pre-industrial society, there was no need for such a word, as most were self-employed peasant farmers, small shopkeepers, tradesmen, or serfs.

The term *entrepreneur* first appeared in a French dictionary in 1723 to describe an individual who organizes and operates a business by taking a financial risk.[2] The term *employee* emerged a century later to describe someone who works for a business in exchange for pay. Over time, this distinction would become a deeply ingrained societal norm as rapid advancements in manufacturing, production, and infrastructure gave rise to the "great" industrialist entrepreneurs of the late nineteenth and early twentieth centuries who wielded enormous power and created millions of jobs. Despite the power and dominance of these entrepreneurs, by the mid-twentieth century, amid a thriving industrial economy, the subject of entrepreneurship had become irrelevant as large, established companies were now run by risk-averse managers who were focused on efficiency, productivity, and growth. While some economists were beginning to recognize the importance of entrepreneurial activity, entrepreneurs themselves were seen as mavericks or misfits who refused to play by the rules. Meanwhile, the popularity of the MBA was on the rise.

Today, the economic value of entrepreneurial activity is abundantly clear, yet the subject of entrepreneurship remains shrouded in myths and misperceptions that prevent us from embracing it more broadly as an essential life skill. For many, entrepreneurship is perceived in ways that are either misleading, irrelevant, or out of reach. Meanwhile, as the world continues to change, the distinction between entrepreneur and employee is increasingly becoming obsolete.

For some, the term *entrepreneur* evokes the image of the iconic billionaires we so often see in the media. For others, it is synonymous with the small business owners we encounter in our day-to-day lives. Some associate entrepreneurship with hucksterism and greed, seeing entrepreneurs as those who exploit others for their own gain. For those who languish in low-paying jobs or unsatisfying careers, entrepreneurship is often a dream that seems out of reach. Yet for those who pursue traditional careers, the subject of entrepreneurship may be of no interest at all.

Certainly, there are good reasons for each of these perspectives, yet they betray a narrow understanding of entrepreneurship and do not accurately reflect the mindset, the motivation, and the methods of a typical entrepreneur. Nor do they allow for a broader application beyond those who have an interest in starting a business. Instead, these narrow definitions skew our thinking, not only about *how* to be entrepreneurial but also about *who* can be entrepreneurial. Therefore, if we are to redefine entrepreneurship in a way that everyone can embrace, we must look beneath the surface to examine the processes and the methods that a typical entrepreneur undertakes. By doing so, a very compelling story—and a new definition—begins to emerge.

In his book *The Origin and Evolution of New Businesses*, Amar Bhidé not only finds that well-planned, venture-backed startups are, *by far*, the exception rather than the rule, he also finds that large, established companies like Hewlett-Packard, Waste Management, and Walmart were likely to be founded by "enthusiastic and somewhat inexperienced" entrepreneurs who initially set out in pursuit of small, uncertain, niche opportunities. And, rather than writing business plans, conducting in-depth market research, and investor presentations, they seemed to be taking a much more iterative experimental approach. Bhidé noted that in the early stages of an entrepreneurial venture, "Coping with ambiguity and surprises, face-to-face selling, and making do with second-tier employees is more important than foresight, deal-making, or recruiting top-notch teams." Moreover, Bhidé and his colleagues observed that these highly successful entrepreneurs did not set out with big ideas with obvious high-growth potential. Instead, they were more likely to be replicating or modifying an existing idea they encountered through previous work. They were also likely to be cash strapped, leveraging, on average, approximately $10,000 they had cobbled together through a combination of personal savings, second mortgages, credit cards, and whatever they could scrape together from family and friends. He also noted that few experienced overnight success. For most, it took decades to develop the assets, the know-how, and the brands that eventually led them to become leading players in their field. In other words, these large, established companies had what Bhidé described as "humble, improvised origins."[3]

Surprisingly, the people, processes, and methods Bhidé observed in the founders of these large, established companies very closely resembled those of the everyday entrepreneurs I encountered through my own research; they seemed to be ordinary people pursuing small niche opportunities without much planning, research, money, or expertise. Nor did they appear to be driven by a desire to get rich. They were ordinary people who had no discernable advantage over others, yet they somehow managed to accomplish extraordinary things.

The question is: *How does this happen? How does an inexperienced, unfunded entrepreneur, without much planning or research, manage to transform a simple idea into a sustainable endeavor? How do they manage to not only recognize opportunities that others overlook but also make things happen in spite of their lack of resources, experience, planning, and research?* After all, if they aren't pursuing big ideas, writing business plans, and attracting outside investors, *what, exactly, are they doing?*

On the surface, these findings seem to reaffirm the idea that successful entrepreneurs are either lucky or that they have been endowed with mysterious traits. Yet when we look more closely at the behavior of everyday entrepreneurs, a very different understanding begins to emerge. Since its origin, the term *entrepreneurship* has been used to describe the process of organizing and managing a business, which is a common frame of reference that brings with it a set of *managerial* assumptions. However, the mindset and methods of a typical entrepreneur stand in stark contrast to the careful planning and analytical skills that are taught in business schools. In our attempts to understand entrepreneurship as a business discipline, we may be limiting our ability to truly comprehend the entrepreneurial person as well as the processes and methods they undertake. We may also be overlooking a powerful cognitive framework that has much broader implications beyond small business creation or the venture-backed startup world. In many ways, we are still using the term *entrepreneur* to distinguish between employer and employee in an age where this distinction is blurring more every day. Therefore, if we are to redefine entrepreneurship in a way that everyone can embrace, we must explore it as a behavioral phenomenon rather than a business discipline.

In order to do that, we'll borrow from a concept known as "transformation theory," which was developed by systems scientist Dr. George Land to explain the nature of change within any living system, be it an individual, organization, or community. Here we find Land's theory quite useful, not only to understand the nature of change but also to better understand the distinction between entrepreneurial and non-entrepreneurial attitudes, behaviors, and skills. Here's how it works.

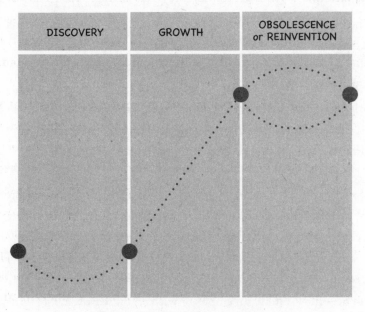

Figure 2.1 | Transformation Theory

According to Land's theory, there are three distinct phases of change within any living system, be it an individual, an organization, or community. The first is a discovery phase, whereby the system is searching for a connection with its environment. The second is a growth phase, whereby the system begins to replicate the connection it found in phase one in order to grow. The third phase is obsolescence, whereby the growth begins to slow. Here the system must reinvent itself by searching for a new connection or it becomes obsolete. Central to Land's theory is the idea that, while each of these three phases is unavoidable, each requires a distinct set of rules for survival. The key to survival, according to Land, is to understand which phase you are in so that you know which rules to apply. The dots represent break points, which are the moments in time when the rules for survival change as the system shifts from one phase to the next. It is worth noting that, while the break points are clearly represented in this diagram, in the real world the indicators that the rules for survival have changed are often easy to overlook. It is also worth noting that the inability to recognize that the rules for survival have changed is to be maladaptive.[4]

So what does transformation theory look like from a human perspective? As Adam Smith observed, we all live by exchanging, and, in that regard, we are all merchants in some sense.[5] The question is: What is the useful thing that we exchange, and with whom do we exchange it? More importantly, what is the process through which we learn how to become useful to others?

As humans, we connect with our environment by making ourselves useful to other humans. As children or young adults, as we undergo the discovery phase, we are typically consuming more resources than we are generating and therefore must rely on parents or guardians to provide our basic needs. And, within the context of modern society, we typically learn how to become useful to an employer with whom we exchange our knowledge and skills for a monthly salary or an hourly wage. We learn how to become useful through formal learning processes in which we are guided by professional teachers through a predetermined set of subjects that are designed to prepare us with the knowledge and skills that will enable us to become a productive member of society. Our academic credentials then signal our usefulness to a potential employer who agrees to pay us a commensurate salary or an hourly wage in exchange for the value we bring to the organization.

Within this prevailing paradigm, the connection is found, and the first break point is reached when we graduate from school and land our first "real" job, whereby an employer agrees to pay us a living wage so that we can now support ourselves. In this way, our first "real" job represents evidence of the usefulness of the knowledge and skills we have acquired. Having reached the first break point, we transition from the discovery phase to the growth phase, whereby the rules for survival change. Now, we must stop searching and begin to apply the knowledge and skills we have acquired in phase one in order to grow during phase two. We now begin to specialize by focusing on incremental improvements within the boundaries of a particular path, becoming more proficient as we become familiar with organizational culture, best practices, and industry norms. Hopefully, over time, we develop expertise that enables us to advance our careers, which is evidence of our becoming increasingly useful.

Then, at some point, the growth inevitably begins to slow, which is an indication that we are nearing the second break point, where once again the rules for survival change. For some, the slowed growth is an indication that we are nearing retirement, at which point our focus begins to shift from productivity and growth to recreation and leisure. In many cases, the slowed growth comes about as a result of boredom, burnout, or complacency. In some cases, the slowed growth may be the result of a temporary condition or a technical challenge that can be remedied with knowledge, resources, and experience. Yet for many, the slowed growth is an indication of an adaptive challenge brought about by broader economic, technological, or geopolitical shifts. When that happens, we must either reinvent ourselves or become obsolete.

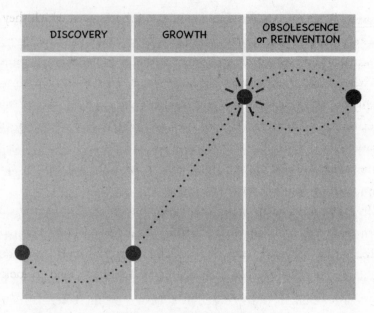

Figure 2.2 | Transformation Theory

Yet, central to Land's theory is that when faced with an adaptive challenge, we often struggle. Rather than recognizing that the rules for survival have changed, we often respond inappropriately with anger or denial, blaming others or dismissing the change as a passing fad. Often, the instinctual response to change is to embrace what Land refers to as a back-to-basics siege mentality, whereby we double down on prior beliefs. Rather than embracing change, we respond with belt-tightening measures that focus on increased productivity rather than reinvention. We try to do more and more for less and less in an attempt to keep up, all while clinging to the underlying values and assumptions that once enabled us to succeed, oblivious to the ways in which they may now be preventing us from adapting in the face of change.

Central to Land's theory is the idea that when faced with an adaptive challenge, we often struggle to adapt, not in spite of but *because of* the underlying values and assumptions that once enabled us to succeed. Without realizing it, these values and assumptions become so deeply ingrained that we are no longer aware of them, much less of the ways in which they may now be inhibiting our ability to adapt.[6] Researchers sometimes refer to this as the "Einstellung effect," which is the negative effect of prior beliefs when faced with new problems. (*Einstellung* is a German term that roughly translates to "attitude.") This phenomenon affects individuals, organizations, and communities alike. Indeed, as Jared Diamond observed, this phenomenon can even cause entire societies to collapse as they cling to the values and assumptions that once enabled them to succeed.[7] Here again, nothing fails like success.[8]

In many ways we struggle to adapt because we fail to distinguish between technical problems and adaptive challenges. What many do not realize is that different types of challenges require different approaches. Yet, if all we have is a hammer, all of our problems tend to look like nails. Identifying the type of problem we are facing is key to determining an effective solution. Ronald Heifetz of the Harvard Kennedy School was among the first to to distinguish between adaptive challenges and technical problems.[9] As he and others have observed, technical problems are easy to identify based on experience. They often lend themselves to quick and concrete solutions that rely on prior knowledge and technical expertise, and the responsibility for finding technical solutions lies with authority figures who then implement them by decree. The obstacles to implementing technical solutions are likely to be time and resources.

Central to Land's theory is the idea that when faced with an adaptive challenge, we often struggle to adapt, not in spite of but *because of* the underlying values and assumptions that once enabled us to succeed.

By contrast, adaptive challenges are ill structured, difficult to identify, and highly complex. They are also easy to deny. Rather than relying on industry experts, solving adaptive challenges requires an iterative, experimental approach that leads to new discoveries. It may also require values, beliefs, and assumptions that are different from those that once enabled success. Responsibility for solving such challenges requires input and participation from those who are affected by the challenge rather than outside consultants, industry experts, or the CEO. In many cases, although people will acknowledge the existence of the adaptive challenge, they will resist the changes necessary to make progress toward a solution. As such, the obstacles to implementing solutions to adaptive problems are likely to be hearts and minds, individual and collective values, loyalties, and relationships, rather than the time, money, and expertise that are typically used to solve technical problems. In short, we struggle to adapt because we lack entrepreneurial attitudes and abilities.

As you will see, the mindset, processes, and methods essential for success in formal learning settings differ markedly from those required for success as a typical entrepreneur. Although the objective in both scenarios is to acquire knowledge and skills that are useful to others, the circumstances in which entrepreneurial discovery occurs differ significantly from those in which traditional learning occurs.

The differences between traditional learning processes and entrepreneurial discovery are significant. For example, whereas traditional learning is likely to be an other-directed process that occurs within highly stable learning environments, entrepreneurial discovery is a self-directed process that occurs within highly ambiguous, resource-constrained circumstances. Whereas traditional learning requires us to memorize facts and follow rules, entrepreneurial discovery requires creativity and critical thinking, experimentation, and adaptation. Whereas traditional learning prepares us to function within known systems with established processes and procedures, entrepreneurial discovery requires us to function outside of known systems where the path is not known and the rules are not clear. Whereas traditional learning is an error-reducing process that punishes failure, entrepreneurial discovery is an error-inducing process that demands it.

Understanding these contextual differences is essential to understanding the distinction between entrepreneurial and non-entrepreneurial attitudes and skills. Three such factors that distinguish entrepreneurial discovery from traditional learning are the high degree of ambiguity involved, the resource constraints, and the self-directed nature of the process itself. A closer look at each of these factors illustrates the differences between entrepreneurial and non-entrepreneurial attitudes, behaviors, and skills.

Highly ambiguous: Unlike traditional learning, entrepreneurial discovery occurs within highly ambiguous circumstances and, for the typical entrepreneur, there are no definitive answers. After all, unmet needs are likely to be latent, unarticulated, and highly complex. As such, the individual must learn to function outside of known systems, without the benefit of predetermined pathways and predictable outcomes. Rather than solving well-structured problems presented by an instructor, the entrepreneurial discovery process requires us to identify and solve ill-structured problems, the solutions to which are multifaceted and unclear. Instead of memorizing facts and following rules, the entrepreneur must learn to think and act like a detective who is searching for clues. To further complicate matters, ambiguity can easily interfere with our ability to think rationally. In many cases we will choose a known path, even when the outcomes may not be ideal, rather than pursuing a less predictable path where the outcomes are not assured. As the saying goes, "better the devil you know than the devil you don't."

Resource constrained: Another important contextual factor to consider is the resource-constrained nature of the discovery process. Unlike traditional learning, whereby our basic needs for food, clothing, and shelter are likely to be provided by parents or guardians, the nascent entrepreneur is likely to be cash strapped, often juggling financial and familial obligations while also undertaking the opportunity discovery process. As such, the resource-constrained nature of the discovery process forces them to become resource-*ful*: to start where they are and make things happen using whatever discretionary time and resources are at hand. More importantly, the lack of resources combined with the high degree of ambiguity forces the fledgling entrepreneur to embrace an error-based learning process through which they learn through trial and error rather than by taking big risks. This iterative, experimental, error-based learning process, which is forced upon them by the lack of resources, provides a vital feedback loop that enables them to home in on opportunities that others overlook.

Self-direction: The self-directed nature of entrepreneurial discovery is also distinct from the other-directed nature of traditional learning. Whereas traditional learning is generally an other-directed process guided by professional teachers who tell us what to learn and do, entrepreneurial discovery is a self-directed learning process where the individual must discover for themselves what they need to learn and do in order to succeed. This is not to say that entrepreneurs function as lone wolves who figure everything out for themselves; rather, they must take it upon themselves to find the knowledge they need. In many cases, the problems entrepreneurs endeavor to solve are ill-structured problems or adaptive challenges for which there are no clear-cut answers, much less professional teachers or subject-matter experts to tell them what to do. As such, entrepreneurs tend to learn by doing, through experimentation and adaptation, thus creating a vital feedback loop that enables them to identify opportunities that cannot otherwise be seen. Here again, where traditional learning discourages failure, entrepreneurial discovery demands it.

What are the rules for survival within such conditions? How does one learn how to make oneself useful to others within such highly ambiguous, resource-constrained circumstances without the guidance of a professional teacher, without the benefit of a predetermined path or a predictable outcome?

Entrepreneurial discovery begins with finding problems to be solved, which, of course, requires problem-finding skills. After all, in order to become useful to others, the entrepreneur must set out in search of problems to be solved or unmet needs to be fulfilled. Rather than assuming that someone else will tell them what is useful, entrepreneurs must take it upon themselves to figure out what other people want and need. This is not to say that they ignore established norms but that they are more likely to also go above and beyond to look for ways to improve them. Doing so requires curiosity, observation and inquiry, exploration, and experimentation. Perhaps more importantly, it requires empathy—the ability to understand the needs of others and not only the functional dimensions, but also the deeper social and emotional dimensions of unmet needs, which are likely to be unarticulated and therefore much more difficult to detect. Think of these as the three dimensions of human needs.

Entrepreneurial discovery also requires effective problem-solving skills. Once a problem has been identified and properly diagnosed, solving the problem requires creativity, imagination, and divergent thinking, which is the ability to explore many possible solutions. It requires learning by doing through an interactive process of experimentation and adaptation. It requires skepticism, the ability to think critically in order to guard against predictable errors of judgment. The resource-constrained nature of the entrepreneurial discovery process also requires resourcefulness, the ability to make things happen in the margins, using whatever discretionary resources are at hand to test an idea on a small scale before going all in. Entrepreneurial discovery requires collaboration and teamwork, the ability to function within small self-organized teams amid chaos and complexity. It requires networking skills, not only as a means of finding customers but as a means of finding knowledge and building support systems. It requires effective communication skills, as good ideas rarely sell themselves. The entrepreneurial discovery process requires emotional self-regulation and resilience, the ability to respond appropriately to the ongoing demands of learning through trial and error so as to develop the ability to persevere in the face of challenges and setbacks one is sure to encounter along the way.

For those engaged in entrepreneurial discovery, a phase-one connection is found not when we are hired by an employer but when sufficient evidence of usefulness has been established. Such evidence typically comes in the form of currency; that is, when someone (other than friends and relatives) agrees to pay for a product or service, they are providing evidence of the usefulness of that product or service. To be clear, currency is not the only means of validating an idea. For example, evidence may come in the form of buy-in from coworkers, colleagues, or the boss. Evidence might be reflected in the number of downloads, followers, readers, or subscribers on social media. It might be the popularity of a poem or a song. The point here is that entrepreneurial discovery is an evidence-based learning process. Contrary to what many believe, the typical entrepreneur is behaving more like a scientist or a detective searching for evidence rather than a high-stakes gambler with an innate propensity for risk. Once sufficient evidence of usefulness has been established, the first break point is reached, and the rules for survival change. The entrepreneur must now embrace a managerial mindset to begin replicating the "useful thing" they discovered in order to grow.

Now that we have illustrated the differences between traditional learning and entrepreneurial discovery, let's return to the question of how inexperienced, unfunded entrepreneurs manage to identify, evaluate, and actualize opportunities that the rest of us overlook. As you will see, when we consider the contextual factors within which entrepreneurial discovery occurs, what was once described as a "scientifically unfathomable mystery of life and mind"* begins to unfold:

- **No breakthrough ideas:** The vast majority of entrepreneurs initially set out in pursuit of small niche opportunities that are unremarkable. For some, through experimentation and adaptation, a greater opportunity emerges over time, and in many cases, they are opportunities the entrepreneurs themselves did not originally foresee.

---

* In his 1921 book, *Risk, Uncertainty, and Profit*, the renowned economist Frank Knight described the decision-making process of entrepreneurs as follows: "The ultimate logic, or psychology, of these deliberations is obscure, a part of the scientifically unfathomable mystery of life and mind" (p. 227).

- **Not much formal planning or market research:** The opportunities entrepreneurs initially pursue are often hidden in the form of unarticulated, unmet needs. As such, they cannot be identified through traditional planning and market research. Instead, the entrepreneur learns by doing through experimentation and adaptation as a way to tease out latent opportunities that others overlook.

- **Not much money:** Within the discovery phase, the lack of resources works to the advantage of everyday entrepreneurs by forcing them to start small with a minimally viable product or service that not only provides feedback but also generates revenue that enables them to grow organically.

- **Lack of experience:** Naiveté can also work to the advantage of the nascent entrepreneur, creating an ability to see things that experts with years of experience may overlook. As Zen Master Shunryū Suzuki stated: "In the beginner's mind there are many possibilities, but in the expert's there are few."[10]

Among the great paradoxes that arise from the observation and analysis of everyday entrepreneurs is that they succeed not in spite of their circumstances but because of them. The highly ambiguous, resource-constrained, self-directed nature of entrepreneurial discovery creates the conditions whereby the lack of experience, the lack of formal planning, and the lack of resources work together in ways that actually create an advantage for the typical inexperienced, unfunded entrepreneur. The distinction between an entrepreneur and a non-entrepreneur lies not in their dispositional traits but in their subtle, underlying beliefs.

From this perspective, we can now redefine entrepreneurship as the self-directed pursuit of opportunities to create value for others. When viewed from this perspective, we no longer see entrepreneurs as distinguished by their traits but as entrepreneurial people who simply take it upon themselves to figure out how to make themselves useful to others, in whatever situation they find themselves, be it within a traditional job or by starting a business of their own. And by embracing this way of thinking, they empower themselves.

Entrepreneurship is the self-directed pursuit of opportunities to create value for others. By doing so, we can empower ourselves.

This is a simple definition that anyone can embrace, regardless of their circumstances or chosen path. Embracing this perspective does not require breakthrough ideas, access to venture capital, or an advanced degree. Nor does it require a unique personality or a propensity for risk. In fact, being entrepreneurial does not require an interest in starting a business at all. It simply requires us to develop attitudes and skills that have historically been discouraged or ignored within traditional learning environments and organizational structures.

Entrepreneurship is the self-directed pursuit of opportunities to create value for others. By doing so, we can empower ourselves.

As Land's theory illustrates, the mindset and methods required to discover opportunities are distinct from those required to exploit them. As the rate of change in our world continues to increase, it is becoming increasingly evident that the managerial mindset that once enabled us to succeed is no longer sufficient. The evolving landscape now requires us to embrace both entrepreneurial and managerial thinking. The key to survival, as Land suggests, is to know which situation we are in so that we know which rules to apply.

Chapter Three

Are Entrepreneurs Made or Born?

At no point in my life did I ever think of myself as being an entrepreneur.

—Dawn Halfaker[1]

As a young graduate of the US Military Academy at West Point, Dawn Halfaker had a promising military career ahead of her. Yet, a few weeks shy of her twenty-fifth birthday, while serving in Iraq, she was severely injured when the Humvee she was riding in was hit by a rocket-propelled grenade. By the time she arrived at Walter Reed army hospital in Washington, DC, the nurses did not expect her to live. A few weeks later, she awoke from a coma to discover that her right arm had been lost. "I thought my life was over," she told me when we met in 2010. "I felt like I was going to lose everything I had worked for. I was feeling sorry for myself; I was focused on what I had lost; I didn't think that I could ever amount to much."

Weeks later, still bound to a wheelchair and feeling somewhat depressed, Dawn's mindset suddenly changed as she was wheeled into the rehabilitation center to begin physical therapy. It was there that she witnessed a young staff sergeant who had lost both legs learning to walk again on his new prosthetic limbs. As she watched the young man struggle to take his first steps, she began to see things in a different light. "My mindset changed forever," she told me. "I was just missing an arm. At that moment, I began to focus on what I had rather than what I had lost. I felt empowered."

As Dawn progressed in her recovery, she was offered a number of desk jobs, yet none of them seemed to suit her needs. Although she desperately wanted to stay connected to her fellow soldiers who were still in harm's way, it soon became clear that her military career, which she had worked so hard to achieve, had come to an end. Now, at the age of twenty-seven, she would have to chart a new course in her life. She had no idea what the future might hold.

Yet despite her challenges, she connected with an idea that would enable her to build on the knowledge and experience she had gained in Iraq in a way that might help protect her fellow soldiers who were still "down range." Maybe she could leverage the knowledge and experience she had gained on the battlefield in ways that might influence policymakers in Washington, DC. With nothing more than a laptop and a business card, Dawn sat down at her dining room table and got to work. Before she knew it, her fledgling consulting firm began to grow, and she was hanging on for dear life. "I wound up with a business through survival," she told me. "Necessity breeds innovation. Adversity can empower people to do amazing things. I feel lucky to be alive. I feel as though I owe it to those who did not come home to make the most of my life." After recently selling her business, Dawn has now shifted her attention to supporting veteran entrepreneurs through her nonprofit, Continuing to Serve Foundation.

For much of the last century, entrepreneurs were seen as enigmatic figures: bold risk-takers who are supremely confident, brilliant, creative, and charismatic, born with unique personality traits that enable them to accomplish extraordinary things. Meanwhile, the rest of humanity seemed destined to be employees who worked in established organizations. This way of thinking was perhaps bolstered by the "great man theory" of the late nineteenth century, which promoted the idea that great advances come about as the result of "great men" who were born with extraordinary abilities. To this day, many assume that successful entrepreneurs are similarly endowed with superlative characteristics that will enable them to accomplish the extraordinary.

More recently, as the economic value of entrepreneurial activity has become abundantly clear, researchers have sought to identify specific personality traits that might reliably predict entrepreneurial behavior.* While numerous studies have attempted to figure out "who" an entrepreneur is, thus far the results have been inconclusive at best. The challenge of this approach begins with the way in which the term *entrepreneur* is defined. For example, while some studies focus exclusively on high-growth entrepreneurs, others broaden the definition to include small business owners. That is where things begin to get complicated. After all, is a small business owner the same as an entrepreneur? If so, would you consider a farmer to be an entrepreneur? And if so, what personality traits are required to be a successful farmer? Are these the same traits that are required to be a successful entrepreneur? The same goes for inventors, franchise owners, freelancers, or anyone who is self-employed. As you can see, the more broadly we define the term *entrepreneurship*, the further we diminish the relevance of trait-based assumptions as the underlying cause of entrepreneurial behavior.

The widespread popularity of the Myers-Briggs (MBTI) assessment—and other similar personality tests—seems to perpetuate the

---

* Here I am referring to dispositional traits such as openness, conscientiousness, extroversion, agreeableness, and neuroticism as distinct from characteristics that refer to how people modify their actions, attitudes, and feelings in response to a particular environment or circumstance.

idea that we can all be grouped into a handful of personality types despite the fact that psychological research has largely proven this concept to be a myth. Numerous studies have questioned the validity of such tests. In her book *The Cult of Personality: How Personality Tests Are Leading Us to Miseducate Our Children, Mismanage Our Companies, and Misunderstand Ourselves,* author Annie Murphy Paul describes the sixteen distinctive types classified by the Myers-Briggs as having "no scientific basis whatsoever."[2]

Nevertheless, we continue to rely on such tests as a way to predict how people are likely to behave. What these tests fail to account for, however, are the ways in which subtle yet powerful situational variables also influence our behavior, often negating the influence of our personality traits. After all, our personality traits are the tendencies that influence our conduct in the absence of other situational influences. While our personality traits certainly influence our behavior, they don't adequately explain the causes of entrepreneurial behavior.

In the field of social psychology, this tendency to overemphasize the influence of dispositional traits when explaining a person's behavior, while ignoring the situational variables that are also at play, is known as the "fundamental attribution error." In other words, it is the tendency to attribute a person's behavior to "who they are" without considering the ways in which the situation also affects their behavior.

Darly and Batson's Good Samaritan study provides a powerful example. Seminary students were asked to prepare a sermon on the parable of the Good Samaritan. Some students were told they were running late to deliver their sermon, creating time pressure, while others were informed that they had more time. On their way to a separate building to deliver their sermons, each student encountered a person in distress who was actually an actor pretending to be in need. What the researchers discovered is that, despite the seminarians' moral beliefs and religious training, the factor that most significantly influenced their likelihood of helping was the perceived time pressure. Those who believed they were running late were significantly less likely to stop and help the person in distress, while those who thought they had sufficient time were much more likely to offer assistance. The Good Samaritan study is but one of many that illustrate how the situation impacts our behavior in ways that override the influence of our personality traits.[3] Nevertheless, we continue to emphasize the importance of dispositional traits when explaining the behavior of others while ignoring the power of situational factors.

Nowhere is this fundamental attribution error more prevalent than in our attempts to explain the causes of entrepreneurial behavior. For example, entrepreneurs are commonly characterized as risk-takers, as if they were born with an innate propensity for risk. In fact, the term *entrepreneur* is often defined as a person who is willing to take a risk in exchange for a profit. And yet while openness to experience is among the "big five" personality traits, our willingness to tolerate risk can be influenced by a host of cognitive, motivational, and situational variables that have very little to do with our personality traits. For example, our capacity for risk may be influenced by our beliefs about our own abilities more than by our personality traits. The more confident we are in our abilities, the more likely we are to accept risks. The extent to which we value the outcome of a particular behavior is also a factor that might influence our propensity for risk. The higher the value we place on the outcome of a particular behavior, the more likely we are to take risks in order to achieve it.

As Ted Moore's story demonstrates, there are any number of situational variables that might influence our propensity for risk. For example, in some situations, we may have everything to lose and little to gain by taking risks, while in others we may have little to lose and everything to gain. Is it fair to characterize Ted Moore as a natural-born risk-taker, or did his lack of viable alternatives influence his willingness to take risks? More importantly, how much risk was he actually assuming? Like so many everyday entrepreneurs, he started with a few hundred dollars in his spare time while maintaining his full-time job. The truth is, he had very little to lose and everything to gain.

In his book *Innovation and Entrepreneurship*, the legendary management consultant Peter Drucker relayed the following story:

> I once attended a university symposium on entrepreneurship at which a number of psychologists spoke. Although their papers disagreed on everything else, they all talked about an "entrepreneurial personality," which was characterized by a "propensity for risk-taking." A well-known and successful innovator and entrepreneur who had built a process-based innovation into a substantial worldwide business in the space of twenty-five years was then asked to comment. He said: "I find myself baffled by your papers. I think I know as many successful innovators and entrepreneurs as anyone, beginning with myself. I have never come across an 'entrepreneurial personality.' The successful ones I know all have, however, one thing—and only one thing—in common: they are not 'risk takers.' They try to define the risks they have to take and to minimize them as much as possible. Otherwise, none of us could have succeeded."[4]

The idea that entrepreneurs are "born" suggests that their behavior is determined by their personality traits, thus implying that some of us are natural-born entrepreneurs while the rest of us are destined to function as employees. While it is clear that our personality traits influence our behavior, they certainly aren't the only factors of influence. What these trait-based assumptions overlook is that our behavior is a function of who we are and where we are: the person *and* the situation. Therefore, we must look beyond personality traits to explain the causes of entrepreneurial behavior. In the remainder of this chapter, we will explore the ways in which subtle yet powerful situational factors can influence our behavior, often without our awareness.

———

We begin with a basic question: Where does motivation come from? We are all born with the innate capacity and desire to reach our full potential.

This self-actualizing tendency is in all living things. Like acorns, we all have within us the capacity to become all that we can become, yet this tendency can easily be thwarted by a host of subtle, underlying cognitive, motivational, and situational factors of which we may or may not be aware. While many of these factors are within our control, control is contingent upon our being aware of them. Therefore, if we are to reach our full potential, we must understand the host of factors driving our behavior so that we can consciously and deliberately create conditions that are conducive to self-actualization.

The term *self-actualization* was first introduced by the German neurologist and psychiatrist Kurt Goldstein to illustrate the tendency of an organism's innate motivation to self-actualize as much as possible, referring to this innate drive as the "master motive."[5] The psychologist Carl Rogers also recognized the self-actualizing tendency as "man's tendency to actualize himself, to become his potentialities... to express and activate all the capacities of the organism."[6] The theory of self-actualization was made most prominent by the psychologist Abraham Maslow, who likewise believed that humans are "energized by a self-actualizing tendency" and that "well-being occurs to the extent people can freely express their inherent potentials."[7]

Nevertheless, in the 1950s and 1960s, the study of motivation was dominated by behaviorists who believed that motivation came from outside the person in the form of punishment and rewards. Among the most prominent was B. F. Skinner's theory of operant conditioning, which is a method of learning that occurs through extrinsic rewards and punishments.[8] This view of externally driven motivation was widely accepted and soon became a deeply embedded cultural norm, most notably within our systems of education and organizational structures.

Nevertheless, there were aspects of human motivation that did not fit with popular behaviorist ideas about extrinsic motivation. Over time, researchers began to notice that different types of goals elicited different levels of motivation from the same individual. In his 1959 article in the

Psychological Review, "Motivation Reconsidered," Harvard psychologist Robert White observed that "organisms engage in exploratory, playful, and curiosity-driven behaviors even in the absence of reinforcement or reward," further stating that "these spontaneous behaviors, although clearly bestowing adaptive benefits on the organism, appear not to be done for any such instrumental reason, but rather for the positive experiences associated with exercising and extending one's capacities."[9] Soon, researchers began to distinguish between two types of motivation: intrinsic motivation, which comes from within, and extrinsic motivation, which is brought about from outside of ourselves. More recently, the social psychologists Edward Deci and Richard Ryan described intrinsic motivation this way:

> From birth onward, humans, in their healthiest states, are active, inquisitive, curious, and playful creatures, displaying a ubiquitous readiness to learn and explore, and they do not require extraneous incentives to do so. This natural motivational tendency is a critical element in cognitive, social, and physical development because it is through acting on one's inherent interests that one grows in knowledge and skills.[10]

They also began to notice that intrinsic motivation elicited significantly higher levels of engagement, as well as higher quality learning and creativity, than extrinsic motivation. More importantly, they observed that extrinsic rewards (or threat of punishment) tend to undermine intrinsic motivation. While extrinsic rewards may work in the short term, in the long term, they have been shown to have the opposite of their intended effect. (A meta-analysis of 128 studies concluded that the effects of extrinsic rewards had a significant negative impact on intrinsic motivation.)[11]

"Organisms engage in exploratory, playful, and curiosity-driven behaviors even in the absence of reinforcement or reward."

Building on these findings, Deci and Ryan introduced a new theory of motivation known as "self-determination theory," which stands in stark contrast to the carrot-and-stick motivational theories that had by then become widely accepted as the norm. According to self-determination theory, all humans have an innate organismic tendency toward growth and vitality, and this self-actualizing tendency will occur as long as certain psychological "nourishments" are attainable. However, in the absence of such nourishments, this self-actualizing tendency will be thwarted and, as a result, suboptimal functioning will occur. What Deci and Ryan discovered is that, in the same way that we are all driven to satisfy our basic physiological needs for essentials such as food, clothing, and shelter, we are also driven by basic psychological needs, and these needs are necessary for lifelong growth, social integration, and psychological well-being. What are those basic psychological needs? Autonomy, competency, and relatedness—or more familiarly, autonomy, competency, and purpose:

- **Autonomy** is the need to be free and to have the freedom to make our own choices, to exercise our free will, to determine our day-to-day actions, and ultimately to chart our own course without being controlled or coerced by others.
- **Competency** is the need to be effective, the need to develop the knowledge and skills necessary to engage in and master challenging tasks so as to be effective in the pursuit of our goals.
- **Relatedness** is the need to feel connected and a sense of belonging, to have a sense of meaning and purpose in our lives, and to be meaningfully involved with the broader social world.

Deci and Ryan also found that the absence of any one of these nutrients will undermine the self-actualizing tendency. Unlike our basic physiological needs, these psychological needs are much more subtle and therefore easy to neglect, particularly within cultural and familial paradigms that do not recognize them as essential for lifelong growth and well-being. In the absence of these basic psychological needs, we tend to seek alternatives, which Deci and Ryan refer to as "need-substitutes," the pursuit of which tends to frustrate rather than facilitate the self-actualizing tendency.[12]

For example, those who find themselves in unfulfilling careers often saddle themselves with debt by purchasing an expensive car that serves as a proxy for relatedness. By doing so, they often find themselves on a hedonistic treadmill whereby they burden themselves with debt, thus surrendering their autonomy while further indenturing themselves to unfulfilling careers. Perhaps this is a modern-day reference to what Henry David Thoreau once referred to as "lives of quiet desperation."[13]

To summarize, Deci and Ryan's theory suggests that we all have the capacity and desire to become all that we can become; however, this self-actualizing tendency requires autonomy, competency, and relatedness. Awareness of these psychological needs is essential for understanding the hidden situational factors that facilitate the development of entrepreneurial attitudes and skills. Yet the attainment of these psychological nutrients may be easier said than done, especially since we have a tendency to get in our own way.

As humans, we are all growth-oriented, opportunity-seeking organisms driven by the innate capacity and desire to realize our full potential. Yet, at the same time, we are also stability-seeking, uncertainty-avoiding organisms, born with an innate need for safety, stability, and a desire to conform to societal and group norms. These compelling and constraining forces create a conflict of interests whereby a constellation of cognitive, motivational, and situational factors act upon us in ways of which we may not be aware. While these forces are often subtle, non-obvious, and easy to overlook, they exert enormous influence on our behavior. In the remainder of this chapter, we will explore some of the ways these cognitive, motivational, and situational factors can either encourage or inhibit our innate tendency toward growth and vitality. Once understood, we begin to see how small changes can make a big difference in our lives.

1. Cognitive Factors

As we have seen, everyday entrepreneurs are not always the best and the brightest, at least in terms of academic achievement scores or standard IQ tests. In fact, many report being mediocre students who struggled within formal learning environments. Yet it is not individual differences in intellect or personality traits that seem to set them apart; rather, it is their underlying beliefs and assumptions—*beliefs and assumptions of which they themselves may not be aware.* For example, our perceived self-efficacy beliefs exert enormous influence on our behavior. Our beliefs about our self-efficacy affect every aspect of our lives, including the goals we set for ourselves, as well as the extent to which we persist in the face of difficulty in the pursuit of our goals. In a 1994 paper, psychologist Albert Bandura describes the effects of our perceived self-efficacy in no uncertain terms:

> People with high assurance in their capabilities approach difficult tasks as challenges to be mastered rather than as threats to be avoided. They set for themselves challenging goals and maintain a strong commitment to them. They heighten and sustain their efforts in the face of failure. They quickly recover their sense of efficacy after failures or setbacks. They attribute failure to insufficient effort or deficient knowledge and skills which are acquirable. Such an efficacious outlook produces personal accomplishments, reduces stress, and lowers vulnerability to depression.

He goes on to say that:

> In contrast, people who doubt their capabilities shy away from difficult tasks which they view as personal threats. They have low aspirations and weak commitment to the goals they choose to pursue. When faced with difficult tasks, they dwell on their personal deficiencies, on the obstacles

they will encounter, and all kinds of adverse outcomes rather than concentrate on how to perform successfully. They slacken their efforts and give up quickly in the face of difficulties. They are slow to recover their sense of efficacy following failure or setbacks. Because they view insufficient performance as deficient aptitude it does not require much failure for them to lose faith in their capabilities. They fall easy victim to stress and depression.[14]

Perceived Locus of Control

Another important underlying cognitive influence is the degree to which we believe that we have control over the events and outcomes in our lives. The psychologist Julian Rotter first introduced the concept of perceived locus of control to describe the underlying beliefs we hold about control over the outcome of events in our lives. Those with an internal perceived locus of control assume that events in their lives are primarily a result of their own actions, while those with an external perceived locus of control are more likely to assume that external factors such as fate, luck, circumstances, or powerful others control the events and outcomes of their lives.[15] As you can imagine, the difference in these unconscious assumptions can have an enormous impact on our behavior.

Construal

Construal is the cognitive process through which we make sense of the world around us. Yet, our construal of a given situation involves our individual interpretations and perceptions and is therefore inherently subjective. After all, different people may construe the same situation in very different ways, leading to very different responses. The problem is that, very often, we are not aware that we are interpreting our circumstances and events, and that it is our subjective interpretation, rather than the event itself, that is causing us to feel, think, and act in a particular way.

As Dawn Halfaker's story so powerfully illustrates, what happens to us matters much less than how we interpret what happens to us.

Consider the ways in which two people might interpret a negative event; one person might view it optimistically while another might adopt a pessimistic perspective. Psychologists refer to this as our explanatory style. In the face of challenges, those with an optimistic explanatory style see setbacks as temporary and fixable, whereas individuals with a more pessimistic style perceive similar situations as permanent or unfixable. Numerous studies indicate that optimism enhances psychological resilience, enabling individuals to swiftly recover or even benefit from adverse experiences. Additionally, research suggests that those who optimistically interpret adversity often emerge healthier, happier, and stronger than those who never face adversity. As Buddha once said, "Your worst enemy cannot harm you as much as your own thoughts, unguarded. But once mastered, no one can help you as much, not even your father or your mother."

> "Your worst enemy cannot harm you as much as your own thoughts, unguarded. But once mastered, no one can help you as much, not even your father or your mother."

2. Motivational Factors

Among the most noticeable and consistent characteristics of an entrepreneur are that they are enthusiastic, intrinsically motivated, and highly engaged. While on the surface such behavior is often attributed to their personality traits, what many fail to realize is the extent to which the entrepreneur's goal itself is eliciting those characteristics and behaviors from the entrepreneur. Just as gravity is an invisible force that acts on an object, the compelling nature of a goal can become a powerful influence that acts upon us in ways of which we may not be aware. One of the most common themes that emerged from my observation of everyday entrepreneurs is the articulation of a vision or a compelling goal, something on the horizon that was pulling them into the future in a way that enabled them not only to break from the past but also to activate the full range of their faculties. For some, the compelling goal may be to escape poverty or to create a more meaningful and prosperous life. For others, it may be to solve a particular problem or to bring a new invention to life. Whatever their motivation, the compelling nature of their goals acts upon them in ways that elicit higher levels of engagement.

To be *compelled* means to be irresistibly drawn toward something, a source of intrinsic motivation, whereas to be *coerced* is to be extrinsically motivated by the prospect of a separable reward or fear of punishment. Goals that are inherently interesting, enjoyable, and rewarding enable us to access higher levels of engagement, creativity, and problem-solving abilities than those that are motivated by money, letter grades, or other extrinsic rewards.

The psychologist Mihaly Csikszentmihalyi described those who are optimally engaged as autotelic. In his book *Finding Flow: The Psychology of Engagement with Everyday Life*, Csikszentmihalyi describes an autotelic person as someone who is less motivated by material possessions, power, or fame because so much of what they do is inherently rewarding. As a result, they are more autonomous and independent and cannot be easily manipulated with the threat of punishment or the promise of rewards.[16]

The desire to fulfill human needs through our own effort is a powerful motivational force that provides a sense of meaning and purpose in our lives. Despite what we see in popular culture, the most powerful motivating forces aren't money, power, or material wealth, but rather to pursue our interests and develop our innate abilities in ways that contribute to the greater good. When that happens, our psyche produces the energy, enthusiasm, focus, and fortitude that can empower us to accomplish extraordinary things. As a result, the distinction between work and play begins to disappear. In his landmark book *Man's Search for Meaning*, Viktor Frankl describes the striving to find meaning in life as the most powerful motivating force in human nature, in contrast to the lack of meaning, which is the greatest source of stress and anxiety.[17] Without realizing it, everyday entrepreneurs unwittingly create the conditions whereby they are able to satisfy their basic psychological need for autonomy, competency, and purpose. As a result, they are much more likely to become optimally engaged.

By contrast, the absence of a compelling goal creates a vulnerability that also influences our behavior. Without realizing it, we often default to stability-seeking, uncertainty-avoiding behavior while ignoring our need for exploration and growth. We come to assume that we are who we are and the world is the way it is, and there is nothing we can do to change it. When that happens, we become alienated and disengaged, we stop learning and become more easily distracted, more vulnerable to anxiety and depression. We become more likely to *spend* our discretionary time and effort pursuing need-substitutes rather than *invest* our time in exploration and growth.

3. Situational Factors

Cognitive and motivational factors are not the only variables that influence our behavior. An endless array of subtle yet powerful situational factors can also hinder or enhance the development of entrepreneurial attitudes and skills. Among the most potent of these situational factors is the influence of our peers. How much do your friends and family determine how entrepreneurial you are? It turns out, a lot.

For example, exposure to entrepreneurial behavior through our social networks of family and friends greatly increases the probability that we will act similarly. Group conformity also affects our behavior in ways that may surprise you. Numerous studies have demonstrated the extent to which we will alter our beliefs and behaviors in order to conform to a group. Other forces of socialization such as school, mass media, public opinion, and religion also act upon us in ways that can either hinder or enhance the likelihood that we will embrace entrepreneurial behavior.

Another situational factor that influences entrepreneurial behavior is our level of satisfaction with the status quo. For example, those who are meaningfully employed and well paid may be much less inclined to be entrepreneurial than those who may be less satisfied in their careers. As the saying goes, if it ain't broke, don't fix it.

On the other hand, a higher level of dissatisfaction may increase the probability of embracing entrepreneurial behavior. For entrepreneurs like Ted Moore, a lack of viable alternatives increases this likelihood. In this case, the status quo becomes so intolerable that the entrepreneur is forced to seek alternative paths. Perhaps this is why so many entrepreneurs hail from some form of adversity. Yet hardship alone does not necessarily predict entrepreneurial behavior. After all, many languish in low-paying jobs or unsatisfying careers and yet they do not see entrepreneurship as a path. The question is: Why do some embrace entrepreneurial behavior when others do not?

Some may not see entrepreneurship as a viable option, particularly if they assume it requires big ideas or access to venture capital, things that are beyond their reach. Others may find themselves trapped in a place where "good enough" becomes the enemy of the great, whereby their work may be unsatisfying but the pain isn't bad enough to bring about change. In such cases, the pursuit of need-substitutes may suffice.

When faced with an adverse condition, such as a low-paying job or an unsatisfying career, our subconscious mind relies on our memory to determine whether or not the condition is escapable. If we (unconsciously) construe the situation to be escapable, our brains will activate and engage us in ways that cause us to explore new strategies or pursue alternative pathways. Simply put, our subconscious minds will decide to invest the energy toward finding solutions. However, if we interpret the situation to be inescapable, our brains will reorient our energy toward coping strategies that enable us to tolerate the adversity rather than wasting energy trying to escape it. This simple internal assessment of our ability to change our circumstances is ultimately a choice, one that is often made automatically and unconsciously yet can have an enormous impact on our lives.

In the field of sociology, the term *agency* is described as our ability to take action in the pursuit of our goals. In contrast, the term *structure* is used to describe the factors of influence such as social class, religion, gender, ethnicity, laws, customs, and societal norms that limit our ability to take action in pursuit of our goals. The concepts of agency and structure can be thought of as compelling and constraining forces that act upon us in ways that influence our ability to set and achieve our desired goals. To what extent do we act as free agents in the pursuit of our goals, and to what extent are our actions determined by social structures? The dominant influence of our individual agency versus that of societal structures is unclear due to the bidirectional nature of the cause-and-effect relationship between the two. One affects the other in a way that neither can be clearly assigned as the cause or the effect.

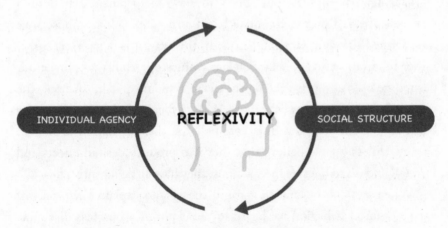

Figure 3.1 | Agency, Structure, and Reflexivity

The term *reflexivity* refers to the capacity of an individual to recognize the forces of socialization and alter their place in the social structure. Reflexivity is the extent to which either we are influenced *by* social structure or *we* influence the social structure. For example, those with lower levels of reflexivity are those who are shaped largely by social structures while those with higher levels of reflexivity would have a greater ability to influence, and alter, their place within the social structure.

In a 1994 interview, Steve Jobs beautifully articulated the idea of agency, structure, and reflexivity in this way:

> When you grow up you tend to get told that the world is the way it is and your life is just to live your life inside the world. Try not to bash into the walls too much. Try to have a nice family life, have fun, save a little money. That's a very limited life. Life can be much broader once you discover one simple fact: Everything around you that you call life was made up by people that were no smarter than you. And you can change it, you can influence it . . . Once you learn that, you'll never be the same again.[18]

Our agency—that is, our ability to act and to pursue our desired goals—is affected by the cognitive belief structures (a.k.a. mindset) we have formed through our experiences. In this way, it is our *sense of agency* rather than our actual agency that determines our ability to pursue our desired goals. As the psychologist Albert Bandura put it, "Among the mechanisms of human agency, none is more focal or pervading than the belief in personal efficacy. This core belief is the foundation of human agency. Unless people believe that they can produce desired effects and forestall undesired ones by their actions, they have little incentive to act."[19]

When we look beyond trait-based theories to explain the causes of entrepreneurial behavior, we begin to see it not as a business discipline but as an expression of the self-actualizing tendency that resides within us all. We begin to see that, while not everyone may want to start a business, we are all born with the innate desire to have control over our day-to-day lives, to fulfill human needs through our own efforts, and to be recognized for our contribution to the greater good. In that sense, the entrepreneurial spirit is the human spirit—it is not just in some of us; it resides within us all. When we begin to recognize the ways in which subtle yet powerful cognitive, motivational, and situational factors influence our behavior, we begin to see that *non*-entrepreneurial behavior is learned. By overemphasizing the influence of personality traits as the underlying cause of entrepreneurial behavior, we may be blinding ourselves to the ways in which the forces of socialization, most notably our systems of education and organizational structures, inhibit the development of entrepreneurial behavior. To assume that entrepreneurs are "great men" (or women) who are somehow born with extraordinary abilities is to overlook the ability of ordinary people to accomplish extraordinary things. By assuming that an entrepreneurial mindset is something we either have or we don't, we may be overlooking untapped potential that remains hidden within ourselves.

Sometimes, small changes can make a big difference in our lives. However, as author Peter Senge suggests, the areas of highest leverage are often subtle, nonobvious, and easy to overlook.[20] Once we become aware of the ways in which these subtle, underlying factors influence our behavior, we have the power to change them. We now have the ability to consciously and deliberately create the conditions that are conducive to exploration and experimentation, vitality, and growth. In the next chapter we will explore the mindset as the missing link.

Chapter Four

Mindset: The Hidden Mechanism That Guides Our Behavior

Until you make the unconscious conscious, it will direct your life and you will call it fate.

—Carl Jung

What is a mindset, where does it come from, and how does it shape our lives? We all have a mindset, but most of the time we are not consciously aware of it or the profound effect it can have on our lives. For some, mindset becomes a hidden mechanism that optimizes our ability to self-actualize. It guides our behavior in ways that enable us to thrive. It becomes a source of confidence, hope, and optimism that cultivates the curiosity, creativity, and critical thinking that encourages us to try new things, to learn and to grow, to develop new skills. It enables us to leverage our strengths and optimize our circumstances in ways that cause us to flourish and thrive.

Yet our mindset can also lead us astray, hijacking our emotions in ways that sabotage our efforts and limit our ability to learn and grow. It can blind us to opportunities and discourage our efforts, clouding our judgment and affecting our reasoning in ways that keep us tethered to familiar yet unproductive patterns of thoughts, feelings, and actions. In other words, our mindset can either hinder or enhance our ability to reach our full potential.

To be clear, mindset is not the same as intelligence. It cannot be measured with IQ tests or academic achievement scores. Nor can it be seen on an fMRI. It is a hypothetical construct used to explain the ways in which our deeply held values and taken-for-granted assumptions influence our behavior in ways of which we may not be aware. And, while it may not be tangible, it is subtle, powerful, and pervasive, influencing every aspect of our lives. Our mindset impacts our ability to think clearly, to reason, and to make judgments. It influences our perception and awareness; it determines what we notice and what we overlook. Our mindset also affects our interpretation of circumstances and events, which in turn impacts our emotions and behavior. It also influences our willingness to take action, the intensity of our efforts, and our willingness to persist in the face of challenges and setbacks. Our mindset also impacts the choices we make, including the goals we set and the people with whom we surround ourselves. And it does much of this without our awareness.

In many ways, our mindset is the mechanism that determines the output we get from whatever capabilities we might have. Drawing from an analogy Warren Buffett once used, a person might have a 400-horsepower engine, yet their mindset is such that they may only be able to get 100 horsepower of output, whereas another person may have a 200-horsepower engine, yet their mindset is such that they are able to get all 200 horsepower of output. Thus the highly optimized mindset of the person with the lower capabilities gives them a distinct advantage over others with greater capabilities who are producing lower output. While some of us may indeed be engaged in ways that optimize our full potential, the truth is that most of us find ourselves somewhere between flourishing and floundering, driven by our innate tendency toward growth, yet hindered in some ways by underlying beliefs and taken-for-granted assumptions of which we may not be aware. The study of culture provides a useful framework for understanding the mindset. The term *culture* refers to a pattern of underlying values and assumptions that guide the behavior of a particular group, be it a family, an organization, or a society. Similarly, our mindset is a collection of underlying values, taken-for-granted assumptions, and habitual patterns of thought that enable us to navigate our day-to-day lives. Simply put, a mindset is to an individual what culture is to a group.

A mindset is to an individual what culture is to a group.

The psychologist Edgar Schein defines culture as "a pattern of shared basic assumptions that was learned by a group as it solved its problems of external adaptation and internal integration, that has worked well enough to be considered valid and therefore, to be taught to new members as the correct way to perceive, think, and feel in relation to those problems." As Schein points out, "the nature of any given culture is such that we can see the outcomes it produces, yet we cannot see the underlying values and deeply held assumptions that ultimately drive the behaviors that produce them."[1] The same is true with entrepreneurs: we can see the businesses, the jobs, and the wealth they create, yet we cannot see the underlying values and assumptions that drive the behaviors that produce those outcomes.

"The nature of any given culture is such that we can see the outcomes it produces, yet we cannot see the underlying values and deeply held assumptions that ultimately drive the behaviors that produce them."

And, like culture, our mindset is powerful in its influence, yet invisible and, to a considerable degree, unconscious. Simply put, a mindset is a pattern of basic assumptions learned by an individual that has worked well enough to be considered valid and therefore assumed to be the correct way to perceive, think, and feel.

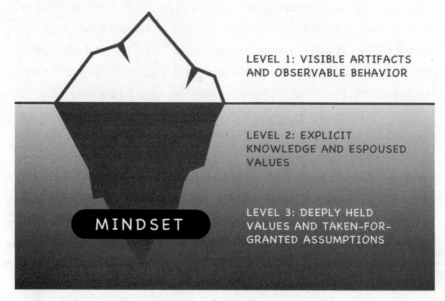

LEVEL 1: VISIBLE ARTIFACTS AND OBSERVABLE BEHAVIOR

LEVEL 2: EXPLICIT KNOWLEDGE AND ESPOUSED VALUES

MINDSET

LEVEL 3: DEEPLY HELD VALUES AND TAKEN-FOR-GRANTED ASSUMPTIONS

Figure 4.1 | Mindset Model

A mindset is a pattern of basic assumptions learned by an individual that has worked well enough to be considered valid and therefore assumed to be the correct way to perceive, think, and feel.

The image of an iceberg provides a useful metaphor for understanding the mindset. On the surface (level one), we can see visible artifacts and observable behaviors, yet we cannot see the underlying values and beliefs that produced them. For example, we can see that an entrepreneur has a successful business that produces products and services, generates revenue, and employs people, yet we cannot see the underlying values and assumptions that ultimately led to those outcomes. We can ask the entrepreneur to explain their underlying values and assumptions that led to their success; however, the answers they provide are only likely to reveal their espoused values and explicit beliefs (level two) rather than their deeply held values and taken-for-granted assumptions (level three), of which they are not likely to be aware. "I worked really hard and never gave up" or "I am really passionate about my work" may represent their conscious rationalizations for their behavior (level two) rather than the true underlying cause. As Schein points out, the true causes of our behavior often remain hidden beneath our conscious awareness. Because we are not consciously aware of these level-three values and assumptions, we often struggle to see the correlation between them and the outcomes they produce. In other words, the level-one outcomes of our lives—the visible artifacts and observable behaviors—are likely to be the result of the deeply held values and taken-for-granted (level three) assumptions of which we are largely unaware. Since we are not aware of them, we fail to see the ways in which they are contributing to the outcomes in our lives. Whether we realize it or not, our mindset is a belief system that is perfectly designed to create the outcomes it creates. (See figure 4.2.)

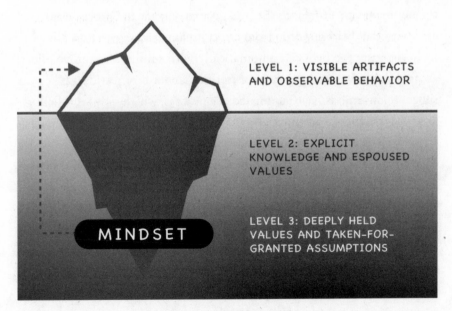

Figure 4.2 | Mindset Model

Why is so much of our mindset unconscious? Like culture, the purpose of a mindset is to enable us to think without thinking. Our brains are inundated with millions of bits of data that pour in through our five senses each second, yet our conscious minds are only capable of processing a few. Therefore, in order to function, our brains must rely on a variety of filtering mechanisms, simplification systems, and coping strategies that enable us to conserve energy and reduce the cognitive burden required to navigate our daily lives. In many ways, our mindset is a simplification system that enables us to function with minimal cognitive effort.

Here's how it works. All behavior begins as goal-directed behavior, whether we're trying to figure out how to navigate unfamiliar terrain or learn a new skill. At first, we're in a learning phase whereby our minds are actively engaged and keenly attuned to what is working and what is not. Remember how difficult it was to learn how to ride a bicycle? Yet, over time, as the new behavior is deemed successful, the mental processes associated with that behavior shift to habitual control so as to reduce the cognitive load on our conscious brains. When that change happens and the new behavior shifts into the background, the mental processes associated with that behavior drop from our conscious awareness, thus allowing us to replicate the behavior automatically with minimal cognitive effort. At that point, we don't really have to think about how to ride a bike; our subconscious minds have automated the process, which now seems effortless. This enables us to function on autopilot, to think without thinking. Psychologists refer to this simplification process as "automaticity."

In his book *Thinking, Fast and Slow*, Nobel laureate Daniel Kahneman describes two separate systems of the mind: system one and system two. System one is the fast-thinking part of our brain that relies on rules and heuristics, intuition, emotions, and other mental shortcuts to make decisions quickly and effortlessly as we navigate our daily lives. In contrast, system two is the slower, more deliberate, and therefore more effortful part of our brain that we engage to solve more complex problems. The fast-thinking part of our brain works reasonably well in most situations, but it can also keep us tethered to familiar yet unproductive ways of thinking because the slower, more contemplative part of our brain tends to overrely on the fast-thinking brain. In this way, our brain's need for efficiency overrides our ability to be effective.[2] On one hand, employing these unconscious mental habits enables us to make judgments with minimal effort, and as long as they are effective, the benefits are obvious. We save time and energy, and nothing important is lost. But there is a price to be paid for overrelying on mental habits, specifically when they turn out to be inaccurate or obsolete or when we use them inappropriately.

From an evolutionary standpoint, our mindset serves as a mechanism that enhances our ability to function within stable environments where the future is similar to the past. It enables us to acquire knowledge and experience that increase our ability to navigate within familiar terrain. However, when faced with changes in our environment or when we want to create a future that looks different from the past, our mindset can hinder our ability to adapt. The unconscious nature of our mindset, coupled with the predictable errors in judgment inherent in our fast-thinking brains, generates a formidable mental inertia. This inertia relies on past experiences to navigate the future, thereby entrenching us in belief systems that impede our capacity to adapt in dynamic situations. As we discussed earlier in this chapter, our mindset can either hinder or enhance our ability to reach our full potential.

Our mindset is consciously and unconsciously acquired. Much of our mindset is made up of beliefs, values, and assumptions that we acquired through both formal and informal learning experiences. These are things we learned through deliberate effort that we accepted as the correct way to perceive, think, and feel and subsequently relegated to habitual control—for example, things we may have been taught by our parents or that we learned in school. Yet, much of our mindset is unconsciously acquired through the forces of socialization as well as our subjective interpretation of our life experiences and events. After all, we are active interpreters of our environment, but we often do so unconsciously and therefore uncritically. Sometimes we accept things as true without really thinking about them at all. As such, our brains are not very good at distinguishing between beliefs, assumptions, and facts. Nevertheless, they become deeply ingrained mental habits that we *assume* to be the correct way to perceive, think, and feel in relation to our problems or in the pursuit of our goals. It is these deeply held values and taken-for-granted assumptions that are the most difficult to uproot.

Here, it is worth noting that the unconscious nature of the mindset also speaks to the tacit, underlying nature of human needs. In the same way that we are not aware of the underlying values and assumptions that drive our behavior, we are often not aware of our underlying wants and needs. Very often what people say they want (level two) differs from what they actually want (level three), a fact that contributes to the highly ambiguous nature of the opportunity discovery process we discussed in chapter 2. (See figure 4.3.)

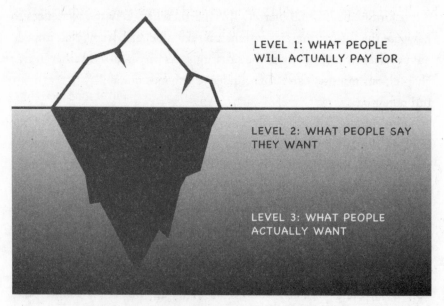

LEVEL 1: WHAT PEOPLE WILL ACTUALLY PAY FOR

LEVEL 2: WHAT PEOPLE SAY THEY WANT

LEVEL 3: WHAT PEOPLE ACTUALLY WANT

Figure 4.3 | The Unconscious Nature of Unmet Needs

A mindset in motion tends to stay in motion. Regardless of whether our mindset is consciously or unconsciously acquired, over time it becomes a fixed way of thinking—*a mind-set*—that creates a powerful incentive to draw from the past in order to navigate the future. Our brains are sense-making machines, constantly searching for patterns that can help us understand how the world works. These patterns then become beliefs. Once that happens, our brains begin to look for—and find—confirming evidence to support those beliefs while simultaneously ignoring or rejecting information that might conflict with our beliefs. This in turn increases our confidence in our beliefs, thereby reinforcing them. Our deeply held values and taken-for-granted assumptions then become part of our identity, causing us to see what we want to see and hear what we want to hear, thus trapping us in familiar yet suboptimal patterns of thought and action. As the psychologist William James said, "The hell to be endured hereafter, of which theology tells, is no worse than the hell we make for ourselves in this world by habitually fashioning our characters in the wrong way. Could the young but realize how soon they will become mere walking bundles of habits, they would give more heed to their conduct while in the plastic state." In other words, don't believe everything you think.

Our mindset is made up of everything we believe to be true—the values, beliefs, and assumptions that we accumulate over time. Unfortunately, while many of our beliefs are well justified and unquestionably true, others may be poorly justified, inaccurate, or obsolete. Nevertheless, we unwittingly rely on them to guide our decisions and regulate our behavior. As the economist Thomas Sowell once said, "It takes considerable knowledge just to realize the extent of our own ignorance."

Sometimes these guiding beliefs may steer us astray. And in some cases, our deeply held beliefs and taken-for-granted assumptions become obsolete. We might acquire a particular belief at a time and place where it made sense, yet once we relegate it to habitual control, our brains are not very good at recognizing the degree to which such a belief may become obsolete over time. Although it is possible to acquire our beliefs mindfully, we often cling to them mindlessly. In other cases, we cling to assumptions and habitual patterns of thought that are inaccurate. For example, we may convince ourselves that "it takes money to make money," which is a common catchphrase that is often interpreted to mean that only those who have access to resources can get ahead. As a result, those who accept such a belief as a fact may be blinding themselves to opportunities that are indeed within their reach.

Regardless of our intellectual abilities, we are all highly susceptible to a host of cognitive biases and predictable errors of judgment that can lead us astray. For example, *confirmation bias* is the tendency to search for or interpret information in ways that confirm our preconceptions while overlooking or dismissing information that does not. Similarly, *selective attention* causes us to see what we are looking for while blinding us to things deemed to be redundant, non-threatening, or irrelevant. Perhaps this is why so many overlook opportunities that are hiding in plain sight. Another predictable error in judgment is the *availability heuristic*, which is the tendency to make decisions quickly by drawing from easily retrieved information. Here again, our slower-thinking brains overrely on the fast-thinking part of our brain, thus causing us to think and act as we always have. Similarly, the *affect heuristic* is the tendency to overrely on emotional responses rather than engaging our slower-thinking brain when making decisions. For example, we often reject new ideas offhand based on an immediate negative emotional response, which, in turn, prevents any further consideration. At the same time, *ambiguity aversion* discourages us from deviating from the norm or taking calculated risks. When faced with an adaptive challenge, *cognitive entrenchment* causes us to cling to prior beliefs rather than exploring alternatives. Perhaps the most pernicious of these cognitive biases is the *self-serving bias*, which is the tendency to attribute our successes to internal factors and our failures to external, situational factors. In other words, it is the tendency to take credit for our triumphs, while blaming others or circumstances for our shortcomings. These examples offer but a brief glimpse into the myriad ways in which our mindset can distort our judgment and lead us astray. While perhaps less relevant when functioning within other-directed stable environments, awareness of our vulnerability to predictable errors in judgment will become particularly relevant when navigating the highly ambiguous nature of the entrepreneurial discovery process.

In this chapter we have begun to explore the mindset as a hidden mechanism that influences our behavior in ways of which we may not be aware. In the next chapter we will explore the origins and evolution of the *managerial* mindset as the dominant cultural paradigm. As you will see, we cannot truly understand the entrepreneurial mindset until we recognize that we are looking at the world through a managerial lens.

Chapter Five

The Origins and Evolution of the Managerial Mindset

Sometimes the most obvious, important realities are the ones that are hardest to see.

—David Foster Wallace

What the Hell Is Water?

Addressing the graduating class of 2005 at Kenyon College, the novelist David Foster Wallace began with a parable. "There are these two young fish swimming along and they happen to meet an older fish swimming the other way, who nods at them and says, 'Morning, boys. How's the water?' And the two young fish swim on for a bit, and then eventually one of them looks over at the other and goes, 'What the hell is water?'"[1]

If we are to develop an entrepreneurial mindset, it is essential to stop and examine the lens through which we currently view the world so that we can excavate the deeply held values and taken-for-granted assumptions that shape our thoughts and deeds. It is here we begin to see that we may be looking at the world through a managerial lens. And, as Wallace points out, sometimes the most obvious, important realities are often the ones that are hardest to see.

A Brief History of Work

For much of the Western world, the Industrial Revolution marked a major turning point for mankind. The invention of steam-powered machines combined with the division of labor created a new economic model that lifted much of humanity from economic stagnation. By all accounts, it was a stark departure from the way life had been lived for previous centuries during which the options for earning a livelihood were generally constrained to agricultural labor and a few specialized trades. Production was confined to the output of skilled craftsmen, which, given the absence of machinery and the reliance on human and animal labor, was barely sufficient for survival. Not only was production limited, but there was also minimal demand for goods and services, as very few possessed the discretionary income required to purchase them. The majority of humans eked out a living as self-employed farmers or landless agricultural workers. This subsistence-based existence persisted for centuries with limited technological advancements and economic growth. During this time period, individual thought was actively discouraged, and people were trained to conform to rigid religious doctrines or the directives of the ruling elite. Those who dared to dissent faced severe punishments, or in some cases, even death.

Yet, things started to change as new ways of thinking slowly began to challenge established norms. A renewed interest in classical humanistic ideals gave rise to philosophical movements that emphasized the value of the individual, affirming that all humans have both the right and the responsibility to lead ethical lives of personal fulfillment that aspire to the greater good. The invention of the printing press in the mid-fifteenth century played a pivotal role in the rapid dissemination of ideas during the Renaissance and the Scientific Revolution of the sixteenth and seventeenth centuries. This technological advancement made it much easier and more affordable to produce books and pamphlets, thus enabling the spread of knowledge, philosophical ideas, scientific discoveries, and cultural developments. This increased access to information contributed to the intellectual climate that eventually led to the Age of Enlightenment in the seventeenth and eighteenth centuries.

The Age of Enlightenment was a philosophical movement that emphasized human reason, rationality, and the capacity for individuals to think for themselves. Enlightenment thinkers advocated for the idea that logic and reason could replace the dogma and superstition that had traditionally been imposed by religious and ruling authorities. The Enlightenment also promoted the concept of self-governance, encouraging people to question authority and to make decisions based on their own understanding. The phrase *"Have the courage to use your own understanding"*[2] encapsulated the Enlightenment's emphasis on individual intellectual autonomy. As these Enlightenment ideas spread, they contributed to a climate of intellectual freedom, which in turn led to a surge in creativity and innovation. People were empowered to use their own reason and logic to understand and improve the world around them. This intellectual freedom and creative potential laid the groundwork for technological advancements and new ways of thinking about society and the economy and were key factors leading to the Industrial Revolution.

The Industrial Revolution combined a number of significant technological and economic developments in a short period of time with truly dramatic results for the Western world. The combination of steam-powered machinery and the division of labor now allowed a single individual to perform tasks that once required the efforts of many. The division of labor, with its focus on highly specialized and repetitive tasks, demanded less knowledge and skill, rendering lengthy apprenticeships and extensive training unnecessary. Products that formerly required the expertise of a master craftsman could now be manufactured by relatively unskilled and, consequently, lower-paid workers, which resulted in more affordable products. This transformation not only significantly reduced production costs, thereby enhancing affordability, but in many cases, it also markedly improved the quality of production. This method of organizing labor enabled workers to generate income beyond mere subsistence, resulting in a surplus that not only liberated them from a hand-to-mouth existence but also generated greater demand for products and services. Ultimately, this economic shift lifted substantial portions of humanity from centuries of abject poverty and economic stagnation.

In *The Wealth of Nations*, Adam Smith illustrates the concept of the division of labor and its profound impact on productivity. Using the example of a pin factory, Smith illustrates how breaking down the production process into specialized tasks can significantly enhance efficiency and output. He contrasts the limited output of a single worker attempting to create a pin entirely on their own with the remarkable productivity achieved when tasks are divided among ten workers, each specializing in a specific aspect of production. This division allows each worker to master their assigned task, resulting in heightened efficiency. The principle extends beyond pin manufacturing and has become a foundational concept in economics and industrial organization, emphasizing the advantages of specialization in fostering increased economic output and overall prosperity.[3]

Yet for all the advances in productivity and prosperity, there were trade-offs to be made. While this new way of organizing work was looked upon as an economic miracle, there were disadvantages, some of which were immediately obvious, while others would reveal themselves over time. For example, while factory work offered higher wages and the promise of greater economic stability, working conditions were often abysmal. Workers toiled for long hours and low wages in dangerous and dirty working conditions with few or no rights. Because there was an abundance of low-skilled workers, employers were likely to offer the lowest possible wage. With few alternatives for earning a living, many were bound to undertake such work as a means of survival.

However, low wages and deplorable working conditions were not the only trade-offs to be made. The routinized, other-directed nature of industrial work also led to a sense of alienation and a lack of worker engagement. The highly structured and routinized nature of the work hindered workers' ability to cultivate judgment and develop effective problem-solving skills. On one hand, Smith emphasized the need to divide work into simple tasks and to assign these tasks as the lifelong occupation of the individual in order to maximize their proficiency in performing their assigned tasks. And yet, on the other hand, he acknowledged the unintended consequences of restricting workers to such a narrow field of experience:

> The man whose whole life is spent in performing a few simple operations, of which the effects too are, perhaps, always the same, or very nearly the same, has no occasion to exert his understanding or to exercise his invention in finding out expedients for removing difficulties which never occur. He naturally loses, therefore, the habit of such exertion, and generally becomes as stupid and ignorant as it is possible for a human creature to become.[4]

Smith also observed that the individual worker, immersed in such narrowly defined tasks, was less likely to understand how the whole pin was made. Nor were they likely to derive any sense of purpose or meaning from their work. The economic gains that were produced by this new way of organizing work came at the expense of the individual worker's ability to think for themselves. In other words, while the division of labor had economic advantages in terms of increased productivity and efficiency, it often clashed with the Enlightenment's emphasis on individual autonomy, creativity, intellectual development, and human flourishing.

Keep in mind, as we transitioned from an agricultural to an industrial economy, the ways in which one could earn a living were limited. For the vast majority, the barriers to becoming an entrepreneur were likely to be insurmountable, as most were uneducated peasant farmers who did not have access to the resources required to purchase the land, buildings, machinery, and raw materials necessary to set up a factory system. Besides, debtors' prison or social ostracism awaited those who tried and failed. Moreover, most people had little or no formal education, thus leaving them with few options but to work in the fields or trade their labor for a salary or hourly wage.

By the late 1800s, the factory system of assembly lines and mass production was well underway. Enabled by the onset of infrastructure such as the telegraph system, railroads, electricity, gas, water, and sewage systems, industrialist entrepreneurs such as Andrew Carnegie, John D. Rockefeller, and Henry Ford began to emerge, creating enormous economic impact while also generating immense influence and wealth. These industrialists were regarded as the "great men" who were assumed to have been born with a superior intelligence that enabled them to build such vast organizations and were therefore never to be questioned. Over time, the idea that the average person was destined to function as an employee would soon become a widely accepted societal norm.

This shift toward industrialization and mass production underscored the growing need for effective management of both people and processes. By the late nineteenth century, the development of transportation and other essential infrastructure played a pivotal role in shaping the industrial landscape. Over time, the field of management began to emerge. Alongside these advancements, the emergence of large-scale factory systems became increasingly prominent. The sheer scale and complexity of these factory systems made it evident that structured management practices were essential to ensure efficient production and the coordination of a large workforce. It was about this time that the term *employee* began to appear.

Among the first to propose management theories was a French mining engineer named Henri Fayol, who outlined five main functions of effective management: planning, organizing, commanding, coordinating, and controlling.[5] Around the same period, a mechanical engineer named

Frederick Winslow Taylor played a significant role in the development of what he referred to as "scientific management principles." Rather than relying on the discretion of the individual worker, Taylor believed that there was "one best way" to perform any task, and his goal was to design systems and standardized processes that would maximize efficiency by eliminating the need for judgment on behalf of the worker. Using time and motion studies, Taylor began to meticulously deconstruct and document processes in ways that would optimize production methods, which included calculations of exactly how much time it should take for the worker to perform a particular task. These new management methods required a higher level of managerial control, which drastically increased the number of managers required to achieve maximum productivity. From Taylor's perspective, the job of the worker was not to think but to execute movements that had been scientifically calculated for them. Bonuses, piecework, and other monetary rewards were offered as incentives to maximize productivity.

Taylor also believed that the average worker should be discouraged from any attempts to improve a particular process or to do things their own way. In his book *The Principles of Scientific Management*, he wrote, "It is thoroughly illegitimate for the average man to start out to make a radically new machine, or method, or process to replace one which is already successful." Not surprisingly, he also advocated for a distant relationship between management and labor. In Taylor's view, the worker's need to think should be eliminated, leaving managers the responsibility of planning and organizing tasks.[6] As you can imagine, workers became increasingly alienated and disengaged. Performing an endless sequence of repetitive tasks offered little satisfaction, thereby alienating the worker from any sense of autonomy, much less a sense of meaning and purpose in their lives. Despite receiving punishments or rewards according to performance, workers continued to demonstrate a lack of engagement. This lack of engagement was often perceived by management as the result of laziness, dishonesty, or a lack of character rather than predictable outcomes of the systems they had established. This perception also reinforced the need for managerial oversight, thus creating a vicious cycle whereby the greater the managerial oversight, the more alienated and disengaged the workers were likely to become, leading to further increases in managerial control.

> In Taylor's view, the worker's need to think should be eliminated, leaving managers the responsibility of planning and organizing tasks.

The ways in which these factory models systematically alienated workers were not lost on everyone. Adam Smith was perhaps the first of many who noted the detrimental effects of other-directed, repetitive labor. Among the vocal critics of such systems was Karl Marx, who observed that under these factory systems, workers became estranged from their "species essence," in part because they had little or no control over the products they were creating.[7] As a result, they did not have a meaningful connection to or sense of ownership over the goods and services they produced. Like Smith, Marx saw a connection between the routinized nature of the work and workers' sense of isolation from the creative or intellectual aspects of their work. He observed that these systems often fostered competition among workers, creating an even greater sense of isolation and division. Marx believed that meaningful work is an essential part of human nature, arguing that "our essential nature can only be actualized when we are free to pursue the internal demands that we impose upon ourselves rather than the external demands imposed upon us by others." In essence, Marx's theory of alienation argued that these industrialized economic systems create conditions whereby workers feel estranged from the products they produce, the processes they engage in, their fellow workers, their own human nature, and society as a whole.[8] While Marx may have become a polarizing figure, research suggests the sense of alienation and lack of engagement he described clearly persists in much of the modern workforce.

"Our essential nature can only be actualized when we are free to pursue the internal demands that we impose upon ourselves rather than the external demands imposed upon us by others."

Nevertheless, as industrialized economies expanded, there arose a demand for standardized compulsory education that was designed to align with the emerging industrial model. In much the same way that factories were designed to systematize tasks for optimal efficiency, schools were similarly designed for learning. This approach involved regimented schedules, standardized curricula, and an emphasis on uniformity, mirroring the principles of industrial production. The focus on routine and conformity in education was seen as a way to prepare students for roles within the industrial workforce. By the early twentieth century, the prevailing model in American schools began to reflect Taylorism, treating every student as if they were an average student and striving to offer a uniform, standardized education to all. As the evolutionary psychologist Peter Gray observed, "For the sake of efficiency, children were divided into separate classrooms by age and passed along, from grade to grade, like products on an assembly line. The task of each teacher was to add bits of officially approved knowledge to the product, in accordance with a preplanned schedule, and then to test that product before passing it on to the next station."[9]

In much the same way that the highly controlled, routinized nature of factory work alienated the worker, standardized education had, and continues to have, a similar effect on students. As Gray put it, "The assumption that children are incompetent, irresponsible, and in need of constant direction and supervision becomes a self-fulfilling prophecy. The children themselves become convinced of their incompetence and irresponsibility and may act accordingly."[10]

By the mid-twentieth century, the postwar Industrial Revolution was in full stride. The economy was booming, as was a burgeoning middle class. By now, it was widely believed that large organizations, with vast resources and capital to invest, were the most efficient mechanisms for driving economic progress. Labor unions were able to negotiate living wages with pensions and benefits while government policies helped to provide safer working conditions. After nearly two centuries, rising levels of education and income made it seem as though we had finally found the correct way to think about learning and work.

In his book *The Organization Man*, William Whyte argues that we became immersed in a dominant cultural paradigm where large organizations were the most efficient means of production that would produce maximum benefit to society, thus making it not only economically prudent but a moral obligation for individuals to subvert themselves to the needs of the organization.[11] Within this paradigm, the social contract was such that workers willingly gave up their autonomy in exchange for economic stability. By this point, large organizations that had once been built by entrepreneurs were now likely to be run by risk-averse managers. Meanwhile, small businesses were seen as insignificant and largely ignored. The dominant focus of business was replication and efficiency, which led to the widespread popularity of business management degrees. Within this prevailing paradigm, the subject of entrepreneurship was largely ignored.

By the 1970s, things were beginning to change as globalization began to disrupt the stability of large, established corporations, many of which responded by outsourcing the higher-paying low-skilled jobs to other countries in order to remain competitive. In response, many began to double down on attempts to improve quality and increase efficiency by embracing a variety of management practices such as "total quality management," ISO 9000, "lean manufacturing," Six Sigma, and others. Those who were unable to adapt began to disappear. Meanwhile, the social contract between workers and their employers began to dissolve. Where once, large organizations saw themselves as corporate citizens with broad responsibilities, many began to embrace a singular focus on shareholder value. As a result, productivity continued to rise while wages began to stagnate. At the same time, the promise of job security with a pension, benefits, and a living wage was beginning to disappear.

By the late twentieth century, the transition from mass production to a knowledge-based economy was well underway. As stable, well-paying medium- and low-skilled jobs were either automated or outsourced, millions of workers now needed to develop new skills. Not only new technical skills but adaptive skills to meet the demands of employers who increasingly sought workers who could think critically and creatively, and who could work in small teams to identify and solve problems amid complexity and change. Where jobs were once designed to eliminate judgment on behalf of the worker, we now needed workers who could think for themselves. As a result of these shifts, college enrollment began to increase. Nevertheless, a skills gap began to emerge as our systems of education and workforce development initiatives struggled to keep pace with the changing nature of work. Not only did workers lack the technical skills employers now demanded, but they also lacked the so-called soft skills such as curiosity and creativity, critical thinking, communication, and effective problem-solving required to function in the new world of work. Where workers were once encouraged to adhere to routinized, other-directed tasks, they were now being asked to use reason and logic to identify and solve problems, to think creatively and critically, and to work independently in small teams. In other words, they were being increasingly asked to think and act like entrepreneurs.

However, by now, the foundational assumptions of the industrial era—which were once foundational to the creation of a thriving economy—had become deeply ingrained in our individual and collective consciousness. By this time, these foundational assumptions had worked well enough to be considered valid and were therefore assumed to be the correct way to think about learning and work. As a result, this top-down managerial way of thinking became a deeply embedded cultural norm. Because we were born and raised within this dominant cultural paradigm, it became the water in which we were all swimming. And in the same way that our individual mindset prevents us from adapting when faced with change, the same phenomenon occurs within a cultural paradigm. And, in the same way that our individual mindset prevents us from adapting when faced with an adaptive challenge, the same phenomenon occurs within a collective cultural paradigm; we collectively cling to the deeply held values that were once the source of our strengths, thus preventing us from adapting to change. Nowhere is this more evident than within our systems of education and organizational structures.

Managerial systems give rise to managerial mindsets. Managerial systems are inherently designed to efficiently replicate and disseminate established products and services. Embedded within such systems are deeply held values and taken-for-granted (level three) assumptions that emphasize efficiency, productivity, routine, linearity, stability, and external control. Additionally, these managerial systems continue to rely on extrinsic rewards (or threat of punishment) to motivate workers. Our educational systems are also managerial in nature and are similarly constructed to transfer explicit knowledge and teach technical skills in an efficient manner, underpinned by principles of hierarchy, routine, linearity, and extrinsic incentives. Almost from the moment a student enters school, their curiosity begins to wane as they quickly discern that others will dictate what they must learn and do in order to be successful. Throughout their entire education, students are guided by professional educators through established curricula with predictable processes and outcomes. They find themselves immersed in externally directed, routinized learning systems where memorization and following the rules are expected norms. These formal learning environments were designed to replicate the top-down, repetitive nature of work, presuming that the student is destined to work in an established organization where the product or service has already been defined, and they will be expected to fulfill a predetermined role in the replication and distribution of established products and services. The outcomes of these paradigms are likely to be managerial mindsets.

Managerial systems give rise to managerial mindsets.

This is water. Through the process of socialization, we unwittingly assume that learning and work are other-directed processes, that education is a onetime event, and that our ability to make ourselves useful to others is determined by our academic credentials. Without realizing it, we learn to assume that we will work as employees, that someone else will determine what is useful, and we will fulfill a predetermined role in exchange for a salary or an hourly wage and that, as long as we diligently perform this role, we can expect stability in exchange. Within this cultural paradigm, it is assumed that we will participate in the delivery rather than the discovery of useful things. This is the water in which we all swim: simply put, managerial systems produce managerial mindsets.

What got us here won't get us there. As a result of functioning within these managerial systems, we've become quite adept at using our managerial mindsets to navigate within highly stable, other-directed circumstances with known pathways, known processes, rule structures, and predictable outcomes. The problem is these conditions are becoming much less prevelant, yet we lack the attitudes and skills required to function effectively within ambiguity, dynamism, and complexity. In other words, the managerial mindset that once enabled us to succeed within highly stable environments is rapidly becoming maladaptive in today's rapidly changing world. We must now learn to function amid volatility, complexity, and ambiguity and develop the capacity to forge ahead, to navigate the future rather than being tethered to the past. We must learn how to learn, unlearn, and relearn on our own. We must learn how to make ourselves useful outside of known systems without the guidance of professional teachers, established curricula, and predictable outcomes. We must learn to understand the distinction between a technical problem and an adaptive challenge. Our changing environment demands a different mindset. In other words, we must learn how to think like entrepreneurs.

To be clear, managerial systems, and the mindsets they produce, are essential for the efficient replication and distribution of useful things. Yet, *because* managerial systems by their very nature are focused on replication and efficiency, and because they are routine and hierarchical, they are not conducive to exploration and experimentation, creative and critical thinking, and other entrepreneurial attitudes, behaviors, and skills. Just as Adam Smith once observed the ways in which routinized labor interfered with the worker's ability to develop problem-solving skills, more recently, the cognitive psychologist Gary Klein described the ways in which the overreliance on rule structures and artificial intelligence interferes with our ability to develop judgment, reason, and expertise. And, as Klein also points out, the more reliant an organization is upon policies and rule structures, the less the likelihood that those who work in such an organization are to have insights.[12] In many ways, the managerial paradigm, with its focus on routinization, replication, and efficiency, is at odds with our individual and collective ability to adapt in the face of change.

> *Because* managerial systems by their very nature are focused on replication and efficiency, and because they are routine and hierarchical, they are not conducive to exploration and experimentation, creative and critical thinking, and other entrepreneurial attitudes, behaviors, and skills.

In many ways, we're trying to solve adaptive challenges with technical skills. At the same time, we cannot solve our problems with the same thinking we used when we created them. If we are to embrace entrepreneurial thinking, we must recognize the extent to which managerial systems that are overreliant on rule structures are likely to inhibit the development of entrepreneurial attitudes, behaviors, and skills. We must recognize the ways in which overly invasive parenting styles that seek to eliminate obstacles may undermine a child's ability to develop the skills necessary to flourish amid complexity and change. Similarly, we must recognize the ways in which formal education systems that are overly reliant on standardized processes and procedures are also likely to inhibit the development of the attitudes and skills necessary for self-direction, exploration, experimentation, and discovery. Sure, we're teaching new skills, but we're not fostering new attitudes; we're not encouraging new methods of teaching and learning; we're not encouraging students to learn, unlearn, and relearn on their own. Technological advancements are happening in leaps and bounds, yet our systems of education and managerial structures remain tethered to nineteenth-century assumptions about learning and work. As parents and educators, we're tasked with preparing the next generation to adapt and thrive in a world we can barely comprehend, to work in jobs that don't yet exist using technologies that have not yet been invented, and yet we're attempting to do so using outmoded methods of teaching that are based on an outdated understanding of motivation and human potential. As Richard Hamming once said, "Teachers should prepare the student for the student's future, not the teacher's past."[13] In many ways, we're stuck because we're steeped in a managerial paradigm that prevents us from adapting in the face of change. As author and management consultant Gary Hamel put it, "Right now, your company has 21st-century internet-enabled business processes, mid-20th-century management processes, all built atop 19th-century management principles."[14] Moreover, systems that rely upon extrinsic rewards and the threat of punishment are likely to undermine the intrinsic desire to learn. Regardless of our position on the organizational ladder, by adhering singularly to these managerial paradigms, we may be blinding ourselves to a vast reservoir of untapped potential.

To be clear, I am not suggesting that we abandon traditional learning methods or management theories. Rather, in today's rapidly changing world, we all need both managerial and entrepreneurial mindsets. One without the other will no longer suffice. In order to do so, we must recognize that the attitudes and skills required to discover useful things are almost entirely distinct from those required to exploit them. Perhaps more importantly, we must recognize that we are not likely to develop entrepreneurial attitudes and skills within managerial systems that are steeped in managerial values and assumptions. If we are to truly understand the entrepreneurial mindset, we must begin by recognizing that we are likely looking at the world through a managerial lens. By illuminating their differences, and exploring the underlying values and assumptions of each, we can better understand not only how to cultivate an entrepreneurial mindset within ourselves but also how to create the conditions that are conducive to both.

Part Two

The Entrepreneurial Process

Chapter Six

In Search of Opportunity

The range of what we think and do is limited by what we fail to notice. And because we fail to notice that we fail to notice, there is little we can do to change; until we notice how failing to notice shapes our thoughts and deeds.

—R. D. Laing

Elias Ruiz is a soft-spoken, unassuming man in his midthirties, a sixth-grade science teacher who likes to bowfish in his spare time. Although he never thought of himself as an entrepreneur, he liked to tinker, and when access to the river near his home posed a challenge, he decided he needed a stable yet lightweight watercraft that would be light enough for him to carry alone, yet stable enough to allow him to stand up while bowfishing. Small kayaks and other collapsible boats were either too cumbersome or not stable enough to accommodate his needs. Unable to find an existing solution, he decided to try to create something on his own.

His original idea was to lash empty two-liter plastic bottles to a sheet of plywood as a way to create a lightweight flotation device that could be easily carried while also providing the stability to support him while standing. Being a science teacher, he engaged his students in the process of determining how many two-liter bottles would be required to provide the buoyancy he needed. To build his first prototype, he used nylon cording to strap a few dozen empty two-liter bottles to a sheet of plywood. He then tested his contraption in his friend's swimming pool to make sure that it would provide the stability and support he needed. Once confirmed, he decided to put his idea to the test by taking his prototype to his favorite fishing spot. What he discovered was that, while lightweight and stable, it was difficult to navigate due to the drag created by the gaps between the plastic bottles. In order to solve this problem, he tried spraying expanding foam between the bottles to eliminate the drag. Back in the river he soon discovered that while the foam did help minimize the drag, it would easily separate from the bottles, thus becoming unreliable while also creating an environmental hazard. After several iterations, he decided to abandon the plywood-and-plastic-bottle method and try using a solid foam slab. Because the foam was only available in four-inch thicknesses, he glued two slabs together to create a platform that would provide the buoyancy and stability he needed. Throughout this trial-and-error process, he would occasionally encounter other fishermen who would ask him how he built his fledgling flotation device.

After an initial trial with his latest iteration, he realized that the foam could easily be damaged by scraping on rocks or submerged trees. Upon further exploration, he found a polymer coating that he could apply with a brush to create a hard outer shell. It wasn't pretty, but it worked, creating a sturdy outer protection while also providing the lightweight stability he was trying to achieve. Eventually, he figured out how to apply the polymer with a spray gun, which made the finish much more even, giving his raft a much more professional, manufactured look. As he was taking his latest iteration to the river for a test run, a stranger asked him, "Where did you *buy* that?"

That was the moment Elias realized that not only would his new invention satisfy his need, but it might also be useful to others who were searching for an inexpensive, lightweight watercraft. To test this assumption, he decided to place a simple ad on social media to see if anyone would actually be willing to pay for his newly developed lightweight raft. Almost immediately he found a paying customer, thus providing initial evidence that his idea was indeed useful to others. From there, he soon found other customers who provided more evidence of the usefulness of his idea. Little did he know that his desire to solve a problem for himself would lead to the creation of a thriving business, all of which he created in his spare time.

To the casual observer, Elias's story appears to be the result of a rare occurrence or random luck. Yet when we look more closely, we begin to see that opportunities exist in our everyday lives, yet they are rarely obvious and therefore difficult to detect with an untrained eye. Instead, they lie hidden in the form of unarticulated, unmet needs. And if we are not attuned to the subtle nature of such needs, we are likely to overlook the opportunities that are hiding in plain sight. In other words, it's not that opportunities are difficult to find; it's that they are easy to overlook.

In many ways, we overlook opportunities because we are viewing the world through a managerial lens. As we discussed in the previous chapter, most of us have become habituated to managerial paradigms whereby we expect to function within known systems with established processes and predictable outcomes. As a result, we've become quite adept at functioning in broad daylight where the path is clear and the rules are well defined yet we're much less likely to be proficient when it comes to operating in the shadows of ambiguity, complexity, and change. As a result, we often overlook the subtle underlying nature of unmet human needs.

Among the many ways in which a managerial mindset can blind us to opportunities is the unconscious filtering process that causes our brains to ignore input deemed non-threatening or irrelevant. One example of this is inattentional blindness, a cognitive phenomenon that occurs when we fail to see something in our visual field because our attention is focused elsewhere, thus "blinding" us to something that is "hiding" in plain sight. A classic example of inattentional blindness is the "invisible gorilla" experiment, in which participants are asked to watch a video of people passing basketballs and to count the number of passes made by a specific team. In the midst of this task, a person dressed as a gorilla walks through the scene, even stops and beats their chest, yet many participants fail to notice the gorilla because their attention is concentrated on counting the passes.[1] Simply put, we all fail to recognize the opportunities that exist in our everyday lives when we are focused on narrowly defined tasks. Pattern recognition also plays a pivotal role in our ability to recognize opportunities. Our brains are inherently wired to make sense of the world around us, but if we lack entrepreneurial experience, our capacity to identify unarticulated, unmet needs is likely to be underdeveloped. Pattern recognition is the cognitive process of matching information from our surrounding environment with information already stored in our long-term memory. This process, which often occurs effortlessly, without conscious awareness, allows us to make sense of our surroundings so that we can make predictions about what to expect in the future. The problem is: pattern recognition requires experience. Everything we see, we understand only through past exposure, which then informs our future perception of the external world. However, without previous entrepreneurial experience, we are much less likely to recognize the opportunities that are hiding in plain sight. This subtle, underlying cognitive process helps to explain why experienced entrepreneurs are able to recognize opportunities that exist even in the most opportunity-constrained environments while those who lack entrepreneurial experience are likely to overlook them even where they abound.

There are many reasons we overlook the opportunities that are hiding in plain sight. In some cases, we do so because we simply do not understand the process that enables everyday entrepreneurs to identify, evaluate, and actualize opportunities. In some cases, we overlook opportunities because we don't realize how small, seemingly insignificant ideas can be transformed into viable products or services that not only create value for others but also for ourselves. Sometimes we overlook opportunities because we are overly focused on our own needs, and by doing so overlook the most basic principle of entrepreneurship: by solving problems—*for others*—we can empower ourselves. While this other-oriented way of thinking may seem counterintuitive, especially for those who may be struggling to get their own needs met, it is the key to exposing opportunities that exist in our everyday lives. This is perhaps the most important insight to be gleaned from the observation of everyday entrepreneurs. It is this subtle cognitive shift that enables them to recognize opportunities that others overlook.

Some overlook opportunities because they are seeking a magic bullet. Many aspiring entrepreneurs set out in search of breakthrough ideas that will lead to overnight success. They mistakenly believe that being entrepreneurial requires a new invention or a great idea that will catapult them to success. In other words, they erroneously assume that in order to win the race, they don't need to be a good jockey; they just need a really fast horse. Yet, in reality, the opposite is more likely to be true. By starting where they are, using what they have, and focusing on what people actually want and need, an ordinary idea can be transformed into a successful enterprise. For everyday entrepreneurs, the jockey is more important than the horse.

In other cases, we overlook opportunities because we stop looking altogether. As we discussed in chapter 5, an unintended consequence of top-down managerial paradigms is that, when we become focused on narrowly defined tasks, we are likely to miss opportunities that exist in our day-to-day lives. In many cases, we develop an external locus of control; without realizing it, we unwittingly assume that our circumstances are beyond our control and that there is nothing we can do to change. As a result, we stop looking for answers; we stop looking for opportunities for growth.

Thus far, I have attempted to illustrate some of the ways in which our mindset can blind us to the opportunities that exist in our everyday lives. In the remainder of this chapter, we will expose some of the common myths and misperceptions that hinder our ability to transform a simple idea into a sustainable success.

Among the most common of these myths is the entrepreneur as a bold visionary willing to risk it all. After all, entrepreneurship, as the saying goes, is about jumping off a cliff and building a parachute on the way down. While this daring narrative might captivate our imagination, for the typical cash-strapped entrepreneur, this screw-it-let's-do-it mentality is likely to lead to disaster. As Drucker observed, if there is anything successful entrepreneurs have in common, it is that they are risk averse.[2]

Another common misconception revolves around the idea of a meticulously planned startup supported by external investments or bank loans. Despite its prevalence in popular culture, this model is, to a large extent, a myth. Nevertheless, many aspiring entrepreneurs are still encouraged to write a carefully crafted business plan detailing every aspect of how their business will unfold, which is then used to pitch outside investors or pursue bank loans. At first glance, this plan-and-pitch approach may seem prudent, yet when we look more closely, it does not reflect the mindset or the methods a typical entrepreneur undertakes. Nor does it make sense when we consider the highly ambiguous and unpredictable nature of the opportunity discovery process itself. As we have seen, even the founders of large, established companies don't start by writing business plans, conducting market research, or pursuing outside funding. What many fail to realize is that the process of *opening* a business is different from that of discovering opportunities. In many ways, this plan-and-pitch approach is more reflective of a managerial rather than an entrepreneurial mindset.

Why Business Planning Doesn't Work

Entrepreneurs are often encouraged to write business plans, not only as a means of evaluating the feasibility of their ideas but also to convince potential lenders or investors to provide the funding necessary to transform their ideas into viable businesses. Such plans typically require the aspiring entrepreneur to describe their idea, the target market, the total market size, the competitive landscape, their competitive advantage, the cost of goods sold, overhead requirements, a break-even analysis, a marketing plan, cash flow projections, as well as the up-front investment required to launch the business. While perhaps daunting, this may seem like a reasonable approach. After all, the nascent entrepreneur must carefully consider every aspect of starting and running their business before they take the leap. And yet, for the inexperienced, unfunded entrepreneur, this plan-and-pitch approach is likely to be misleading and counterproductive, if not premature. Here's why.

For one thing, the road map is not the terrain. Inherent in the plan-and-pitch approach is the assumption that, through careful planning, one can mitigate the risks that are inherent in the entrepreneurial discovery process. After all, as the saying goes, failing to plan is planning to fail. Yet the business planning process tends to overrely on assumptions derived from statistical analysis rather than empirical evidence. And, in their eagerness to secure funding, the aspiring entrepreneur often conflates their beliefs and assumptions with facts. By doing so, they do not account for the highly unpredictable and complex nature of human needs, much less the complexity of the entrepreneurial terrain. As a result, the planning process can easily lull the inexperienced entrepreneur into assuming that the road map *is* the terrain and that, through careful planning, they can accurately assess the customer's needs and thereby determine the correct course of action. However, for the vast majority of everyday entrepreneurs, the road map rarely matches the terrain.

Formal business planning relies on a know-before-you-go strategy

85

that is reflective of a managerial mindset. This way of thinking, which is known as causal reasoning,[3] is typical of managers in large, established organizations who are tasked with launching new products and services, acquiring new businesses, or opening new locations in order to expand their reach. These circumstances tend to be relatively clear, with little ambiguity, and the organizations typically have ample resources to pursue such actions. Within these circumstances, this plan-and-pitch way of thinking is prudent, as these types of undertakings tend to be large-scale initiatives where the cost of failure is high, the customer is likely to be known, the brand is well established, and the opportunity being pursued is therefore quantifiable through careful planning and in-depth research. In other words, with causal reasoning, the manager is able to draw from the past in order to predict the future. Within such circumstances, this approach makes perfect sense. Yet for the typical inexperienced, unfunded entrepreneur, none of these conditions are likely to exist. As such, this know-before-you-go strategy is maladaptive within the highly ambiguous, resource-constrained circumstances that typify those of an inexperienced, unfunded entrepreneur. After all, the opportunities they pursue are likely to be small niche opportunities that are latent and therefore cannot be identified through careful planning and in-depth research. Any data that does support their initial ideas are likely to be speculative at best. Moreover, the fact that a particular product or service represents a multibillion-dollar market does not equate to evidence that a business that offers that particular product or service will succeed. Besides, in the beginning, the typical entrepreneur is not likely to have a track record, much less an established brand. As such, the formal planning process undertaken by large, established companies is not effective as a means of evaluating an opportunity for the typical entrepreneur.

Another reason formal planning is counterproductive is that good ideas rarely arrive fully formed. Rather than a flash of insight, good ideas are more likely to evolve over time through an ongoing process of experimentation and adaptation. This process is only possible through extended interactions with the people whose problems the entrepreneur is trying to solve. Formal planning often hinders this crucial process by giving the entrepreneur a false sense of certainty that they can accurately predict what their customers truly want and need. More often than not, those who do succeed do so in ways they did not anticipate when they began. When it comes to entrepreneurship, the first trick is not to fool yourself.

The business planning process is not only encouraged as a means of evaluating an idea but also to persuade potential investors or lenders of the viability of the idea. As such, the nascent entrepreneur may be inclined to exaggerate the upside potential while downplaying unknown variables and risks. What's worse, inexperienced entrepreneurs, eager to chart their own path, are likely to become highly vulnerable to a host of cognitive biases that can lead them astray. In the process of trying to persuade others, they can easily fool themselves.

When it comes to entrepreneurship, the first trick is not to fool yourself.

The idea that it takes money to make money is among the most persistent myths of entrepreneurship. Inherent in the plan-and-pitch approach is the assumption that outside investment or bank loans are necessary for starting a business. The aspiring entrepreneur mistakenly assumes that the only thing that stands in the way of launching a successful business is the funding required to actualize their idea. Yet there is an important distinction to be made between *opening* a business, which is a managerial function, and discovering opportunities, which is an entrepreneurial function. While opening a business with known products and services, paying customers, and an established brand may indeed require significant up-front investment, the opportunity discovery process does not. In fact, access to resources can easily thwart the opportunity discovery process by encouraging a build-it-and-they-will-come mentality, which, for the typical entrepreneur, is more akin to gambling than it is a practical method for identifying, evaluating, and actualizing opportunities.

Here again, the difference between success and failure lies in the underlying assumptions of which the nascent entrepreneur is not likely to be aware. Those who set out to *open* a business tend to embrace a managerial mindset, approaching their startup as if it were simply a smaller version of an established organization. They unwittingly assume (or are told) that through careful planning they now have the correct course of action and that access to funding is the only obstacle that stands in their way when, in fact, access to resources is likely to thwart rather than facilitate the opportunity discovery process. Those who do manage to secure outside funding are likely to set about executing their plan, which they are now likely to assume to be the correct course of action. In many cases, they mistake the approval of a funder as further validation of their ideas. As such, they are more likely to become committed to a particular course of action. In their eagerness to execute their plan, they unwittingly overlook the need for ongoing experimentation and adaptation, which is not only vital for validating their idea but also for minimizing the risks. In their eagerness to chart their own path, they become highly susceptible to confirmation bias, which causes them to ignore evidence that conflicts with their original plan. Not only that, with their focus on the execution of their plan, they are more likely to suffer from inattentional blindness, thus overlooking adjacent opportunities that they were not aware of when they began. In other words, they attempt to start at the first break point, unwittingly assuming they can avoid the iterative, experimental opportunity discovery process through careful planning and in-depth research. Here again, this way of thinking is reflective of a managerial rather than an entrepreneurial mindset. (See figure 6.1.)

Those who set out to *open* a business tend to embrace a managerial mindset, approaching their startup as if it were simply a smaller version of an established organization.

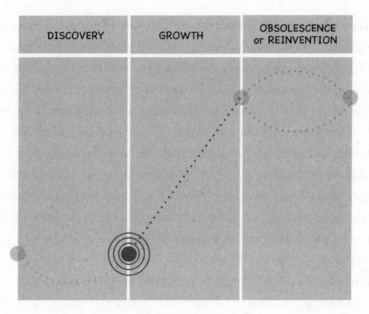

Figure 6.1 | Opening a Business

For example, had I managed to secure outside funding for my gutter-cleaning business, I would likely have purchased a truck and ladders and hired a graphic designer to create a logo that I would then apply to my truck, embroider on my shirts, and use in other promotional materials. By doing so, I would have not only burdened myself with unnecessary debt, but I would also have likely ignored requests to solve other adjacent problems for my customers, thus blinding myself to the greater opportunity that would eventually unfold. Moreover, seeing my steadfast commitment to gutter cleaning, my customers may have been less inclined to ask me to solve other problems, which ultimately revealed a much greater latent opportunity that no amount of planning could have predicted.

The truth is that the vast majority of new ideas (and nascent entrepreneurs) do not warrant outside investment or bank loans when they begin. Therefore, the plan-and-pitch methods embraced by high-growth entrepreneurs or corporate managers are maladaptive for everyday entrepreneurs. In the beginning, both the feasibility of the idea and the capability of the entrepreneur are likely to be unknown, specifically for the everyday entrepreneur. At this stage, they are still trying to figure out what their customers actually want. And the best way to do that is through customer interaction rather than careful planning and the pursuit of outside funding. Not only does the business plan have the potential to mislead the aspiring entrepreneur in terms of the feasibility of their idea, but it also presumes the capability of the entrepreneur. As Y-Combinator cofounder Jessica Livingston once said, "At the beginning of his career, an actor is a waiter who goes to auditions."[4] The same is true for everyday entrepreneurs; in the beginning they are explorers and experimenters who test their ideas on a small scale as a way to figure out what works.

"At the beginning of his career, an actor is a waiter who goes to auditions."

What many fail to realize is that a lack of resources actually works to the advantage of the nascent entrepreneur. Without access to resources, they are not in a position to take significant risks. Instead, they are forced to micro-experiment, to start at a point where they are using whatever discretionary resources they have to test their ideas on real customers and learn from the results. Because they are strapped for cash, they are forced to focus on a customer discovery process, which provides a vital feedback loop that enables them to zero in on unarticulated, unmet needs that cannot be detected through formal planning and in-depth research. And, over time, through continuous experimentation and adaptation, new insights are gained, and in many cases, greater unforeseen opportunities emerge.

When undertaking entrepreneurial initiatives, one must acknowledge the tacit nature of unmet needs as well as the unpredictable nature of the terrain. People are not always consciously aware of what they want. Therefore, they can only demonstrate their needs through their willingness to pay for a particular solution. Just as we may not be aware of the level-three values and assumptions that influence our behavior, we may also not be aware of our unmet needs. And in many cases, opportunities lie hidden not in the functional dimension of unmet needs, but in the deeper social and emotional dimensions. Indeed, many of the entrepreneurs I've interviewed succeeded not because they invented anything new but because they delivered an existing product or service exceptionally well by focusing intently on their customers' needs.

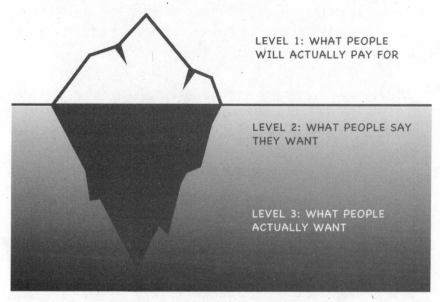

LEVEL 1: WHAT PEOPLE WILL ACTUALLY PAY FOR

LEVEL 2: WHAT PEOPLE SAY THEY WANT

LEVEL 3: WHAT PEOPLE ACTUALLY WANT

Figure 6.2 | The Unconscious Nature of Unmet Needs

It's not that planning isn't prudent; it's that it's premature. The know-before-you-go logic inherent in the business planning process may become useful once the first break point has been reached (see figure 6.2), and both the idea and the entrepreneur have been validated through an ongoing iterative experimental discovery process. After all, evidence of usefulness in the form of paying customers is not only evidence of the feasibility of an idea but also the capability of the entrepreneur. For the typical entrepreneur, permission to succeed does not come from the opinions of investors, lenders, or industry experts; rather, permission to succeed comes from those whose problems they endeavor to solve.

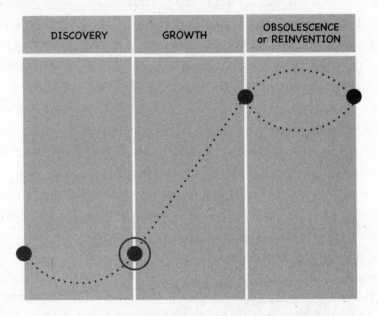

Figure 6.3 | Planning Becomes Prudent

As we discussed in previous chapters, the managerial mindset is essential for replicating and distributing useful things, yet the abilities required to discover new opportunities are almost entirely distinct from those required to exploit them. The great insight from Land's theory of transformation is that the attitudes and skills required to succeed in the growth phase are maladaptive to the discovery phase.[5] Similarly, the attitudes and skills required to succeed in traditional learning environments are very different from those required to discover new opportunities. Among the most important insights to be gleaned from the study of everyday entrepreneurs is that the managerial mindset is maladaptive to the opportunity discovery process. Whereas careful planning, access to resources, and industry experience are essential for success during the growth phase, they can easily hinder our ability to discover new opportunities. At the same time, the lack of planning, resources, and experience can thwart our ability to grow. Here again, the key to survival is to know which phase we are in so that we know which rules to apply. Yet, if all we have is a hammer, everything looks like a nail.

For the typical entrepreneur, permission to succeed does not come from the opinions of investors, lenders, or industry experts; rather, permission to succeed comes from those whose problems they endeavor to solve.

In many ways, business planning and the pursuit of outside funding is a classic example of treating an adaptive challenge as if it were a technical problem. It comes as no surprise as most of us learned how to function within highly stable, other-directed environments and are therefore unlikely to be familiar with the entrepreneurial processes and methods required to solve adaptive challenges. In other words, if all we have is a managerial mindset, all our problems tend to look like technical problems.

For the typical entrepreneur, permission to succeed does not come from the opinions of investors, lenders, or industry experts; rather, permission to succeed comes from those whose problems they endeavor to solve.

When we look beyond the popular myths and common misperceptions to explore the mindset and the methods of everyday entrepreneurs, we begin to demystify the process that enables them to recognize, evaluate, and actualize opportunities that others overlook. We see that they possess no extraordinary dispositional traits. We see that they are not gamblers who undertake significant risks. Nor are they careful planners who conduct in-depth market research. Instead, they are simply embracing a way of thinking and acting that is unfamiliar to the managerial mindset. Rather than taking big risks or engaging in careful planning and in-depth market research, these everyday entrepreneurs learn by doing through a process of experimentation and adaptation. In other words, they embrace a *go-in-order-to-know* strategy that enables them to tease out latent opportunities with minimal risk. This way of thinking, which is known as "effectual reasoning,"[6] stands in stark contrast to the *know-before-you-go* strategies that are characteristic of managerial systems. And it is precisely this go-in-order-to-know strategy that enables them not only to identify opportunities that others overlook but also to reduce the cost of failure through micro-experimentation and adaptation, thereby creating an effective feedback loop that increases the probability that a connection will be found. In doing so, they not only minimize the risk, but their ideas become much more robust. At the same time, paying customers not only provide evidence of usefulness but also a source of revenue (and credibility) on which the aspiring entrepreneur can build, thus eliminating the need for up-front investment or bank loans.

When Elias Ruiz set out to create a lightweight watercraft suitable for bowfishing, he did not start by writing a business plan and pursuing outside funding. Nor did he quit his job or mortgage his home. Instead, he created a minimally viable product with nothing more than a sheet of plywood and a few dozen two-liter bottles. Through trial and error, he eventually emerged with a viable solution. Using social media, he was able to quickly confirm that others were interested in his ideas. From there, he was able to repeat his experiment while reinvesting whatever he earned to transform his fledgling idea into a viable business, all of which he accomplished in his spare time. Ted Moore followed a similar path, using whatever discretionary time and resources he could find to test his ideas on a small scale before going all in.

To be clear, everyday entrepreneurs like Elias Ruiz and Ted Moore are not likely to embrace these strategies because they are particularly clever or because they possess any particular personality traits. This go-in-order-to-know strategy is a predictable pattern of behavior that is brought about by a combination of cognitive, motivational, and situational factors of which the entrepreneurs themselves are largely unaware. In fact, most of the entrepreneurs I interviewed were dismayed to learn that they had actually followed a predictable pattern of beliefs and behaviors.

Nevertheless, their journeys all began with a simple assumption: "It is up to me to figure out how to make myself useful to others, and by doing so, I can empower myself." The compelling nature of this assumption enabled them to become optimally engaged, while it was the highly ambiguous, resource-constrained nature of the opportunity discovery process itself that gave rise to the iterative experimental nature of their behavior.

In many ways, entrepreneurial behavior is merely an expression of the self-actualizing tendency that resides within us all. When we look at the attitudes and behaviors that drive everyday entrepreneurs, we see an organic process at play. It is the process by which an organism orients itself to unfamiliar terrain—not through careful planning or taking big risks—but by trying lots of things on a small scale as a way to see what works. Through this process of micro-experimentation and adaptation, the organism not only creates a vital feedback mechanism that enables it to navigate unfamiliar terrain but also greatly increases the probability that a connection will be found. While these examples draw from the observations of traditional everyday entrepreneurs, one need not have an interest in starting a business to embrace the mindset and the methods that enable them to succeed.

As Adam Smith observed at the dawn of the Industrial Revolution, we all live by exchanging useful things,[7] and in that way, we all have customers in one form or another, be they employers or employees, colleagues or constituents, students or subscribers, donors, followers, or paying customers. The question we should all be asking ourselves is: *What is the useful thing that we exchange? And with whom do we exchange it?* In the next chapter we will explore the mindset and the methods that enable everyday entrepreneurs to do just that.

Chapter Seven

The Method Behind the Madness

Every practice rests on theory, even if the practitioners themselves are unaware of it.

—Peter Drucker[1]

A t first glance, the seemingly haphazard behavior of a typical entrepreneur appears disorganized and chaotic, the result of unbridled enthusiasm, a lack of experience, or a propensity for risk. Yet, when we begin to look more closely at the behavior of those who manage to succeed, predictable patterns of thought and behavior begin to emerge. Amid the chaos, we begin to see a method behind the madness; a method of which the entrepreneurs themselves are largely unaware. As we discussed in previous chapters, the everyday entrepreneurs I observed weren't taking big risks, nor were they writing business plans or pursuing outside investment or bank loans. In this chapter, we will not only examine the processes and methods that enable everyday unfunded entrepreneurs to recognize, evaluate, and bring new ideas to life, but we'll also explore the situational factors that cause them to think and act as they do.

Let's begin by defining entrepreneurship as the self-directed pursuit of opportunities to create value for others. At its essence, it is a discovery process by which an individual or small group of individuals searches for a connection with their environment by making themselves useful to other humans. It is an informal learning process that typically occurs outside of known systems, without the guidance of a professional teacher, a predetermined path, or a predictable outcome. This type of discovery learning is nothing new. In fact, discovery is an organic learning process for which we are innately designed. In many ways, discovery learning is reflective of the ways in which humans have learned for hundreds of thousands of years, long before we had written language, classrooms, or professional teachers, much less the internet, audiobooks, and YouTube. Unlike formal learning, discovery learning relies on our innate curiosity, a desire to explore, to pursue our interests, and to discover knowledge through our own efforts.

To be clear, the knowledge acquired through discovery learning does not need to be new to mankind. After all, the entrepreneur as an inventor is largely a myth. What is important is that nascent entrepreneurs acquire knowledge for themselves through the use of their own intellect by following their own interests and by developing their own abilities. In the process of doing so, they discover not only new opportunities that exist in their everyday lives but also the untapped potential within themselves.

The opportunity discovery process is an evidence-based process. As we discussed, opportunities exist in virtually any circumstance, yet they are often latent, unarticulated, and complex, and are therefore difficult to detect. More importantly, opportunities are also easy to misdiagnose. Countless failures can be attributed to those who set out to solve a problem they either don't understand or, worse, a problem that doesn't exist. The ability to properly identify, evaluate, and actualize latent opportunities requires the aspiring entrepreneur to embrace an evidence-based learning process, one that requires them to balance enthusiasm with skepticism and doubt.

On one hand, the opportunity discovery process can activate a powerful motivational force that can enable ordinary people to accomplish extraordinary things. And yet, at the same time, this same motivational force can also leave the aspiring entrepreneur extremely vulnerable to all manner of cognitive biases that can easily lead them astray. As such, they must learn to balance their enthusiasm with a healthy dose of skepticism so as to minimize the likelihood of fooling themselves. Without realizing it, they do so by embracing an evidence-based approach, one that very closely resembles the scientific method.

THE OPPORTUNITY DISCOVERY PROCESS

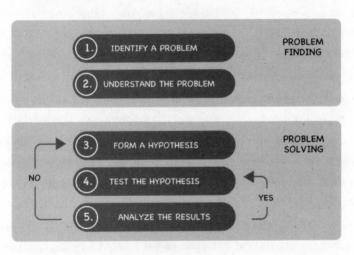

Figure 7.1 | The Opportunity Discovery Process

Science, my boy, is made up of mistakes, but they are mistakes which it is useful to make, because they lead little by little to the truth.

—Jules Verne[2]

Like the scientific method, the opportunity discovery process begins with the awareness of a potential problem or unmet need. This leads to the formulation of a hypothesis for a potential solution to that problem. This hypothesis then leads to a series of small-scale experiments that enable the aspiring entrepreneur to test their ideas and learn from the results. To be clear, a hypothesis is simply a guess made on the basis of limited evidence as a starting point for further investigation. If the experiment fails, the entrepreneur is forced to reconsider their original hypothesis and start anew. If the experiment is a success, they continue to repeat it in a way that provides further insights into the true nature of their customers' needs. In many cases, it also provides a source of revenue they can use to grow. For example, had I not found a paying customer on the first day of my gutter-cleaning experiment, in all likelihood I would not have continued to pursue the idea. However, because I did find a paying customer, I confirmed my original hypothesis that people in wealthier neighborhoods would indeed be willing to pay to have their gutters cleaned. In other words, I found evidence of the usefulness of my idea. The point here is that, like scientists, everyday entrepreneurs tend to approach their ideas as assumptions rather than facts. By embracing this iterative, experimental, evidence-based process, they not only reduce the likelihood of failure but also greatly increase their probability of success. Yet they embrace this experimental, evidence-based strategy not because of specialized knowledge or unique personality traits but because of situational factors that prompt them to think and act this way. After all, in the beginning, the typical entrepreneur is likely to be highly motivated yet inexperienced. Nevertheless, their behavior reveals a very effective process for identifying, evaluating, and actualizing opportunities that exist in our everyday lives. As you will see in part 3, "The Entrepreneurial Situation," this process is not only effective for starting and growing new businesses, but as a framework for thinking that has become essential for individuals, organizations, and communities to adapt and thrive in a changing world. Broadly speaking, the opportunity discovery process gleaned from the observation and analysis of hundreds of everyday entrepreneurs occurs in three distinct phases: exploration, experimentation, and replication. Each of these three phases occurs within the discovery phase described in Land's transformation theory explained in chapter 2 (see figure 7.2). In the remainder of this chapter, we will explore these phases in greater detail.

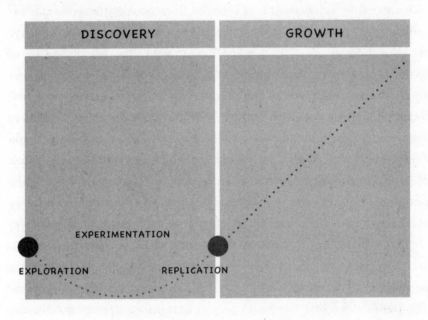

Figure 7.2 | *Three Phases of Discovery*

Phase One: Exploration

Exploration is the problem-finding phase, which is probably the most important aspect of the opportunity discovery process. It is also the most likely to be overlooked. As we now know, the basic premise of entrepreneurship is that, by solving problems for others, we can empower ourselves. As such, the opportunity discovery process begins with finding problems to be solved. Many aspiring entrepreneurs fail because they overlook this fundamental first step. Without realizing it, they offer a solution without properly diagnosing the problem they are trying to solve. In some cases, they fail because they set out to solve a problem for themselves. Rather than creating value for others, they unwittingly pursue opportunities to create value for themselves. They embrace entrepreneurship as a way to make money or to escape the tyranny of an unfulfilling career, yet they unwittingly prioritize their own needs over those of their potential customers. By doing so, they blind themselves to the opportunities that lie hidden in the form of unarticulated, unmet needs. Some entrepreneurs, like Elias Ruiz, stumble into opportunities by initially trying to solve a problem for themselves, yet in the process of doing so, they realize that others may also be interested in the solution they initially created for themselves. Others, like Ted Moore or Dawn Halfaker, deliberately set out in search of problems to be solved. The point here is that the problem-finding process requires problem-finding skills.

Among the most overlooked aspects of the entrepreneurial mindset is empathy—the ability to understand the needs of others from *their* perspective. And not only the functional dimensions of their needs but also the deeper social and emotional dimensions, which are often deeply rooted level-three needs that cannot otherwise be identified through careful planning and in-depth research. In fact, they are often needs that a potential customer might struggle to articulate. Unearthing these unarticulated needs begins with observation and inquiry, the willingness to understand before being understood. In order to increase the probability of success, the entrepreneur must accurately diagnose the problem *before* prescribing a solution. Understanding the problem from the perspective of their potential customers also helps the aspiring entrepreneur stimulate new ideas, stories, and images that generate new possibilities for action. In many ways, it is the emphasis on solving problems for others that enables them to recognize opportunities that are hiding in plain sight. While prioritizing the needs of others over our own immediate interests may seem counterintuitive, it is an essential aspect of the hidden logic that enables everyday entrepreneurs to identify opportunities that others overlook.

Phase Two: Experimentation

This is the problem-solving phase of the opportunity discovery process whereby the aspiring entrepreneur tests their ideas in the real world. Once the entrepreneur has made a reasonable attempt to understand the problem from their potential customer's perspective, they are now in a better position to propose a solution. Rather than going all in on their ideas, the lack of resources forces them to adopt an interactive, experimental process that enables them to test their assumptions on a small scale and learn from the results. They typically do so by using whatever available resources they have to build a minimally viable product or service (MVP/S). Like a scientist designing a laboratory experiment, the aspiring entrepreneur develops a low-fidelity version of their idea that enables them to test their ideas in the real world. For example, Ted Moore started in his spare time with a few hundred dollars and some used office equipment he found in the trash. When it came to gutter cleaning, my minimally viable product was a borrowed ladder strapped to the roof of my car.

For the everyday entrepreneur, the value of creating an MVP/S is difficult to overstate. First and foremost, it enables them to engage in an iterative experimental process that provides a vital feedback loop, which enables them to learn what their customers actually want and need. Because they have limited access to resources, they must focus their efforts on finding evidence of the usefulness of their ideas—evidence in the form of paying customers, that is. Here again, this enables the aspiring entrepreneur to identify latent opportunities that cannot otherwise be identified through careful planning and in-depth research. And by paying for the product or service, their early customers not only provide empirical evidence of the usefulness of their ideas, but a source of revenue that enables the fledgling entrepreneur to grow. The MVP/S becomes a mechanism that provides vital feedback not only for testing the feasibility of an idea but also for developing the capabilities of the entrepreneur. Yet, here again, the everyday entrepreneur is likely to behave this way not because they are a brilliant strategist who understands the principles of risk management but because they simply do not have access to the resources that would enable them to go all in. While some might perceive the lack of resources as a barrier, when we begin to understand the iterative, experimental nature of the opportunity discovery process, we can see how it becomes an advantage for the everyday entrepreneur. More importantly, it provides a powerful example of the ways in which the situation influences our behavior in ways of which we might not be aware.

> The MVP/S becomes a mechanism that provides vital feedback not only for testing the feasibility of an idea but also for developing the capabilities of the entrepreneur.

In some cases, the problem-finding and problem-solving phases can be accomplished simultaneously using an MVP/S, but only when the cost of developing an MVP/S is low. For example, rather than spending an inordinate amount of time and effort talking to potential customers to understand the problem from their perspective, the aspiring entrepreneur can develop an MVP/S to accomplish both simultaneously. After all, what people say they value (level two) and what they actually value (level three) and are therefore willing to pay for (level one) are often two different things. (See figure 7.3.)

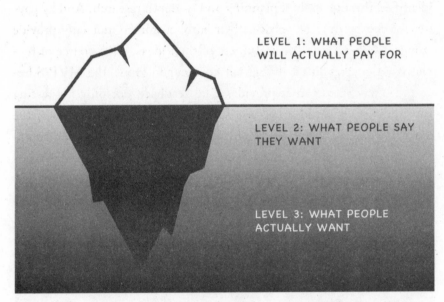

Figure 7.3 | The Unconscious Nature of Unmet Needs

However, one should only combine the problem-finding and the problem-solving phases when the cost of building an MVP/S is inexpensive and easy to produce. Economists refer to this as an "affordable loss." Simply put, the cost of building an MVP/S is correlated to the amount of time one should spend in the problem-finding phase; the higher the cost of building an MVP/S, the more time and effort one should invest in diagnosing the problem from the customer's point of view. (See figure 7.4.)

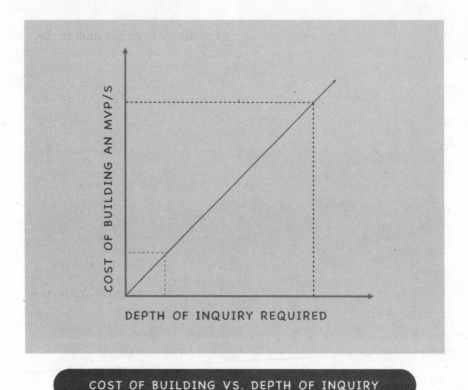

COST OF BUILDING VS. DEPTH OF INQUIRY

Figure 7.4 | Depth of Inquiry vs. Cost of Building an MVP/S

For example, when starting Clio Muse Tours as a way to promote the world's cultural heritage using modern technology, Yiannis Nikolopoulos and his partners spent months interviewing potential customers before building their MVP/S. They did so because building an MVP/S would require months of programming that would be potentially wasted if they misdiagnosed their customers' needs. They realized that the more time spent diagnosing the problem from their customers' perspective, the greater the likelihood their solution would actually fulfill a need. While they were certainly passionate about the problem they were trying to solve, they also realized how easy it would be to develop a product or service that their customers may not want or need. As a result of their painstaking diligence, their business became successful almost from the minute they launched.

In my case, a low-cost MVP/S—a borrowed ladder—became a powerful mechanism that enabled me to test my idea quickly and inexpensively, in a way that would enable me to learn from the results. Since the experiment was a low-cost undertaking, there would be no point in spending time conducting market research or surveying potential customers to determine whether or not they would pay to have their gutters cleaned. It was simply more effective to test my idea on real customers and learn from the results. By doing so, I not only found evidence of usefulness, but I also soon found greater opportunities that I could not have foreseen when I began.

By reducing their ideas to the most basic experiment possible and using only whatever discretionary time and effort they have to experiment in the margins, risking only what they can afford to lose (discretionary time, effort, resources), aspiring entrepreneurs greatly increase the probability that a connection will be found before either giving up or going broke. If there is one thing I've learned from everyday entrepreneurs, it is that testing an idea with an MVP/S is a much more effective strategy than writing business plans, pursuing outside funding, or taking big risks.

Phase Three: Replication

Once an idea has been validated through customer interaction, the aspiring entrepreneur now begins the third phase of the opportunity discovery process, where they must replicate and refine their ideas in a way that is sustainable, both in terms of creating value for others and capturing value for themselves. Once evidence of usefulness has been established, what remains to be determined is whether the idea is sustainable: Are there enough potential customers to support a profitable business? Does the entrepreneur care enough about the idea to invest the time and energy required to sustain their ideas? Perhaps more importantly, is the nascent entrepreneur capable of transforming their ideas into a sustainable endeavor that creates value for others while also capturing value for themselves? The opportunity discovery process not only determines the feasibility of the product or service being offered but also the capability of the entrepreneur. At this point, the entrepreneur is nearing the first break point, where the rules for survival will change from those required to discover the opportunity to those required for sustainability and growth. Yet they have not reached the break-even point. Before they are ready to fully commit to their ideas, there is more work to be done. This is where many begin to engage with other, more experienced entrepreneurs who can share their knowledge while also providing ongoing encouragement and support.

The opportunity discovery process not only determines the feasibility of the product or service being offered but also the capability of the entrepreneur.

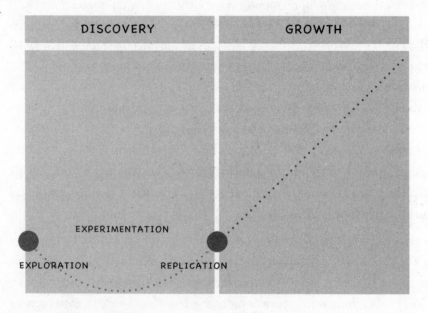

Figure 7.5 | Three Phases of Discovery

For many, this can be the most difficult stage of the entrepreneurial process, as they must now learn how to communicate the value of their ideas to others. What they may not realize is that, contrary to what many believe, good ideas rarely sell themselves. Enamored of their ideas, inexperienced entrepreneurs often fall prey to the myth of overnight success, expecting customers to beat a path to their door. Unfortunately, this is rarely the case. A few early customers often create a false positive that is difficult to replicate in a sustainable way. The more likely scenario is that it will take considerable time and effort to transform a minimally viable product or service into a sustainable endeavor.

The truth is, achieving wide-scale adoption of a new product or service takes time—*sometimes a very long time*. People are generally wary of new products and services, specifically those offered by unfamiliar people or unknown brands. Unless they are in great pain or have an urgent need, most will wait to see others adopt a new product or service before they buy in.

The diffusion of innovations, first introduced by sociologist Everett Rogers, explains the process by which new ideas are adopted by a given group. What Rogers found is that those who are successful in introducing new ideas do so by identifying the early adopters who typically represent a small subset of a given group who are eager to try new things.[3] Over time, these early adopters become the "activating agents" who then communicate the value of the new product or service to their more reluctant peers. (See figure 7.6.) This process of diffusion provides a helpful framework for aspiring entrepreneurs who might otherwise assume that customers will beat a path to their door.

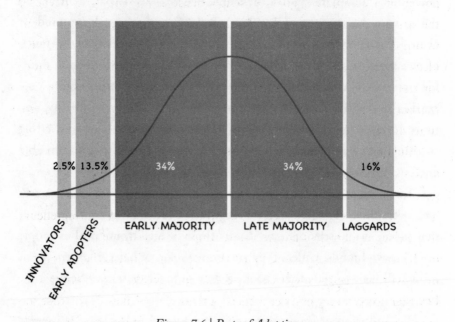

Figure 7.6 | Rate of Adoption

Many of the entrepreneurs I interviewed managed to accelerate this process by delighting their customers. They built a reputation for being reliable and responsive, going out of their way to satisfy their customers, which then helped accelerate the spread of their ideas through word of mouth. Over time, this relentless focus on their customers not only exposed adjacent opportunities that were initially unforeseen but also accelerated their path to sustainability and growth. For most, success was not a result of the inventiveness of their ideas but in the delivery of whatever product or service they offered. Here again, for the typical entrepreneur, being a good jockey is much more important than having a fast horse.

For most, success was not a result of the inventiveness of their ideas but in the delivery of whatever product or service they offered.

The time and effort it takes to transform an idea into a sustainable endeavor also speaks to the importance of intrinsic motivation and the power of a compelling goal. Absent a sense of urgency and purpose, the nascent entrepreneur is less likely to endure the challenges inherent in bringing new ideas to life. More importantly, in the beginning, new ideas are fragile, and, like children, they need strong advocates in order for them to become fully actualized. It is also important to remember that many aspiring entrepreneurs undertake such endeavors in their spare time, enabling them to minimize the risk before going all in.

The opportunity discovery process gleaned from the observation and analysis of hundreds of everyday entrepreneurs reveals a highly effective process for identifying, evaluating, and actualizing opportunities that exist in our day-to-day lives. Yet, it is a "process" of which the entrepreneurs themselves are largely unaware. Most simply assumed that they were flying by the seat of their pants. What they did not realize is that it was the *situation* that was causing them to think and act like entrepreneurs. As Drucker noted, every practice rests on a theory, regardless of whether the practitioners themselves are aware of it. In the case of the everyday entrepreneur, it is a combination of their circumstances—*as well as their subjective interpretation of their circumstances*—that necessitates the development of entrepreneurial attitudes, behaviors, and skills.

The study of everyday entrepreneurs provides a powerful example of the ways in which our behavior is influenced by who we are—the person—and the situation. In order to truly understand entrepreneurial behavior and the mindset that ensues, we must acknowledge the conditions that necessitate the development of entrepreneurial attitudes, behaviors, and skills. We must acknowledge the underlying cognitive and motivational factors within the person, as well as the situational factors that cause them to think and act as they do. While these factors are often subtle and easy to overlook, they shed important light on the true underlying causes of entrepreneurial behavior.

The desire to fulfill human needs through our own efforts creates a powerful motivational force that acts upon the aspiring entrepreneur in ways of which they themselves may not be aware. Without realizing it, the self-directed pursuit of opportunities to create value for others activates their imagination and engages their faculties in ways that other-directed, routinized tasks do not. By pursuing their interests and developing their abilities in ways that contributed to the greater good, everyday entrepreneurs inadvertently tap into the most potent form of human motivation. And by doing so, they become optimally engaged. What many fail to realize is that it is the compelling nature of the goal itself, combined with the self-directed, highly ambiguous, and resource-constrained nature of the entrepreneurial *situation* that causes them to think and act like entrepreneurs.

Because they do not have access to resources, everyday entrepreneurs are likely to pursue niche opportunities that are not suitable for outside funding. As a result, they channel their efforts into figuring out what their customers actually want and need by developing a minimally viable product or service. By doing so, they inadvertently create a powerful mechanism that not only enables them to test their ideas in the real world but also generate revenue on which to build. Moreover, the limited availability of resources prevents them from impulsively adopting a "build-it-and-they-will-come" strategy that is much more likely to fail. While they may not realize it, the lack of resources also works to their advantage by forcing them to take small, calculated risks that increase the likelihood that a connection will be found. Perhaps the most important lesson of all is that, when it comes to opportunity discovery, even those who do have access to resources should act as if they don't.

The self-directed nature of the entrepreneurial process also affects the aspiring entrepreneur in ways that other-directed learning and work do not. Over time, through a series of small wins, their competency and sense of self-efficacy begin to grow, and, as a result, the size and scope of their goals also grow. Self-direction cultivates a greater sense of autonomy and control, thus encouraging them to make choices that lead to a sense of ownership and responsibility. Self-direction also contributes to higher levels of intrinsic motivation as the nascent entrepreneur is driven by their own interests and passions, making their pursuits more enjoyable and fulfilling. Naiveté can also work to the advantage of the everyday entrepreneur as their lack of experience often enables them to see things and try things that experts or those who are less motivated may not.

> Perhaps the most important lesson of all is that, when it comes to opportunity discovery, even those who do have access to resources should act as if they don't.

The Fundamental Attribution Error

To the uninitiated, the entrepreneurial mindset appears to be driven by personality traits when it is simply a result of underlying cognitive, motivational, and situational factors that are acting upon the individual in ways that they themselves are not likely to be aware. Without realizing it, the nascent entrepreneur stumbles into the conditions—the perfect storm, if you will—of human motivation, whereby they satisfy their basic psychological needs for autonomy, competency, and relatedness. In the beginning they are highly motivated yet inexperienced. Most have no idea what they are doing, yet the compelling nature of their goals engages their faculties in ways that enable them to not only break from the past but also to access problem-solving abilities that are otherwise not available. Over time, through a series of small wins, their sense of self-efficacy begins to increase. As their self-efficacy increases, the size and scope of their goals also begin to increase. Because they are self-directed, and because they are solving problems for others, they unwittingly satisfy their innate need for autonomy, competency, and relatedness, which are the three essential nutrients for lifelong learning, growth, and psychological well-being. Slowly but surely, over time, the entrepreneurial mindset emerges—*as a result*—rather than the cause of their behavior. They succeed not in spite of their circumstances but because of them. Quite literally, by creating value for others, they empower themselves.

The observation and analysis of everyday entrepreneurs sheds important light on the ways in which cognitive, motivational, and situational factors can empower ordinary people to accomplish extraordinary things. Clearly, we can now see that their advantage lies not in their personality traits but in their subjective interpretation of their circumstances and the deeply held, taken-for-granted assumptions of which they are largely unaware. We can also see that the entrepreneurial mindset emerges as a result—rather than the cause—of entrepreneurial behavior. Therefore, the only way to develop an entrepreneurial mindset is by undertaking an entrepreneurial project of your own.

Chapter Eight

A Project of Your Own

One learns by doing a thing; for though you think you know it,
you have no certainty until you try.
                                        —Sophocles

As a high school student, Steve Orlando was unsure of what his future might hold. He came from a large working-class family and had watched his father struggle to make ends meet. By all accounts, he was a mediocre student who showed no particular interest in school. During the summers, he worked as a caddie at a local country club, where he was exposed to people who seemed to be better off, some of whom were entrepreneurs. Although he was still in his teens, he connected with the idea that he, too, could one day start a business of his own.

As a senior in high school, he decided to start an office-cleaning business in his spare time. With a vacuum cleaner and a few flyers, he set out in search of customers by knocking on office doors. Yet, his enthusiasm soon began to wane as no one seemed to be willing to give him a chance. Perhaps they had no need of his services, or perhaps his prices were too high, or maybe his target customers were reluctant to allow a high school student unsupervised access to their office. To Steve, the answers to these questions were not clear. Nevertheless, he persisted, knocking on every door that he could on weekends and after school. Little did he know that his persistence would expose an opportunity that he did not foresee. As he continued to canvass local business owners, he encountered a commercial property manager who had a different problem to be solved; rather than cleaning his office, he needed someone to tidy up the parking lots of several shopping centers and strip malls they managed. It was a simple problem that did not require any specialized knowledge or major investment in equipment; they simply needed someone to pick up any litter, sweep the sidewalks, and empty the trash bins several times per week. Steve jumped at the opportunity, and his first business was born. And, by going above and beyond, his business soon began to take off. With nothing more than a broom and some trash bags, he earned $40,000 in his first year, all of which he accomplished in his spare time.

As we have learned throughout this book, being entrepreneurial does not require big ideas, access to venture capital, or an advanced degree. Nor does it require us to quit our jobs, drop out of school, or undertake significant financial risks. It does, however, require us to reappropriate some modicum of our discretionary time and attention toward the self-directed pursuit of opportunities to create value for others. Doing so requires us to set out in search of problems to be solved. In other words, it requires us to undertake an entrepreneurial project of our own. In chapter 2, we redefined the term *entrepreneurship* in a way that anyone can embrace. In this chapter, we will explore the entrepreneurial process in a way that anyone can undertake.

The Entrepreneurial Mindset Challenge

The Entrepreneurial Mindset Challenge is a simple idea: take some small amount of money, an amount that you can easily afford to lose, say, five dollars or fifty dollars, and turn it into ten times that amount by making yourself useful to others. Like a video game, you can take this challenge as far as you like. For example, if you start with five dollars, you can stop at fifty dollars. Or you can try to get to the next level by transforming fifty dollars into five hundred dollars, and so on. The idea is to reappropriate some small amount of your discretionary time, effort, and resources in a way that demonstrates usefulness to others while also providing some benefit to you. The central idea is that it should be simultaneously challenging and rewarding. It should also be fun.

The purpose of the Entrepreneurial Mindset Challenge is not to start a business or to make money per se, although it can certainly be used to accomplish either of those goals. The purpose of the mindset challenge is to create the conditions that will enable you to develop entrepreneurial attitudes and skills. Whatever money is earned should be considered evidence—not only of the usefulness of your ideas but of your capabilities as an entrepreneur. Whether you start with five dollars or fifty is not important. The point is to start with a small amount of money that you can afford to lose, not only as a way to limit the scope of potential failure, but also to create the resource-constrained circumstances that will necessitate the development of entrepreneurial attitudes and skills. The ability to transform five dollars into fifty dollars in your spare time is both an actionable and an achievable first step that anyone can undertake. Whatever your initial investment, the first milestone is to multiply your initial investment by a factor of ten. Once you have reached that goal, you can assess what you have learned to determine how to proceed to the next level, which is to again multiply your earnings by a factor of ten. The further you progress, the more you will develop entrepreneurial attitudes, behaviors, and skills, which you can then apply to other areas of your life, be they personal, professional, or community oriented. In subsequent chapters, we will explore ways to adapt this method in a variety of personal and professional domains.

The Entrepreneurial Mindset Challenge is designed as a learning opportunity to be undertaken in your spare time. It is a straightforward process derived from the observation of everyday entrepreneurs just like you. While this process is similar to the lean startup methodologies embraced by high-growth entrepreneurs, the assumptions inherent in the Entrepreneurial Mindset Challenge are those of everyday entrepreneurs who may not have novel ideas, access to venture capital, or years of experience in their chosen field. Therefore, it is an opportunity discovery process that anyone can undertake, regardless of where they start. Here again, by limiting yourself to a fixed amount of time and money, you are deliberately creating the constraints that necessitate the development of an entrepreneurial mindset. Hopefully, the stories of others who started with little or nothing will increase your willingness to try.

The Entrepreneurial Mindset Challenge is a simplified version of the opportunity discovery process. While it is assumed that you are engaging in this challenge as a learning experience, it is designed to guide you through all three phases of the opportunity discovery process. The extent to which you pursue the challenge is entirely up to you. Hopefully, you will persist until you have experienced some modicum of success. If done properly, it will be a rewarding experience that pushes you beyond the limits of your current capabilities.

While some may choose to go it alone, others may be more comfortable undertaking the challenge with a partner, a colleague, or a friend. Where some may embrace it as a fun way to earn extra money in their spare time, others may do so strictly as a means of professional development, to solve a particular problem or to fulfill a particular need. Regardless of your motives, the point is that you should begin with an end in mind. After all, it is the compelling nature of the goal itself that will activate your imagination and engage your faculties in ways that will ultimately enable you to strengthen your entrepreneurial abilities. The more compelling the goal, the more likely you are to persist in the face of setbacks and failures that you are certain to encounter along the way.

Don't wait for the perfect idea. Start with something simple that isn't too far out of reach. It's good to think big, although for the purpose of this exercise, it is essential that you start small to increase the likelihood that you will get traction before you give up. Over time, as your entrepreneurial efficacy evolves, the scope of your ideas will also likely expand. For example, I don't have a particular affinity for gutter cleaning, yet because I did not have access to resources, I was forced to try things I might not otherwise be willing to try. By doing so, I soon found a greater opportunity that was much better suited to my interests and abilities. The point here is that you don't need the perfect idea to get started; you just need to start. In other words, you need to *go in order to know*. Like any aspiring entrepreneur, in the beginning you are likely to be enthusiastic but inexperienced, yet through trial and error you will begin to develop entrepreneurial attitudes and skills. In the remainder of this chapter, we will introduce the Opportunity Discovery Canvas as a tool to help guide you through the problem-finding and problem-solving phases of the opportunity discovery process.

Please visit GarySchoeniger.com to download the Entrepreneurial Mindset Advantage Opportunity Discovery Guide.

The Opportunity Discovery Canvas is designed to guide you through the process of identifying and evaluating opportunities that exist in your everyday life. It represents a distillation of the mindset and methods gleaned from hundreds of everyday entrepreneurs. Following the basic premise of the scientific method, it is a simple tool that can help you discover new opportunities while also preventing you from fooling yourself. (See figure 8.1.)

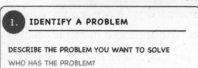

OPPORTUNITY DISCOVERY CANVAS

1. IDENTIFY A PROBLEM

DESCRIBE THE PROBLEM YOU WANT TO SOLVE

WHO HAS THE PROBLEM?

DESCRIBE THE NEED IN 3 DIMENSIONS.

HOW ARE THEY CURRENTLY SOLVING IT?

WHERE ARE THE CURRENT SOLUTIONS FALLING SHORT?

2. UNDERSTAND THE PROBLEM

RECOGNIZE THE CUSTOMER'S PERSPECTIVE

TEST YOUR ASSUMPTIONS BY INTERVIEWING POTENTIAL CUSTOMERS.

CONSIDER THE COST OF BUILDING AN MVP/S AGAINST THE DEPTH OF INQUIRY.

REMEMBER THAT SAMPLE SIZE MATTERS.

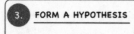
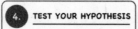

3. FORM A HYPOTHESIS

DESCRIBE A POSSIBLE SOLUTION

HOW WILL YOUR SOLUTION SOLVE THE PROBLEM?

HOW IS YOUR SOLUTION DIFFERENT FROM EXISTING SOLUTIONS?

4. TEST YOUR HYPOTHESIS

DESIGN A MINIMALLY VIABLE PRODUCT OR SERVICE

HOW CAN YOU CREATE A LOW-COST EXPERIMENT TO TEST YOUR ASSUMPTIONS?

WHAT WILL YOU CONSIDER AS EVIDENCE OF USEFULNESS?

5. ANALYZE THE RESULTS

DID YOUR EXPERIMENT CONFIRM YOUR HYPOTHESIS?

IF YES, CONTINUE TO REPLICATE, LEARN, AND GROW. BEWARE OF FALSE POSITIVES.

IF NO, RETURN TO STEP THREE TO REVISE YOUR HYPOTHESIS. REMEMBER THAT SAMPLE SIZE MATTERS.

Figure 8.1 | Opportunity Discovery Canvas

Think of the Opportunity Discovery Canvas as a low-fidelity, back-of-the-napkin guide that enables you to sketch out your initial assumptions, test your ideas, and learn from the results. Here the term *canvas* implies that the process is iterative, creative, and experimental. It also implies that your initial assumptions are likely to be flawed. The canvas is intended to be used as a guide rather than a step-by-step formula. The questions are merely suggestions or things to consider as you navigate the highly ambiguous resource-constrained nature of the entrepreneurial terrain. After all, the Entrepreneurial Mindset Challenge is a self-directed process that requires you to think for yourself. As such, it is best to think of the Opportunity Discovery Canvas as if it were a compass rather than a detailed map.

Here's how it works: Each box contains basic guidelines and a few basic questions (see figure 8.1). You will notice that the upper half of the canvas is concerned with the problem-finding phase of the opportunity discovery process while the bottom half is concerned with the problem-solving phase. Although many of these concepts have appeared in earlier chapters, they are so fundamental to the opportunity discovery process that they are worth repeating here as they will greatly increase the probability of success. Eventually, you won't need the opportunity discovery canvas, as the process will eventually become a (level three) habitual way of thinking. Keep in mind that when undertaking the opportunity discovery process, there are two key variables to be determined: the feasibility of your ideas and your capability as an entrepreneur. Let's begin by finding a problem to be solved. (See figure 8.2.)

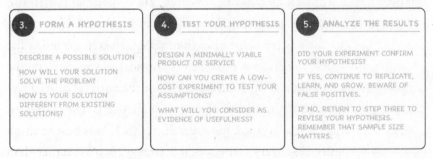

Figure 8.2 | Opportunity Discovery Step 1

Step One: Identify a Problem

As a single father of two young children, John Kendale struggled to make ends meet. His work as a line cook in a local restaurant left him very little discretionary income, much less free time. Yet somewhere, in the back of his mind, he knew there must be a better way to live. One afternoon, while taking a break on the front steps of his apartment building, he watched a young couple struggling to move furniture from their apartment into a rented truck. Being a good neighbor, he offered to assist. After helping load the truck, he realized they would also need help unloading the truck once they arrived at their new apartment, which was only a few miles away, and he offered to assist at the other end as well. Needless to say, his neighbors were extremely grateful, offering to pay him with free pizza and a generous tip. At that moment, he connected with an idea: when people move, finding a rental truck is easy enough, yet they need help loading and unloading the truck. That was his problem-finding moment. Now he had to figure out how to test his idea in the real world. He did that by printing a few hundred flyers, which he then distributed by going door-to-door. Within an hour, his phone began to ring, and a new business idea was born. Not only did John recognize the opportunity by solving problems for others, but he also developed a low-cost MVP/S that enabled him to test his idea quickly to determine if there was actually a need. The moral of the story is that if you aren't looking for problems to solve, you will likely overlook opportunities that are hiding in plain sight.

Problem finding is perhaps the most important aspect of the opportunity discovery process, and yet it is also the most overlooked. Many aspiring entrepreneurs start with an idea for a product or a service without really understanding the problem they are trying to solve. Without realizing it, they prioritize their own needs over others' and by doing so, they not only increase the likelihood of failure, but they also blind themselves to the adjacent opportunities that are often hiding in plain sight. In other words, it is the other-oriented focus that enables everyday entrepreneurs to identify opportunities that others overlook.

Sometimes, a subtle shift in perspective can make a big difference in our lives. An entrepreneur once told me, "The whole world is looking for a great idea, and they trip over one about three times a week. The only thing you need to do to find a great idea is to go through your daily life and wait for something bad to happen and ask yourself, *How could I have avoided that?* Then ask yourself the entrepreneurial question, which is, *How could I help other people avoid that problem?*" In other words, looking for problems to be solved is the key to recognizing opportunities that exist in our everyday lives. It is also a key component of the entrepreneurial mindset.

What problems do you want to solve? Think about problems, frustrations, and unmet needs you have encountered in your own life. Ask yourself: *Why does this happen? How could this be avoided? Why are we doing it this way? Do other people experience the same problem? How does it affect their lives? How would their lives improve if the problem were solved?* Identifying problems requires an empathic perspective, to be observant, to ask questions, and to understand the social and emotional dimensions of human needs. Once we learn to see the world from this perspective, opportunities begin to emerge. And remember, you don't need to invent anything new. Simply start by thinking about what other people need.

Once you have identified a potential problem to be solved, document your basic assumptions about the problem as outlined in step one. For example, had I used the Opportunity Discovery Canvas for my gutter-cleaning idea, it might have looked something like this:

- **Describe the problem you want to solve.** Clogged rain gutters can cause roof leaks, ice damage, and other problems.
- **Describe the people who have the problem.** People who live in upper-middle-class neighborhoods with large houses.
- **How are they currently solving the problem?** They may do it themselves or they may not do it at all.

- **Where are the current solutions falling short?** Inconvenient, unreliable, dangerous ...

Remember, these are assumptions. The answers to each of these questions represent your initial assumptions rather than foregone conclusions or established facts. When it comes to opportunity discovery, "I'm not sure" is an acceptable answer. In fact, it may be an indication that you have identified a missing piece of the puzzle that is yet to be resolved. Now it's time to "get out of the building" in order to understand the problem from your customer's point of view.

Step Two: Understand the Problem

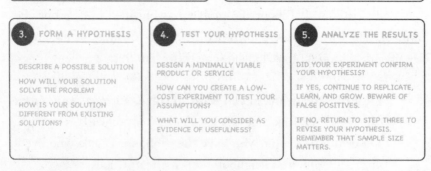

Figure 8.3 | Opportunity Discovery Step 2

The next step of the process is to better understand the problem from the perspective of those who have the problem—your potential customers. One way to begin is to interview people who have the problem you are trying to solve. Think of this as a customer discovery process. This process is similar to the background research phase of the scientific method. This enables you to understand the problem from a potential customer's point of view so as to determine whether the problem is worth solving. After all, if it isn't really a problem, then it might not be worth solving. This customer discovery process also enables you to gauge the scope of the problem to determine if there are enough potential customers to justify the effort of providing a solution. In other words, the process of understanding the problem from the customer's perspective enables you to determine the depth and the breadth of the problem you are trying to solve.

Talking to potential customers can be an intimidating experience, but it can also be very rewarding. Although you may be tempted to do this through social media, there are distinct advantages to face-to-face interaction, as body language, eye contact, and other nonverbal cues often provide important clues. And, as Steve Orlando discovered, face-to-face interaction often reveals adjacent opportunities that you may not have anticipated. Ideally, you can undertake this process with a colleague or a friend, whereby one of you asks questions while the other observes and takes notes. You can also use the "five whys" technique, repeatedly asking "why" in order to better understand the deeper social and emotional dimensions of your customer's need. Remember, you're looking and listening for emotion and frustration as the key to discovering unmet needs. The more people you interact with, the greater the likelihood that an opportunity will unfold.

To be clear, it's okay to start with an idea for a product or service. In fact, many entrepreneurs do just that. Yet, before you go running headlong into an idea, it is important to remember that, at this stage of the process, you are in listening mode rather than pitching mode, which can be particularly difficult for those who already have an idea and are eager to convince others of its value. By going into pitch mode prematurely, you might just miss an adjacent opportunity that is hiding in plain sight. The point here is that, while it's okay to start with a solution, it is important that you take the time to understand the problem from the perspective of potential customers. If you don't understand the problem you are trying to solve from the perspective of those who have it, you may be missing the first principle of entrepreneurship, which is about solving problems *for others* as a way to empower yourself. (See figure 8.4.)

OPPORTUNITY DISCOVERY CANVAS

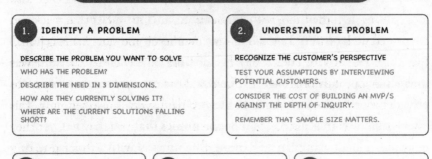

1. IDENTIFY A PROBLEM	**2. UNDERSTAND THE PROBLEM**
DESCRIBE THE PROBLEM YOU WANT TO SOLVE	RECOGNIZE THE CUSTOMER'S PERSPECTIVE
WHO HAS THE PROBLEM?	TEST YOUR ASSUMPTIONS BY INTERVIEWING POTENTIAL CUSTOMERS.
DESCRIBE THE NEED IN 3 DIMENSIONS.	CONSIDER THE COST OF BUILDING AN MVP/S AGAINST THE DEPTH OF INQUIRY.
HOW ARE THEY CURRENTLY SOLVING IT?	REMEMBER THAT SAMPLE SIZE MATTERS.
WHERE ARE THE CURRENT SOLUTIONS FALLING SHORT?	

3. FORM A HYPOTHESIS	**4. TEST YOUR HYPOTHESIS**	**5. ANALYZE THE RESULTS**
DESCRIBE A POSSIBLE SOLUTION	DESIGN A MINIMALLY VIABLE PRODUCT OR SERVICE	DID YOUR EXPERIMENT CONFIRM YOUR HYPOTHESIS?
HOW WILL YOUR SOLUTION SOLVE THE PROBLEM?	HOW CAN YOU CREATE A LOW-COST EXPERIMENT TO TEST YOUR ASSUMPTIONS?	IF YES, CONTINUE TO REPLICATE, LEARN, AND GROW. BEWARE OF FALSE POSITIVES.
HOW IS YOUR SOLUTION DIFFERENT FROM EXISTING SOLUTIONS?	WHAT WILL YOU CONSIDER AS EVIDENCE OF USEFULNESS?	IF NO, RETURN TO STEP THREE TO REVISE YOUR HYPOTHESIS. REMEMBER THAT SAMPLE SIZE MATTERS.

Figure 8.4 | Opportunity Discovery Pause

Empathy and emotional intelligence are the secret weapons of the everyday entrepreneur. One way to identify opportunities that exist in our daily lives is to look beneath the functional dimension of unmet needs to understand the deeper social and emotional dimensions. In the same way that people can know more than they are able to tell, they can also need more than they can say. As such, it is important to consider not only what people say but also what they might think and feel in relation to the problem they are trying to solve.

> Empathy and emotional intelligence are the secret weapons of the everyday entrepreneur.

At the age of eighteen, Brian Scudamore was looking for a way to pay for college. One day, he noticed a beat-up old truck that offered trash hauling services, which someone had haphazardly announced in spray paint on the side. Not only was the truck in rough shape; the two men inside also looked as though they, too, had seen better days. "I looked at that truck and connected with an idea: I should buy my own truck and start hauling junk," Brian told me. His idea was that if he had a reasonably clean truck and was dressed in a professional manner, he could earn enough money to pay for college by going door-to-door, offering to haul away unwanted junk. His assumption was that people might have a need for junk removal, yet they might be reluctant to hire such a rough-looking crew. Without realizing it, he was not only considering the functional dimensions of his customers' needs but also the deeper social and emotional dimensions. Within a week's time, with $1,000 he had saved, he bought a used pickup truck, printed some flyers, and started knocking on doors. Little did he know that his simple idea would become 1-800-GOT-JUNK?, a global brand that now generates more than one hundred million dollars in revenue per year.

The point here is that you don't need to be an inventor to be an entrepreneur. Like Brian Scudamore, many build thriving businesses by delivering an existing product or service in a way that addresses an unmet need. The moral of the story is: when it comes to discovering new opportunities, emotional intelligence is the key.

Step Three: Form a Hypothesis

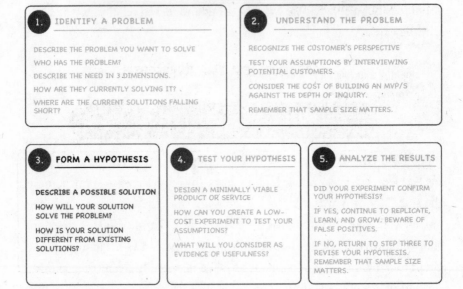

OPPORTUNITY DISCOVERY CANVAS

1. IDENTIFY A PROBLEM

DESCRIBE THE PROBLEM YOU WANT TO SOLVE

WHO HAS THE PROBLEM?

DESCRIBE THE NEED IN 3 DIMENSIONS.

HOW ARE THEY CURRENTLY SOLVING IT?

WHERE ARE THE CURRENT SOLUTIONS FALLING SHORT?

2. UNDERSTAND THE PROBLEM

RECOGNIZE THE CUSTOMER'S PERSPECTIVE

TEST YOUR ASSUMPTIONS BY INTERVIEWING POTENTIAL CUSTOMERS.

CONSIDER THE COST OF BUILDING AN MVP/S AGAINST THE DEPTH OF INQUIRY.

REMEMBER THAT SAMPLE SIZE MATTERS.

3. FORM A HYPOTHESIS

DESCRIBE A POSSIBLE SOLUTION

HOW WILL YOUR SOLUTION SOLVE THE PROBLEM?

HOW IS YOUR SOLUTION DIFFERENT FROM EXISTING SOLUTIONS?

4. TEST YOUR HYPOTHESIS

DESIGN A MINIMALLY VIABLE PRODUCT OR SERVICE

HOW CAN YOU CREATE A LOW-COST EXPERIMENT TO TEST YOUR ASSUMPTIONS?

WHAT WILL YOU CONSIDER AS EVIDENCE OF USEFULNESS?

5. ANALYZE THE RESULTS

DID YOUR EXPERIMENT CONFIRM YOUR HYPOTHESIS?

IF YES, CONTINUE TO REPLICATE, LEARN, AND GROW. BEWARE OF FALSE POSITIVES.

IF NO, RETURN TO STEP THREE TO REVISE YOUR HYPOTHESIS. REMEMBER THAT SAMPLE SIZE MATTERS.

Figure 8.5 | Opportunity Discovery Step 3

This is the problem-solving phase of the opportunity discovery process. Once you have made a reasonable attempt to understand the problem from the customer's perspective, you are now in a much better position to design a solution that meets their needs. In some cases, like that of Steve Orlando, the customer will tell you exactly what they want and need. In other cases, you may need to develop a hypothetical solution using what you have learned. Keep in mind that good ideas rarely come as a flash of insight. Nor do they always arrive fully formed. In fact, many aspiring entrepreneurs start out with bad ideas, but over time, through micro-experimentation and adaptation, better ideas emerge. The opportunity discovery process occurs through ongoing interactions with those whose problems we endeavor to solve. And besides, opportunity discovery is an error-based learning process, and, unlike traditional learning, changing your assumptions is a sign of progress rather than failure. After all, the best time to realize that your assumptions are wrong is before you have invested a significant amount of time, effort, and resources into a solution that nobody really wants.

Step Four: Test Your Hypothesis

OPPORTUNITY DISCOVERY CANVAS

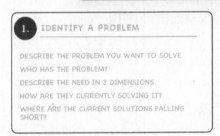

1. IDENTIFY A PROBLEM

DESCRIBE THE PROBLEM YOU WANT TO SOLVE
WHO HAS THE PROBLEM?
DESCRIBE THE NEED IN 3 DIMENSIONS.
HOW ARE THEY CURRENTLY SOLVING IT?
WHERE ARE THE CURRENT SOLUTIONS FALLING SHORT?

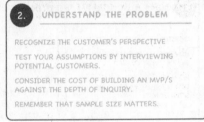

2. UNDERSTAND THE PROBLEM

RECOGNIZE THE CUSTOMER'S PERSPECTIVE
TEST YOUR ASSUMPTIONS BY INTERVIEWING POTENTIAL CUSTOMERS.
CONSIDER THE COST OF BUILDING AN MVP/S AGAINST THE DEPTH OF INQUIRY.
REMEMBER THAT SAMPLE SIZE MATTERS.

3. FORM A HYPOTHESIS

DESCRIBE A POSSIBLE SOLUTION
HOW WILL YOUR SOLUTION SOLVE THE PROBLEM?
HOW IS YOUR SOLUTION DIFFERENT FROM EXISTING SOLUTIONS?

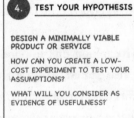

4. TEST YOUR HYPOTHESIS

DESIGN A MINIMALLY VIABLE PRODUCT OR SERVICE
HOW CAN YOU CREATE A LOW-COST EXPERIMENT TO TEST YOUR ASSUMPTIONS?
WHAT WILL YOU CONSIDER AS EVIDENCE OF USEFULNESS?

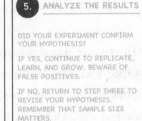

5. ANALYZE THE RESULTS

DID YOUR EXPERIMENT CONFIRM YOUR HYPOTHESIS?
IF YES, CONTINUE TO REPLICATE, LEARN, AND GROW. BEWARE OF FALSE POSITIVES.
IF NO, RETURN TO STEP THREE TO REVISE YOUR HYPOTHESIS. REMEMBER THAT SAMPLE SIZE MATTERS.

Figure 8.6 | Opportunity Discovery Step 4

Interviewing potential customers is a great way to understand the problem you are trying to solve, but the feedback gleaned from these interviews must not be seen as actual evidence of the usefulness of your idea. Remember, the nature of a mindset is such that what we say we want and what we are willing to pay for it may be two different things. Therefore, the best way to prove your concept is to create an MVP/S that will enable you to test your idea quickly and learn from the results. After all, the opportunity discovery process is an evidence-based process whereby a paying customer represents evidence of the usefulness of a product or service. As we discussed, evidence of usefulness may come in other forms of *buy-in*, yet for the purposes of the Entrepreneurial Mindset Challenge we'll use currency as the metric for evaluating the usefulness of an idea. Almost any idea can be reduced to a minimally viable product or service that can then be used as a means of testing the idea on paying customers while also generating revenue that will enable you to grow.

For example, Diana Bezanski and her partner, Jeffrey Tautrim, dreamed of owning a restaurant, yet they didn't have the money to fund their dream. As full-time photographers, they also lacked the culinary experience that might attract outside investment or justify a bank loan. Instead, they began with a minimally viable product for a restaurant: a few hot plates and a pop-up canopy, testing their recipes one serving at a time at farmers markets and local fairs. Over the course of the next several years they worked tirelessly on weekends to perfect their recipes while also generating the extra income that would ultimately enable them to fulfill their dream of opening a restaurant. By the time they were in a position to quit their jobs and go all in, they had not only proven their concept but also generated enough income to give them a solid start. And, because they were listening to their customers, they had also developed a reputation that all but ensured their success. As we have seen throughout this book, the idea that it takes money to make money is largely a myth. Here again, the lack of resources works to the advantage of everyday entrepreneurs, forcing them to test their ideas on a small scale and learn from the results. It also prevents them from taking big risks. Therefore, even if you do have access to resources, you should act as if you don't.

Sample size matters. Whether you start by interviewing potential customers or you start with a low-cost MVP/S, it is important to recognize that the more interactions you have with potential customers, the more likely you are to discover an opportunity. In my case, what started as gutter cleaning quickly evolved into a much greater opportunity that I did not initially foresee. Some, like Steve Orlando, knock on dozens of doors before they find their first customer, while others, like John Kendale, get a more immediate response. The point is to avoid giving up prematurely. For the purpose of the Entrepreneurial Mindset Challenge, I suggest setting a minimum goal of fifty interactions with potential customers before pausing to reevaluate your assumptions and assess what you have learned. Remember, people will show you what they want and need; you just have to look.

Step Five: Analyze the Results

OPPORTUNITY DISCOVERY CANVAS

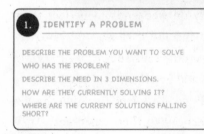

1. IDENTIFY A PROBLEM

DESCRIBE THE PROBLEM YOU WANT TO SOLVE

WHO HAS THE PROBLEM?

DESCRIBE THE NEED IN 3 DIMENSIONS.

HOW ARE THEY CURRENTLY SOLVING IT?

WHERE ARE THE CURRENT SOLUTIONS FALLING SHORT?

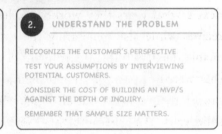

2. UNDERSTAND THE PROBLEM

RECOGNIZE THE CUSTOMER'S PERSPECTIVE

TEST YOUR ASSUMPTIONS BY INTERVIEWING POTENTIAL CUSTOMERS.

CONSIDER THE COST OF BUILDING AN MVP/S AGAINST THE DEPTH OF INQUIRY.

REMEMBER THAT SAMPLE SIZE MATTERS.

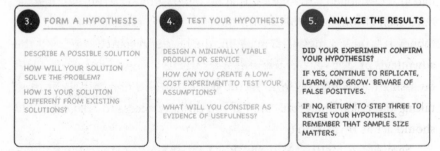

3. FORM A HYPOTHESIS

DESCRIBE A POSSIBLE SOLUTION

HOW WILL YOUR SOLUTION SOLVE THE PROBLEM?

HOW IS YOUR SOLUTION DIFFERENT FROM EXISTING SOLUTIONS?

4. TEST YOUR HYPOTHESIS

DESIGN A MINIMALLY VIABLE PRODUCT OR SERVICE

HOW CAN YOU CREATE A LOW-COST EXPERIMENT TO TEST YOUR ASSUMPTIONS?

WHAT WILL YOU CONSIDER AS EVIDENCE OF USEFULNESS?

5. ANALYZE THE RESULTS

DID YOUR EXPERIMENT CONFIRM YOUR HYPOTHESIS?

IF YES, CONTINUE TO REPLICATE, LEARN, AND GROW. BEWARE OF FALSE POSITIVES.

IF NO, RETURN TO STEP THREE TO REVISE YOUR HYPOTHESIS. REMEMBER THAT SAMPLE SIZE MATTERS.

Figure 8.7 | Opportunity Discovery Step 5

Now that you have interacted with potential customers, what did you learn? Did the outcomes of your experiment confirm or invalidate your assumptions? Or did you land somewhere in between? If you have no evidence of usefulness, do not be discouraged. After all, the opportunity discovery process is an error-based learning process that requires you to not only learn from your mistakes, but also to persist in the face of setbacks and failures. Expecting to get it right on your first attempt is probably a mistake. If the outcomes did not match your expectations, it's time to revisit your original assumptions and start anew. At this point, all you have lost is perhaps a small amount of money and a few hours of your spare time. But do not overlook what you have gained. By getting out of the building and talking to potential customers, you may have overcome the greatest hurdles of all, which are inertia, fear, and self-doubt.

Hopefully your customer interactions led to new insights that will now enable you to modify your assumptions or alter your idea in a way that better fits their needs. The nature of the opportunity discovery process is such that micro-experiments lead to micro-failures, and micro-failures lead to insights that will ultimately enable you to tease out latent opportunities that cannot otherwise be seen. Perhaps this is what Thomas Edison meant when he said, "I have not failed. I've just found 10,000 ways that won't work."[1]

At the same time, persistence can be a double-edged sword. On one hand, the willingness to persist through challenges and setbacks is vital to the success of any entrepreneur. On the other hand, blindly clinging to an idea can also prevent us from understanding what people actually want and need. As the legendary investor David Morgenthaler once told me, "The world doesn't give a damn about what you want to do." Here again, as an aspiring entrepreneur, you are searching for opportunities to create value for *others*. And the first rule is that you must not fool yourself. Those who fall in love with their ideas are perhaps the easiest to fool.

The true power of the opportunity discovery process lies in its iterative, experimental nature, which is distinct from the traditional methods of learning to which so many have become inured. Most notably, traditional learning punishes failure, whereas opportunity discovery demands it. After all, micro-failures lead to the insights that ultimately enable us to discover the hidden opportunities that exist in our everyday lives. Because these micro-experiments are done with minimal investment of time and money, we can pursue opportunities for learning and growth with minimal risk. In other words, the benefits of micro-experimentation far outweigh the costs. The willingness to try things on a small scale and learn from the results is essential to developing entrepreneurial attitudes and skills.

On the other hand, if your initial experiments confirmed your hypothesis, proceed with caution, as you may not be out of the woods just yet. You may have encountered a false positive whereby you stumble across a chance opportunity that cannot be easily replicated in a sustainable way. In other words, you may perceive an opportunity where none exists. Like the scientific method, it is important to replicate the experiment, not only as a means of gaining valuable feedback and reducing risk, but also as a means of generating revenue on which you can build. Through continuous experimentation and adaptation, you may also find an adjacent opportunity you did not initially foresee. In other words, your first idea may not be your best idea, yet through observation, experimentation, and adaptation, opportunities are likely to unfold. The more you are able to replicate your experiments, the more likely you are to eliminate such risks. The point is: proceed with caution, as a few early adopters may not be evidence enough to go all in.

Regardless of your initial outcomes, the idea is to continue the process of experimentation and adaptation until you have managed to validate the usefulness of an idea. It is important to remember that identifying and evaluating opportunities is just the beginning. Once sufficient evidence of the usefulness of your idea has been established, you must then learn to replicate and refine your idea while also learning how to communicate the value of your product or service to others in a sustainable way. This is where we begin to understand the importance of learning to be a good jockey rather than relying on a fast horse. As you will see, good ideas rarely sell themselves.

Among the most pernicious myths of entrepreneurship is that of overnight success. While some may indeed stumble upon an idea that leads to overnight success, such cases are—*by far*—the exception rather than the norm. The truth is that, for most, overnight success takes a long time. And getting there requires psychological resilience, which is not only the ability to recover quickly from setbacks and failure but also to benefit from them in terms of learning and growth.

Delighting your customers is the best way to increase the probability of success. As we have seen, the key to success for the everyday entrepreneur often lies not in the inventiveness of their ideas but in their delivery of a product or service that already exists. As Ted Moore put it, "If I ain't nothin' but a broom sweeper, I'm gonna be the best broom sweeper there is."[2] It is just such an attitude that can enable anyone to succeed. Delighting your customers, whoever they might be, will also increase the likelihood that unforeseen opportunities will emerge.

Above all, beware of the story you tell yourself. The first step in developing resilience is to challenge irrationally pessimistic self-talk that reinforces self-limiting beliefs. Those who learn to optimistically interpret failure and setbacks gain significant advantage over those of equal or greater ability who unwittingly interpret the same situation in a more pessimistic way. As the psychologist Martin Seligman put it, "Failure also can occur when talent and desire are present in abundance but optimism is missing."[3] Simply put, the entrepreneurial mindset advantage requires us to be mindful of our internal thought processes so that we can develop the resilience that will ultimately enable us to succeed.

Creating an entrepreneurial support network is another way to increase the probability of success. Once you begin to gain some traction, surrounding yourself with other, more experienced entrepreneurs is among the most impactful things you can do to increase the probability of success. Experienced entrepreneurs exist in every community: in small towns, big cities, urban centers, and everywhere in between. And they have the knowledge and experience that can help bring your ideas to life. In many cases, they are willing, if not eager, to help. Sometimes all it takes is the courage to ask. Start by attending networking events or visiting a coworking space. Or simply start a conversation with a local business owner by asking, "How did you get started in this business?" and see where the conversation goes. While this can be intimidating, especially for those who are starting from scratch, in many cases you are likely to encounter others who have overcome hardships similar to your own.

The Entrepreneurial Mindset Challenge represents a simplified version of the processes and methods gleaned from the observation of hundreds of everyday entrepreneurs. They were people just like you: they were schoolteachers and broom sweepers, former felons and military veterans, side hustlers and stay-at-home moms. In the beginning, they had no idea what they were doing, but over time, through a combination of experimentation, adaptation, and persistence, they figured out how to create value for others, and by doing so, they empowered themselves. Perhaps the greatest mindset advantage of all is that they set out to create a future that looked different from their past.

You can do the same. By solving problems for others, you can empower yourself. Look for problems to solve. After all, problems are opportunities in disguise. Get out of your comfort zone and try things. Learn how to learn, unlearn, and relearn, on your own. Start where you are and use what you have to create a minimally viable product or service that will enable you to test your ideas. Pay attention to the deeper dimensions of human needs. People will show—rather than tell—you what they want and need. Build a reputation for being reliable and responsible; show up early and stay late. Opportunities will find you. Create a deliberate support network of other, more experienced entrepreneurs who can provide critical guidance and support. Above all, be mindful of the story you tell yourself.

The purpose of the Entrepreneurial Mindset Challenge is not necessarily to start a business but as a means of personal or professional development. While some may use the Entrepreneurial Mindset Challenge to start a business, my hope is that you will persist long enough to recognize that you are indeed capable of being innovative and entrepreneurial. The process of transforming fifty dollars into five hundred can be a life-changing experience that opens our eyes to new possibilities as well as our own untapped potential. Once that happens, you will naturally want to encourage others to do the same.

Part Three

The Entrepreneurial Situation

Chapter Nine

Unlocking the Entrepreneurial Potential in Others

Your diamonds are not in far distant mountains or in yonder seas; they are in your own backyard, if you but dig for them.
—Russell H. Conwell, "Acres of Diamonds"

As a government employee, Rob Vigil had no interest in entrepreneurship. He worked as a sanitation supervisor for the city of Albuquerque—a stable job with a pension, good healthcare, and a living wage. Despite the stability his job provided, Rob had a nagging feeling that he was becoming complacent or that he was somehow falling behind. Nonetheless, when his boss suggested that he attend our Ice House Entrepreneurial Mindset Training, which was being offered at a local community college, his response was indifferent: "I'm not really a classroom guy," he told his boss. After all, he wasn't a great student in high school, and he had never been to college. Besides, why on earth would a city government employee like him need to learn how to think like an entrepreneur? In spite of his reluctance, his boss insisted that he attend. Like many who are asked to take part in mandatory training, Rob did everything he could to let the instructor know that he did not want to be there and had no intention of participating in the class. Then, suddenly, something clicked for Rob when the instructor, Tom Darling, introduced the idea of micro-experimenting as means of exploration and growth. Suddenly Rob realized he didn't need to start a business to embrace an entrepreneurial mindset. Instead, he could apply these principles to his current job. It was an "aha" moment for Rob that shifted his perspective as new possibilities began to unfold, all within the boundaries of his role as a sanitation supervisor. Where he once felt complacent, Rob now became excited about his role. Back on the job, he and his team began to find new ways to improve the services they provided. They also began treating the people they served as customers while also finding ways to save the taxpayers hundreds of thousands of dollars each year. For Rob, a subtle shift in perspective led to a big change in his life.

There exists a vast reservoir of untapped entrepreneurial potential hidden in people and places we might otherwise overlook. There is un-tapped entrepreneurial potential in our children and our students, in our workforce and our communities. It's right there, right in front of our eyes, yet it remains dormant, inaccessible within traditional man-agerial contexts. It is hidden in the millions if not billions of workers around the world who languish in low-paying jobs or unsatisfying ca-reers. It lies idle in millions of students who have become bored and dis-engaged. It is trapped within those who feel stuck, those who have been locked out or left behind. This untapped potential lies dormant in our classrooms, organizations, and communities, yet it cannot be accessed through traditional methods of teaching or the top-down managerial assumptions of the past. The individual and collective costs of this un-tapped potential are incalculable, not only in terms of lost productivity but also in terms of human suffering. Not only do those who languish suffer, but the organizations and communities they inhabit also suffer.

Once we experience the entrepreneurial mindset advantage in our own lives, we sense a greater obligation as parents, teachers, organizational leaders, and community stakeholders to take an active role in creating the conditions that are conducive to unlocking the untapped entrepreneurial potential in others.

As you will see, doing so does not require massive policy changes or radical restructuring of our educational and organizational frameworks. Nor does it require extensive knowledge in the field of entrepreneurship. On the contrary, it requires only small changes that can make a big difference in terms of optimizing engagement and unlocking human potential. Whether a parent, an educator, an organizational leader, or a community stakeholder, the formula for accessing the entrepreneurial potential in others is straightforward: create the conditions that are conducive to exploration and experimentation while also facilitating the entrepreneurial (opportunity discovery) process. As you will see, your belief in the untapped entrepreneurial potential of the individual is far more important than your subject-matter expertise. In the same way that entrepreneurial discovery shows us how to identify latent opportunities that exist in our everyday lives, this chapter shows how to access the latent entrepreneurial potential that lies dormant in others.

The concepts in this chapter combine the observations of hundreds of everyday entrepreneurs with motivation research and human-centered learning. These are actionable ideas that anyone can embrace. I have taught thousands of educators and business and nonprofit leaders around the world how to implement these ideas in their classrooms, organizations, and communities. Again and again, I have seen untapped potential emerge in people and places that have been historically overlooked or ignored. I have seen people, organizations, and communities transformed when entrepreneurial potential is cultivated into entrepreneurial action. Indeed, I have seen the untapped potential that is hiding in plain sight. In this chapter, we'll explore the basic guidelines for unlocking the entrepreneurial potential in others. In the chapters that follow, we'll explore best practices for unlocking this potential in specific groups: children, students, workers, community members, and aspiring entrepreneurs.

Creating the Conditions That Are Conducive to Exploration and Experimentation

As we learned in earlier chapters, entrepreneurial attitudes and skills arise as a result of the self-directed pursuit of opportunities to create value for others. However, creating the conditions that are conducive to entrepreneurial behavior also requires us to consider the social, emotional, and functional dimensions of the participants' needs, including the needs for autonomy, competency, and relatedness, which are essential for human flourishing. Doing so requires not only the physical space where learners can exchange ideas and share experience but also the psychological space that is conducive to discovery. As a facilitator of entrepreneurial behavior, we must create conditions where the learner is free to explore new ideas without fear of ridicule or punishment while at the same time promoting the creative discomfort that encourages them to go beyond their current capabilities. In order to do this, we must create learning environments that encourage exploration and experimentation while also promoting candor and vulnerability, self-direction, and peer-to-peer learning. By doing so, we help to create the conditions whereby learners feel safe to explore and to fail, thereby increasing the probability that new insights will arise.

Allowing the time for discovery is also an important aspect of creating psychological safety. When people feel overwhelmed by their day-to-day responsibilities or the attainment of their basic needs, taking the time to explore new ideas can lead to an increased sense of anxiety that can undermine their capacity to do so. This is not to say that one needs to abandon their day-to-day responsibilities but to suggest that we carve out some modicum of discretionary time to encourage exploration and experimentation. By doing so, you will soon see how small changes can indeed make a big difference.

Facilitating the Opportunity Discovery Process

As we have seen, the entrepreneurial process is a discovery process, one that requires discovery skills—skills of which we are all capable, yet skills that have been historically overlooked or discouraged within formal learning and work environments. Guiding learners—be they adolescents or adults—through the opportunity discovery process requires methods of teaching that are distinct from those required in traditional learning. After all, entrepreneurship is the *self-directed* pursuit of opportunities to create value for others. Yet self-direction can be difficult for those who lack confidence in their ability to navigate the highly ambiguous, resource-constrained nature of the entrepreneurial process. As such, once you introduce the learner to the opportunity discovery process, your role must shift from instructor to that of a facilitator as you guide the learner from a state of dependence to one of self-direction while also helping them develop an ever-increasing sense of self-efficacy. After all, you are not only facilitating the opportunity discovery process but also a self-discovery process.

To be clear, although new insights and perspectives are an important aspect of the opportunity discovery process, as facilitators, we should not limit the learner to discovering things that are new to mankind. As we discussed, the vast majority of entrepreneurs do not invent anything new. When facilitating the opportunity discovery process, the learner should be encouraged to discover for *themselves* what is useful to others and to advance their own understanding of the world and of themselves through their own efforts and initiative, thus shifting their mindset from a state of other direction to one of self-direction.

Some learners may be more motivated than others. For a variety of reasons, not everyone will initially buy into the idea of undertaking an entrepreneurial project of their own. Your role as a facilitator is to win the hearts and minds of the learner. After all, opportunity discovery relies upon intrinsic rather than extrinsic motivation. In many cases, the early adopters who embrace the opportunity discovery process with enthusiasm will help convince their more reluctant peers. In other cases, it just takes a little nudge, a little direction, or a little encouragement for the learner to buy in. With that said, here are some things you can do to increase the likelihood of engaging the learner in the opportunity discovery process.

Start with why. Begin by discussing the broader benefits of an entrepreneurial mindset and the advantages it can provide, regardless of one's chosen path. After all, learners will arrive with a variety of motivations. Some may be motivated to earn more money. Others may embrace these ideas to accelerate their careers or reinvent themselves. Some may be motivated by the chance to solve problems or to contribute more meaningfully. Whatever the learner's motivation, your role as a facilitator is to help them see the advantages of learning how to think like an entrepreneur.

One way to do this is to help the learner see the big picture and to connect an entrepreneurial mindset with their personal and professional goals. Imagination and goal setting are powerful ways to encourage the learner to envision a better future while also taking responsibility for their own learning by confronting the ways in which they are held back by external barriers and even by themselves. Research has shown that imagining our best possible self can have a significant impact on optimism and resilience.[1] It changes the expectations we have of ourselves, allowing us to identify and overcome self-limiting beliefs. Discussing self-limiting beliefs is also a good way to introduce the mindset as a hidden mechanism that can either hinder or enhance our ability to learn and grow and to achieve our desired goals.

In addition, it is important to begin by redefining entrepreneurship in a way that everyone can embrace. After all, most are likely to associate entrepreneurship with starting a business and may therefore be reluctant to engage with the opportunity discovery process if they don't share the goal of owning a business or being a traditional entrepreneur. Redefining entrepreneurship as a self-directed pursuit of opportunities to create value for others (as opposed to a startup-oriented business discipline) may go a long way toward convincing reluctant learners to participate. Keep in mind that, while not everyone may have a desire to start a business, the desire to solve problems and to fulfill human needs through our own effort is a powerful motivational force, and when encouraged to do so, we are much more likely to become engaged.

You can also use stories of everyday entrepreneurs to inspire participants. Introducing examples of people similar to themselves who have created meaningful and prosperous lives by embracing these ideas will go a long way to increasing their willingness to undertake entrepreneurial projects of their own. Seeing people similar to themselves succeed through sustained effort is also likely to increase the learners' beliefs in their own ability to improve their lives through their own actions.

It is also important to manage the learners' expectations by setting the stage for the opportunity discovery process, which is quite distinct from traditional learning. As facilitators, it is our role to prepare the learner to identify and solve ill-structured problems within highly ambiguous resource-constrained circumstances *without* the guidance of a professional teacher or the benefit of a predetermined path. For most learners, these expectations will be far outside what they have experienced in the past. While traditional learning typically involves solving well-structured problems with definitive answers, ill-structured problems have many possible solutions because they are complex and poorly defined. The best possible solutions are dependent on the priorities of the individual learner and the underlying context of the situation. Solving such ill-structured problems requires the development of higher-order thinking skills and the ability to construct a convincing argument for a particular solution as opposed to all other possible solutions. For many, this type of learning may be uncomfortable. Preparing the learner to face a new and challenging type of problem will help set a foundation for success.

Once you have set the stage, the next step is to immerse the learner in the opportunity discovery process described in part 2, "The Entrepreneurial Process." Where appropriate, you can use the Entrepreneurial Mindset Challenge as a guiding framework. Or you can simply use the Opportunity Discovery Canvas as a tool to help the learner identify opportunities that exist within their day-to-day life. In subsequent chapters we'll explore different ways to introduce the opportunity discovery process to specific groups, using appropriate strategies and resources. Whenever possible, it is best to encourage the learner to work with a friend or colleague, or to self-organize into small teams. Here again, once learners become engaged in the opportunity discovery process, your role will shift from that of an instructor to a facilitator of discovery. Rather than a sage on the stage, you will quickly take on the role of a guide on the side.

Self-direction is vital to the development of an entrepreneurial mindset. As such, autonomy support is essential for creating effective entrepreneurial learning environments. As we discussed in chapter 3, autonomy, which is the freedom to make our own choices and to have control over our day-to-day lives, is among the psychological nutrients that are required for optimal engagement and psychological well-being. Yet, despite its importance in our lives, autonomy is largely absent from traditional learning environments. Instead, the subject matter, learning strategies, and evaluations are dictated by a teacher, with little room for a student to exert influence on their own learning. As psychologist Carl Rogers observed, within traditional learning environments, there is an implicit assumption that the student cannot be trusted with their own learning.[2] As facilitators of the opportunity discovery process, we must assume the opposite; we must assume that the learner can indeed be trusted with their own learning. We must recognize the self-actualizing tendency that resides within us all. We must assume that the capacity and desire to be innovative and entrepreneurial are innate, and that it is our job to create the conditions that are conducive to these innate tendencies.

Whether we realize it or not, the lack of autonomy stifles creative and critical thinking, intrinsic motivation, self-reflection, and other essential entrepreneurial attitudes and skills. Therefore, when creating the conditions that are conducive to entrepreneurial behavior, the learner must have a sense of freedom, control, and choice. As facilitators, it is important to allow the learner to choose their own projects and their own teams. We must also allow them to fail. As a facilitator, it is important to resist the temptation to insert ourselves as subject-matter experts. Nor should we judge the feasibility of the learner's ideas. The more prescriptive we are in terms of guiding the learner's behavior or judging the feasibility of their ideas, the more likely we are to undermine their entrepreneurial development. The greater the autonomy, the more likely the learners are to become optimally engaged. More importantly, learners must discover for *themselves* through trial and error, experiencing success and failure not as reward or punishment, but as a feedback loop that will ultimately guide their behavior. As the learner's confidence increases, you may monitor progress to ensure success, but step in to assist only when asked. Holding regular meetings that enable participants to discuss their progress encourages learners to cooperate and consult with each other while maintaining a culture of accountability. It also promotes individual initiative, helping the learner increase their sense of reflexivity as they begin to see themselves as cocreators of the culture in which they are immersed.

Tools for Facilitating the Opportunity Discovery Process

Your role as a facilitator is to help the learner develop an ever-increasing sense of entrepreneurial self-efficacy. In the field of psychology, the term *self-efficacy* refers to our belief in our capacity to act in ways that are necessary to reach our desired goals. The concept of self-efficacy was originally proposed by the psychologist Albert Bandura, who observed that: "Unless people believe they can produce desired effects by their actions, they have little incentive to undertake activities or to persevere in the face of difficulties. Whatever other factors may serve as guides and motivators, they are rooted in the core belief that one can make a difference by one's actions."[3]

As we learned in chapter 4, our sense of self-efficacy influences every aspect of our lives, including the goals we set for ourselves, the amount of energy we invest in our goals, and the extent to which we stick with them in the face of difficulties. A strong sense of self-efficacy promotes accomplishment and well-being, whereas low self-efficacy can be linked to higher levels of stress, anxiety, and depression. Yet it does so largely without our awareness. Keep in mind that self-efficacy is domain specific, meaning that we can have a strong sense of self-efficacy in one area of our life while having a low sense of self-efficacy in others. Although high self-efficacy in one area may influence our performance in other aspects of our lives, it is not necessarily the case.

> "Unless people believe they can produce desired effects by their actions, they have little incentive to undertake activities or to persevere in the face of difficulties. Whatever other factors may serve as guides and motivators, they are rooted in the core belief that one can make a difference by one's actions."

Among the most impactful ways to increase the entrepreneurial self-efficacy in others is to encourage them to start where they are, helping them achieve small wins while prodding them to overcome increasingly difficult challenges through sustained effort. Over time, the cumulative experience of small wins leads to an increased sense of self-efficacy. Your role as a facilitator is to question and listen, encourage and validate, honoring and supporting those who venture beyond their comfort zones. As their sense of self-efficacy begins to increase, learners often experience a paradigm shift or a sense of personal transformation as they begin to see new possibilities and their own untapped potential. Your role as a facilitator is also to persuade the learner to believe in themselves. By doing so, they are likely to exert more effort, thus increasing their chances of success.

Bandura described the impact of encouraging small wins as a means of building self-efficacy: "Successes build a robust efficacy. Failures undermine it, especially in early phases of efficacy development when people feel insecure about their capabilities. If people experience only easy successes, they come to expect quick results and are easily discouraged by failure."[4] As facilitators, our role is to create situations where the learner is encouraged to function in their zone of proximal development: to reach beyond their current capabilities, yet not so far that they give up before achieving small wins. (See figure 9.1.)

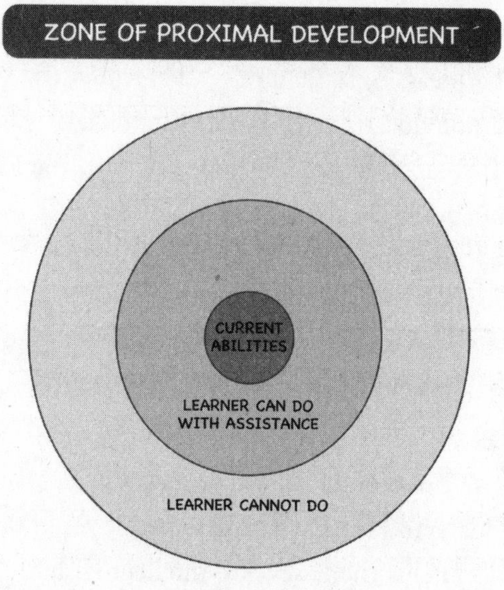

Figure 9.1 | Zone of Proximal Development

Peer-to-peer learning is also an effective means of shifting the learner's mindset from a hierarchical to a horizontal perspective. Holding regular meetings that encourage learners to share their discovery experiences with their peers who are also engaged in the process can be a highly effective means of optimizing engagement. The interaction between equal partners and more capable peers allows learners to gain different perspectives while exchanging and building upon each other's ideas. Seeing firsthand how others face and overcome obstacles can also increase the learner's willingness to persevere in the face of difficulty. Peer-to-peer learning is reflective of the ways in which humans have learned naturally, long before we had written language, classrooms, and professional teachers.

Socratic Questioning

Socratic questioning is an ideal tool for guiding learners through the opportunity discovery process. It is the process of asking open-ended questions without directly offering answers or specific guidance. Socrates believed the disciplined practice of thoughtful questioning enabled students to examine ideas logically and to determine the validity of those ideas. With Socratic questioning, the facilitator feigns ignorance (or reserves judgment) so as to engage in dialogue with the learner, thus promoting independent, higher-level thinking, giving them ownership of what they are learning through discussion, debate, evaluation, and analysis. Socratic questioning also shifts the balance of power from a traditional top-down hierarchy to an egalitarian model where the learner and you, as a facilitator, share responsibility for discovering new opportunities. By asking a series of focused yet open-ended questions, you can help the learner distinguish between beliefs, assumptions, and facts, parsing what they know or understand from what they do not yet know or understand. In that way, it also helps them develop intellectual humility. Below are a few brief examples of Socratic questioning.

Clarification questions help learners sharpen their thinking and explore the origin of their underlying assumptions:

- Why do you say that?
- What do you mean by ... ?

- How does this relate to our discussion?
- What do you think is the main issue?
- Could you expand upon that point further?

Assumption questions are meant to illuminate the learner's underlying presuppositions:

- Why would someone make this assumption?
- What could we assume instead?
- How can you verify or disprove that assumption?

Probing questions are designed to encourage the learner to provide evidence:

- What would be an example?
- What do you think causes that to happen ... ?
- Why ... ?
- What other information do we need?
- By what reasoning did you come to that conclusion?
- Is there reason to doubt that evidence?

Consequence questions explore implications and future developments:

- What generalizations can you make?
- What are the consequences of that assumption?
- What are you implying?
- How does ... affect ... ?
- How does ... tie in with what we learned before?

Viewpoint and perspective questions delve into alternate ways of thinking:

- What would be an alternative?
- What is another way to look at it?
- How would other groups of people respond and why?
- What might someone who believed . . . think?
- Would you explain why it is necessary or beneficial, and who benefits?
- What are the strengths and weaknesses of . . . ?
- How are . . . and . . . similar?
- What is a counterargument?

Questioning the question helps dissect the questioning process:

- Why is this question important?
- What was the point of this question?
- Why do you think I asked this question?
- What does . . . mean?
- How does . . . apply to everyday life?

When using Socratic questioning, it is helpful to draw as many learners as possible into the discussion. Also, it is important to allow time for the learner to follow up on their responses, either with additional questions or by summarizing their responses in their own words.

Engage with Local Entrepreneurs

Inviting local entrepreneurs into the learning experience is among the most effective means of increasing the learner's sense of entrepreneurial self-efficacy. Exposure to successful role models—specifically those with similar interests who come from similar circumstances—helps provide focus and energy, assisting the learner to see that "if they can do it, I should be able to do it too." The greater the similarity to the learners, the more persuasive the local entrepreneurs become as role models. According to Bandura, "Seeing people similar to oneself succeed by sustained effort raises observers' beliefs that they, too, possess the capabilities to master comparable activities to succeed."[5] Local entrepreneurs can also become a vital source of knowledge, mentoring, and ongoing support. As we discussed in the previous chapter, experienced entrepreneurs are in every community and, very often, they are willing, if not eager, to encourage and support others who are engaged in their own opportunity discovery processes. The responsibility for identifying and inviting local entrepreneurs into the learning process should be shared by you as a facilitator as well as the learners themselves.

When inviting local entrepreneurs into the learning environment, keep in mind that they may not know what they know. In other words, much of the knowledge they acquire is tacit knowledge, which is difficult to convey through conventional means. The best way to transfer such knowledge is through sustained face-to-face interactions, which is why it is important for learners to create their own ongoing support networks. With that in mind, when inviting local entrepreneurs to share their experiences, it may be helpful to start by asking them to retrace their steps from the beginnings of their entrepreneurial journeys. Ask them about their motivations, the mistakes they made, the best and worst advice they were given, what obstacles they faced, and how they got through difficult times. Here, too, you can use Socratic questioning as a framework to unearth the deeply held beliefs and taken-for-granted assumptions that drive their behavior.

———

Promote resilience through self-regulation. We all understand the risks associated with overconfidence, yet we rarely think of the debilitating costs associated with negative emotions. The opportunity discovery process can be a roller-coaster ride of emotional highs and lows. In the same way that overconfidence can lead an entrepreneur astray, a lack of optimism can also cause them to give up before a connection is found. As facilitators, we can help the learner build resilience by encouraging them to manage their emotional response to failure in a way that is instructive and empowering rather than destructive and demoralizing.

> Promote resilience through self-regulation. We all understand the risks associated with overconfidence, yet we rarely think of the debilitating costs associated with negative emotions.

As we discussed in earlier chapters, psychological resilience refers to our ability to not only recover quickly from failure or setbacks but also to benefit from them. What many do not realize is that our ability to develop resilience is rooted in our subjective interpretation of our experiences and life events. Those who learn to optimistically interpret adverse experiences become stronger as a result and are more likely to behave in ways that will ultimately lead to success.

As facilitators, we can help the learner develop resilience, not only by making them aware of the impact of their explanatory style, but by helping them replace irrationally pessimistic beliefs with more optimistic ones. The ABC model, which was first introduced by the psychologist Albert Ellis, is a simple yet powerful tool you can use to help learners do just that. (See figure 9.2.)

Figure 9.2 | ABC Model 1.0

Here's how it works: The letter A stands for the activating event. The letter B represents our beliefs about the event. This represents our subjective interpretation of the activating event. The letter C represents the consequences; the emotional and behavioral response to our subjective interpretation of the event. However, we often fail to realize that it is not the activating event itself that is causing our reaction but our *subjective interpretation* of the event that ultimately determines our response. Because we are not aware that we are unconsciously interpreting the event, we mistakenly assume that the activating event itself is causing the emotional response. (See figure 9.3.)

Figure 9.3 | ABC Model 1.1

Here, the role of a facilitator is not only to point out the fact that it is our interpretation rather than the event itself that determines our response but also to challenge the learner's pessimistic beliefs while helping to replace them with more optimistic alternatives. (See figure 9.4.)

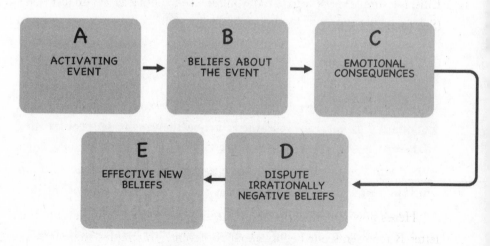

Figure 9.4 | ABC Model 1.2

The ABC model is a powerful tool that can help learners develop the psychological resilience necessary for navigating the emotional ups and downs of the opportunity discovery process. To be clear, it is not designed to promote toxic positivity but rather to help the learner understand the harmful effects of irrationally pessimistic interpretations of circumstances and events. It is a simple tool that shows us how a subtle shift in our thinking can make a big difference in our lives.[6] As the renowned psychiatrist and Holocaust survivor Viktor Frankl once observed, our true power lies in our ability to choose our response to any given set of circumstances.

Encourage self-reflection. Self-reflection brings entrepreneurial learning to life. The learning that comes from opportunity discovery can be greatly enhanced when the learner is encouraged to reflect on what they are learning and how it applies to their personal and professional goals. Reflection encourages the learner to pause—to think about their own thinking and to become more aware of the ways in which their deeply held beliefs might hinder or enhance their ability to set and achieve their goals. Reflection supports a growth-oriented mindset by encouraging the learner to improve and to learn from their mistakes. It also enables them to recognize the ways in which they are influenced by their social environment, ultimately enabling them to consciously and deliberately create the mental habits and environmental conditions that are conducive to growth.

Encourage self-reflection.

As facilitators, our role is to encourage the learner to pause and reflect periodically on what they've learned and how they might apply the learning to their goals. Ask them to volunteer to share their insights and reflections, either with you privately or with the group. Ask them to reflect on any shifts in their underlying beliefs such as perceived locus of control, intrinsic versus extrinsic motivation, and self-efficacy beliefs. Encourage them to apply what they are learning to their vision of their best possible selves.

For many, the opportunity discovery process can be a transformative

experience that alters the course of their lives. Over time, it can also transform the culture of organizations and communities. Like most entrepreneurs, in the beginning the learner is likely to be enthusiastic yet inexperienced. Ideally, by redefining entrepreneurship as an opportunity discovery process and by exposing them to relatable social models, they become willing to engage in the process, willing to reappropriate some modicum of their discretionary time and effort toward exploration, experimentation, and growth. Hopefully the collective experience of others combined with the tools provided here will help reduce the learning curve while also helping to avoid catastrophic mistakes. With proper guidance and support, over time the learner will develop an ever-increasing sense of entrepreneurial self-efficacy, which will eventually become a deeply ingrained pattern of thought and action.

Your role as a facilitator is to create the conditions in which the learner is likely to become optimally engaged. By encouraging the self-directed pursuit of opportunities to create value for others, we consciously and deliberately create the conditions that are conducive to growth and psychological well-being. In other words, by creating the conditions that are conducive to exploration and experimentation and by encouraging the self-directed pursuit of opportunities to create value for others, we are creating the conditions whereby the learner's basic psychological needs for autonomy, competency, and relatedness are more likely to be met. When that happens, the learner is likely to become intrinsically motivated and therefore optimally engaged.

In the beginning, you may not be confident in your ability to cultivate entrepreneurial mindsets in others. Nevertheless, you can use these very principles to develop your ability as a facilitator of the opportunity discovery process. Like any entrepreneurial endeavor, at first you are likely to be enthusiastic yet inexperienced. Nevertheless, as you forge ahead and try things on a small scale, you will learn from the results. As with any new endeavor, you must be willing to fail. If done properly, guiding others through the opportunity discovery process will also become a

transformative experience for you. As a result of guiding others through the opportunity discovery process, you will begin to see your own entrepreneurial mindset emerge.

The American philosopher L. P. Jacks once observed: "A master in the art of living draws no sharp distinction between his work and his play; his labor and his leisure; his mind and his body; his education and his recreation. He hardly knows which is which. He simply pursues his vision of excellence through whatever he is doing, and leaves others to determine whether he is working or playing. To himself, he always appears to be doing both."[7]

The overarching objective of the opportunity discovery process is for the learner to experience learning and work as ongoing, self-directed activities that energize them, awakening their curiosity in ways that engage the full range of their faculties. When that happens, you will begin to see the vast reservoir of untapped potential that lies hidden in people and places we might have otherwise overlooked or ignored.

Raising Entrepreneurial Children

You don't remember the times your dad held your handlebars.
You remember the day he let go.
— Lenore Skenazy[1]

Like many twelve-year-old kids, Robert was becoming increasingly bored with school and, rather than focusing on homework, he seemed to be spending every waking minute of his spare time playing video games with his friend. As you might imagine, his parents were becoming increasingly concerned. When Robert approached his father, asking him for $400 to purchase the newest version of his favorite video game console, his response was emphatic: "No way. If you want a new video game console, you're going to have to earn that money yourself."

"Dad, I'm twelve! How am I going to earn four hundred dollars?" was Robert's reply.

Sensing a teachable moment, the father began to engage his son in a serious discussion of the ways in which he might be able to earn the $400 he needed on his own. Drawing on his son's interest in woodworking, they hatched a plan to build simple birdhouses that he could then sell as a way to earn the money to buy his new video game. Their assumption was that neighbors might be willing to pay twenty dollars for a birdhouse built by a twelve-year-old boy. So they found a simple plan online, made a list of materials they would need to build the first batch of birdhouses, and set off to the nearest home center to purchase the needed supplies. With some initial guidance from his father, Robert eagerly set about to build his first birdhouse. Through trial and error, within a few days, he had figured out how to create a minimally viable product that he might be able to sell. Now confident in his ability, and eager to earn the money he needed, Robert set about to build as many birdhouses as he could.

Seeing the change in his behavior, his fifteen-year-old sister couldn't help but ask in a somewhat cynical tone what on earth he was doing. Barely looking up from his work, Robert replied, "I'm making birdhouses."

"That's the dumbest thing I've ever heard of," was her response.

Despite his sister's dismissal, Robert was undaunted, working diligently to build a presentable prototype that would enable him to test his idea on family members as his first customers. Before long, he managed to sell ten birdhouses, generating $200 in sales. As you can imagine, he was excited and eager to show his father the money that he had earned: "Dad, I'm halfway there!" he announced.

"Well, not quite," his father explained. "You owe me eighty dollars for the up-front investment of the tools and materials."

While somewhat taken aback by this realization, Robert was nevertheless undeterred and determined to forge ahead. Having now exhausted his circle of friends and family members, Robert asked his father about how he might grow his customer base. His father suggested that he go door-to-door, taking a sample birdhouse with him, so that he could then take orders with a down payment. His confidence bolstered by the initial validation of family and friends, Robert set out to do just that. However, it wasn't long before his schoolmates caught wind of his new venture and began to ridicule him, referring to him as "the birdhouse boy." By this point, though, he had enough confidence that he was determined to forge ahead. As his sales continued to grow, he became increasingly self-sufficient, occasionally turning to his father for advice. For example, after exhausting his immediate neighborhood, Robert asked his father how he might expand his reach. Together, they figured out how to modify his bicycle in a way that would enable him to sell and deliver birdhouses to other neighborhoods. By now, Robert had earned well beyond his $400 goal. More importantly, he was no longer interested in video games. Instead, when he wasn't building and selling birdhouses, he was busy learning about local bird species and their habitats so that he could expand his line of birdhouses beyond his initial design. At that point, his sister was now interested and eager to help.

Our children are more capable than we think. Not only are they capable of more, but they are also desirous of more. More importantly, they are capable of more than *they* believe. Robert's story clearly demonstrates that children have both the capacity and the desire to learn on their own, with minimal instruction from adults. In many ways, his story reflects the ways in which we humans learn naturally, as "active learners who participate in learning by choice, and for whom learning is an ongoing, playful activity, not separated from the rest of life."[2] Robert's story also reminds us that raising entrepreneurial children may require us to reexamine our own deeply held assumptions, not only about the capability of our children but also about how best to prepare them to adapt and thrive in a constantly changing world.

Our children are more capable than we think.

And yet, as parents, it is also easy to lose sight of the fact that the desire to learn is innate. Too often we mistakenly assume that children are incapable of learning without explicit, formal training by adults. By teaching children within narrow, structured parameters dictated by adults, we perpetuate circumstances that stifle rather than stimulate their intrinsic desire to learn. For many, video games provide an outlet for self-endorsed challenge and unsupervised play, which is how children have naturally evolved to learn.*

Children are born innately curious and creative, asking endless questions from almost the moment they learn to speak. After all, curiosity is the means by which we orient ourselves to our surrounding environment. Yet, if we're not careful, that inborn desire to learn can be easily thwarted by situational factors of which we may not be aware. For example, studies have shown that almost from the moment children set foot in school, their innate curiosity begins to wane.[3] When that happens, they become increasingly alienated and disengaged. As we discussed in chapter 1, numerous studies have shown that student engagement plummets from grades five through twelve.[4] Sadly, as they progress through school, they become even less engaged. Meanwhile, the rate of change and complexity continues to increase. An entrepreneurial mindset is an adaptive mindset. The purpose of encouraging children to develop entrepreneurial attitudes and skills is not necessarily to become entrepreneurs in the traditional sense, although that may indeed be a desired outcome. The broader imperative is to encourage them to develop the ability to adapt and thrive amid complexity and change. As we have discussed throughout this book, those with an entrepreneurial mindset are creative and critical thinkers who are self-directed, resilient, and resourceful. They not only can navigate complexity and change but also make a greater contribution to the organizations and communities they inhabit. As a result, there is unlimited global demand for those who can think like entrepreneurs. If our children are to adapt and thrive, they, too, must become self-directed lifelong learners who can learn, unlearn, and relearn on their own.

Meanwhile, as the rate of change continues to increase, there is a growing body of evidence that suggests that adolescents lack the essential

---

* While there are certainly things one can do to cultivate entrepreneurial attitudes in younger children, here I am generally referring to adolescent children roughly between the ages of ten and eighteen.

life skills that are crucial for navigating the challenges of adulthood—to say nothing of an increasingly complex and rapidly changing world. This lack of preparedness is due, in part, to a decades-long decline in opportunities to engage in activities that involve some degree of risk and personal responsibility without direct oversight by adults. As opportunities for exploration and experimentation have declined, the rates of anxiety, depression, suicide, and feelings of helplessness have skyrocketed among adolescents and young adults. Somewhere along the way, we went from preparing our children for life to protecting them from life. What children are missing is a sense of freedom to learn and grow on their own, without the constant supervision of adults. According to the social psychologist Jonathan Haidt:

> With every decade children have become less free to play, roam, and explore alone or with other children away from adults, less free to occupy public spaces without an adult guard, and less free to have a part-time job where they can demonstrate their capacity for responsible self-control. Among the causes of this change are a large increase in societal fears that children are in danger if not constantly guarded, a large increase in the time that children must spend in school and at schoolwork at home, and a large increase in the societal view that children's time is best spent in adult-directed school-like activities, such as formal sports and lessons, even when not in school.[5]

We all know that children are much more likely to flourish as adults when they experience themselves as living in accordance with their own internal desires and decisions rather than being driven by rewards, punishments, and demands put upon them by others. Such experiences of effortful control over their circumstances are essential for building the self-efficacy and psychological resilience that are essential for children to flourish as adults.

One way to do that is by encouraging our children to undertake entrepreneurial projects of their own. By doing so, we enable them to develop an internal locus of control that will help them become the kind of self-directed problem solvers who will not only survive but also thrive. According to Haidt:

> Research shows that people of all ages who have a strong internal locus of control (internal LOC), that is, a strong sense of being able to solve their own problems and take charge of their own lives, are much less likely to suffer from anxiety and depression than those with a weaker internal LOC. Obviously, however, to develop a strong internal LOC a person needs considerable experience of actually being in control, which is not possible if you are continuously being monitored and controlled by others.[6]

Raising entrepreneurial children requires us to recognize the ways in which invasive or overcontrolling parenting is detrimental to the development of entrepreneurial attitudes and skills. Such overcontrolling parenting is often associated with a lack of respect for the child's autonomy and independence whereby parents leave little room for their children to make decisions on their own. Instead, such parents constantly monitor and micromanage all aspects of their children's lives, including their academic performance, their friendships, and their extracurricular activities. These parents are constantly pushing their children to achieve specific goals with little consideration for the child's interests or desires. This type of parenting can have negative consequences for a child's emotional well-being, self-esteem, and long-term development. In many cases, it becomes a self-fulfilling prophecy whereby the child becomes passive, unable, or unwilling to think and act for themselves, thus reinforcing the need for constant supervision and direction.

If we are to develop entrepreneurial capabilities in our children, we must create learning opportunities that encourage them to observe and explore, to experiment, to participate in learning by choice as an ongoing, playful activity, not separated from the rest of life. Perhaps more importantly, we must encourage them to learn by doing, through trial and error, and allow them to fail and to learn from their mistakes. The Entrepreneurial Mindset Challenge is an ideal mechanism for doing just that.

Keep in mind that our children are not likely to learn this stuff in school. For most, school is designed for the efficient transmission of knowledge and cultural values from one generation to the next. As we covered in chapter 5, many of these foundational values are predicated upon industrial-era assumptions that stifle rather than stimulate the development of entrepreneurial attitudes, behaviors, and skills. Despite the evolving nature of learning and work, our systems of education remain steeped in one-best-way managerial assumptions of the past, which are generally intolerant of exploration and experimentation. Instead, they rely on top-down methods of teaching and learning that inhibit rather than encourage the creativity and critical thinking that our kids will need to thrive. Within this prevailing paradigm, it is widely assumed that they must learn to function within highly stable, other-directed environments where someone else will determine what they need to learn and do in order to be successful. It is assumed that our children will grow up to work in established organizations where the "useful thing" they contribute is determined by others and that they will be rewarded for following established processes and procedures. Within this prevailing paradigm, it is also assumed that there is no need for children to develop entrepreneurial competencies. Instead, they learn to focus on standardized testing that prioritizes academic achievement over practical knowledge and the so-called soft skills that will allegedly empower them to adapt and thrive. Not only is formal education inadequate in that regard; like invasive parenting, it assumes that students cannot be trusted to learn on their own. As a result, many lose interest in learning, as John Dewey observed, because of the ways in which it was presented to them.

We must remember that school is not the only place where learning occurs. As parents, we must acknowledge that learning can and should take place outside of a classroom. Often, the most important learning occurs as a natural function of everyday life. As Robert's story clearly demonstrates, one way to stimulate such learning is to encourage children to undertake projects of their own as a way for them to experience learning as an ongoing, playful activity, not separated from the rest of life.

Noticing his nine-year-old son's eagerness to engage in a side project that he had undertaken on his own, the entrepreneur and investor Paul Graham described the importance of encouraging children to undertake such hands-on, self-directed projects:

> We treat "playing" and "hobbies" as qualitatively different from "work." It's not clear to a kid building a treehouse that there's a direct (though long) route from that to architecture or engineering. And instead of pointing out the route, we conceal it, by implicitly treating the stuff kids do as different from real work. Instead of telling kids that their treehouses could be on the path to the work they do as adults, we tell them the path goes through school. And unfortunately, schoolwork tends to be very different from working on projects of one's own. It's usually neither a project, nor one's own. So as school gets more serious, working on projects of one's own is something that survives, if at all, as a thin thread off to the side. It's a bit sad to think of all the high school kids turning their backs on building treehouses and sitting in class dutifully learning about Darwin or Newton to pass some exam, when the work that made Darwin and Newton famous was actually closer in spirit to building treehouses than studying for exams.[7]

Children need self-endorsed difficulties; they need to undertake projects of their own choosing, projects that challenge them, projects that encourage them to pursue their interests and develop their abilities without constant supervision by adults. Doing so enables them to experience learning and work as a self-directed process that energizes rather than alienates their innate desire to learn. Activating this innate desire is crucial to developing an entrepreneurial mindset advantage in our children, thus equipping them with the ability to thrive in a dynamic world.

Why a Lemonade Stand Won't Do

Encouraging kids to sell lemonade is an age-old activity designed to spark the entrepreneurial spirit in children, yet this ubiquitous activity may not actually be effective at developing entrepreneurial attitudes and skills. In many ways, the lemonade stand promotes managerial rather than entrepreneurial attitudes and skills. Sure, a lemonade stand can help children absorb basic financial literacy and communication skills, but in reality they are abiding by an other-directed formula that does not allow them to discover for themselves what is useful to others. Instead, someone else is providing the formula, telling the child exactly what to do and even how and when and where to do it. Rather than providing them with a predetermined formula, encourage them, as Robert's father did, to pursue their interests and develop their abilities in ways that create value for others. Rather than building a lemonade stand, encourage them to embrace the Entrepreneurial Mindset Challenge. Encourage them to discover for themselves what people want and need. The objective is for the child to experience learning as a self-directed adventure, a source of meaning and purpose, rather than as other-directed tedium that must be endured.

The best way to do that is to start with a compelling goal. In Robert's case, his father leveraged his need for a new video game console as a way to entice him into undertaking an entrepreneurial project of his own. While helping children develop intrinsic motivation is the ultimate goal, it's okay to initially garner the child's interest using extrinsic rewards. After all, entrepreneurship is an altruistic paradox whereby we get what we want by helping other people get what they want. As parents, our role is to encourage our children to explore the intersection of their interests and abilities in ways that enable them to create value for others. By doing so, they are likely to become more engaged in learning as an ongoing, self-directed process that is not separated from the rest of life.

It is also important to recognize that Robert's birdhouse business was a project that was within his reach. While the idea of building and selling birdhouses was beyond his capabilities when he started, it wasn't so far that he would be likely to give up before he experienced a small win. In other words, it was within his zone of proximal development, the space between what a learner is capable of doing on their own and what they cannot do, even with support. Robert's father initiated the process by helping him find a plan, purchase materials, and build his first birdhouse. Encouraging Robert to start by selling his birdhouses to family and friends gave him the confidence to eventually go beyond his initial zone of safety. Early validation from family and friends may even have increased his willingness to tolerate the ridicule of his peers. Once Robert had proven his concept, his father stepped back, providing guidance and support only when asked. By that time, Robert had become intrinsically motivated to figure things out for himself.

The opportunity discovery process also facilitates incidental learning. For Robert, it became a rich learning opportunity where he not only learned how to build and sell birdhouses but also encountered practical applications for math and geometry, basic financial literacy, creative and critical thinking, communication, effective problem-solving, and other essential life skills. Perhaps the most important lesson of all from Robert's story is that learning can be a self-directed process that is fun and rewarding rather than tedious and boring. When children are encouraged to follow their interests in ways that create value for others, we begin to see that they are indeed capable of more than we might imagine. Robert's story is but one example—one that can be replicated in many ways. The central idea is to encourage exploration and to steer our children in the direction of their own interests and abilities in a way that can benefit others so as to cultivate their innate desire to learn and to become optimally engaged. An entrepreneurial project of their own provides an opportunity for self-endorsed struggle, an opportunity to actively participate in learning as it should be—as an ongoing, playful activity, not separate from the rest of life.

Chapter Eleven

Entrepreneurship in Education

We need to stop asking students what they want to be when they grow up, and instead ask them what problem they want to solve, how they want to solve it, and what they need to learn to solve the problem they are passionate about.

—Jaime Casap, Founder and CEO, Autotelic Solutions, and former Chief Education Evangelist, Google[1]

There is a vast untapped reservoir of human potential that lies dormant within our systems of education. Much of it is hidden within those who may not excel in conventional learning environments, in those our systems of education have traditionally overlooked or ignored. It remains unrealized in those who feel disconnected from traditional education, those who have the potential to make valuable contributions yet have become disengaged and alienated from the learning process. It is untapped potential that cannot be accessed through traditional methods of teaching and learning, nor can it be measured by standardized academic achievement scores.

Education is the most important lever we can pull to unlock the entrepreneurial potential of our communities and societies. It is the most important lever we can pull to promote human flourishing and stimulate economic growth. And now that we understand the underlying causes of entrepreneurial behavior, we know how to create learning environments that stimulate rather than stifle the development of entrepreneurial attitudes, behaviors, and skills. Rather than creating entrepreneurial mindsets by accident, we now know how to create them by design.

Cultivating entrepreneurial mindsets in education is a national imperative. As the rate of technological change continues to accelerate, the mindset that once enabled us to succeed is rapidly becoming obsolete. If we are to adequately prepare the next generation to adapt and thrive in a dynamic world, we must look beyond new business creation to recognize basic entrepreneurial competencies as essential life skills.

As we have discussed throughout this book, entrepreneurial attitudes and skills can be learned. It is crucial to incorporate entrepreneurship education into an individual's lifelong learning journey, starting in adolescence and extending into higher education and through adulthood. Lifelong entrepreneurial learning is imperative for all, and this includes those who have been economically or socially marginalized. Our future depends on shifting *entrepreneurial mindset education* from the perimeter to the core of the way education operates.[2]

The benefits of embracing entrepreneurial mindset education are difficult to overstate.* As numerous economists have noted, entrepreneurs are arguably the most important players in the modern economy. On an individual level, entrepreneurial mindset education cultivates the skills and abilities that have become essential for navigating the challenges of a dynamic and ever-changing world. It promotes creativity and effective problem-solving. It cultivates adaptability, resilience, and a willingness to embrace change. It also promotes critical thinking: the analytical skills

---

* Here I am using the phrase "entrepreneurial mindset education" to distinguish from traditional entrepreneurship education.

necessary to evaluate opportunities, assess risks, and make decisions with limited information. Overall, entrepreneurial mindset education not only promotes the attitudes and skills necessary for individuals to adapt and thrive but also enables them to make a greater contribution to society. Perhaps more importantly, it creates a powerful incentive to learn.

From a broader perspective, entrepreneurial mindset education is essential for creating vibrant, equitable, and sustainable communities. Indeed, it is essential for stimulating economic growth and the overall prosperity of a society. As we discussed in chapter 1, entrepreneurs not only create new jobs that revitalize our communities, they also solve social, economic, and environmental problems that improve the overall quality of our lives. Entrepreneurial mindset education can also greatly enhance global competitiveness. Broadly speaking, entrepreneurial mindset education has the potential to create a positive ripple effect throughout society by fostering economic development, innovation, and a mindset of adaptability, resilience, and human flourishing. The best way to cultivate that potential is through entrepreneurial mindset education.

The long-term consequences of neglecting entrepreneurial mindset education are also difficult to overstate. By doing so, we are likely to perpetuate the widening wealth gap while leaving huge swaths of society ill prepared for the ever-changing nature of work. Neglecting entrepreneurial mindset education can have far-reaching consequences for individuals, organizations, communities, and societies, negatively impacting economic vitality, innovation, job creation, and the overall quality of life. If we are to create vibrant, sustainable communities, stakeholders must recognize the need to infuse entrepreneurial mindset development into our systems of education starting in adolescence and extending into higher education, workforce development, and adult education.

Entrepreneurship education initiatives are on the rise, yet the vast majority are focused on new venture creation and are therefore inadequate to meet the need for all students to develop basic entrepreneurial attitudes and skills. For the most part, traditional entrepreneurship education programs are offered as extracurricular options rather than required learning. We know that exposure to entrepreneurial learning experiences starting from youth and continuing into higher education and throughout adulthood is essential, yet, thus far, our systems of education are creating entrepreneurial mindsets by accident rather than by design. Given the potential societal impact of entrepreneurship education, one wonders why it is treated as an extracurricular activity when it might be the most impactful aspect of education we can promote.

We're stuck on the perimeter because we're steeped in nineteenth-century managerial paradigms that don't recognize the broader societal impact of entrepreneurial thinking as an essential life skill. We're stuck on the perimeter because we fail to recognize the ways in which the rigid structures of standardized education stifle rather than stimulate creativity and curiosity, self-direction, resilience, resourcefulness, and other entrepreneurial abilities. We're stuck on the perimeter because we fail to recognize the ways in which standardized education discourages students from questioning established norms or exploring alternative perspectives. We're stuck on the perimeter because we continue to emphasize standardized test scores and rote memorization over developing students' capacities to analyze, synthesize, and evaluate information critically and independently. We're also stuck on the perimeter because of the ways in which we define entrepreneurship. After all, when entrepreneurship is presented as a business discipline, only a small percentage of students and teachers are likely to engage. By narrowly focusing on high-growth entrepreneurship, we're going to overlook the untapped entrepreneurial potential that lies dormant in those who have been traditionally neglected or ignored.

More importantly, we're stuck on the perimeter because we're treating adaptive challenges as if they were technical problems. As a society, we have reached the second break point, the point at which growth begins to slow, the point at which we either reinvent ourselves or we become obsolete. Yet, in spite of the changes that are happening all around us, our systems of education continue to rely on outdated methods of teaching and learning that leave both students and teachers alienated and disengaged. Rather than exploring the ways in which the deeply held values and assumptions that once enabled us to succeed may now be holding us back, we're blaming others while doubling down on prior beliefs. We're asking teachers to do more and more with less and less while at the same time pointing fingers at parents, politicians, and smartphones as the cause. Here again, if all we have is a hammer, all of our problems tend to look like nails.

Meanwhile, we're falling behind. Despite decades-long efforts and billions of tax dollars spent on initiatives designed to enhance academic standards, boost test scores, encourage college attendance, prolong school hours, expand learning time, and implement other accountability measures, our systems of education continue to fall short. In fact, in the face of such initiatives, student performance has actually decreased, especially in math. According to data collected by the OECD, students in the United States are trending sharply downward in math performance and report average performance in reading and science compared to other OECD countries, despite the significant resources funneled into raising these metrics.[3] Meanwhile, students are largely bored and disengaged. In the United States, approximately two million students between the ages of sixteen and twenty-four drop out each year. At the same time, rates of anxiety, depression, and suicide among young people continue to rise. As author Peter Senge once observed in his analysis of systems, "The harder we push on the system, the harder the system seems to push back."[4]

These challenges are not limited to students. Teachers are also overburdened and struggling to keep pace. Faced with unimaginable workloads, inadequate support, and a lack of autonomy support, many are experiencing emotional exhaustion and high levels of burnout. Teachers are increasingly becoming alienated from teaching for the same reasons that workers become alienated from their work. As Marx pointed out nearly two centuries ago, people become alienated when they have little input into the design and delivery of their work. Instead, they are expected to function within systems that are designed to extract the maximum amount of value while offering increasingly diminished psychological satisfaction, leaving many miserable, unhappy, and drained of the energy to carry on.[5] As a result, teachers are abandoning the profession at an alarming rate. One survey conducted by the National Education Association showed that more than half of all teachers were thinking about leaving the profession.[6]

The long-term consequences of continuing on this path are also difficult to comprehend. Clearly, we've reached a break point whereby the values and assumptions that once enabled us to succeed are becoming increasingly maladaptive in the face of change. Clearly, today's problems are the result of yesterday's solutions. Yet, when faced with an adaptive challenge, we know that sometimes small changes can produce big results. However, the areas of highest leverage are often the least obvious. In other words, the solution to these overwhelming and urgent challenges may be easier than we think.

Here again, shifting entrepreneurial mindset education from the perimeter to the core does not require a major overhaul of our systems of education. It simply requires us to examine our own deeply held beliefs and taken-for-granted assumptions about the capabilities of young people. It also requires us to recognize the ways in which routinized, other-directed learning stifles rather than stimulates the development of entrepreneurial attitudes, behaviors, and skills. If we are to shift entrepreneurial mindset education from the perimeter to the core, we must ensure that all students, throughout their formal educational experience, are encouraged to undertake entrepreneurial projects of their own. In other words, we must embrace entrepreneurial discovery learning as an essential part of every student's educational experience.

As we discussed in previous chapters, the entrepreneurial process is essentially a learning process whereby an individual or small group of individuals searches for the intersection of their interests and abilities and the needs of others. By doing so, they are much more likely to become optimally engaged. I refer to this as Entrepreneurial Discovery Learning

(EDL). EDL is easily accessible and can be widely embraced by students regardless of background, interests, or academic achievement scores. EDL empowers students by activating their imagination while encouraging them to develop creative and critical thinking and the resilience and resourcefulness necessary to navigate and succeed in complex, uncertain environments. Perhaps more importantly, EDL also creates a powerful incentive to learn.

Educators are already familiar with the basic elements of EDL. When viewed through an academic lens, EDL is similar to other well-known methods of teaching and learning, such as problem-based learning, inquiry-based learning, and self-organized learning. EDL is also well aligned with individualized learning, an instructional approach that tailors education to the unique needs, interests, and pace of a targeted learner. This approach recognizes that learners have different backgrounds, interests, and abilities and aims to create a more effective and engaging learning experience for everyone. Like EDL, individualized learning empowers students to take greater control of their education by allowing them to set goals, make choices, and pursue areas of personal interest. EDL also encourages collaboration by immersing students in entrepreneurial projects that promote social learning and the development of collaborative skills. EDL is also similar to Montessori education in that knowledge is constructed rather than passively absorbed. For example, EDL is process oriented rather than content oriented. Rather than memorizing content, the focus in EDL is learning how to identify, evaluate, and solve ill-structured problems. Students learn to analyze and interpret information to understand what is being learned rather than just giving the correct answer from memorization. EDL is also an error-based learning process that pushes students to a deeper level of understanding through trial and error. Like Montessori education, EDL relies on facilitation rather than the teacher acting as a subject-matter expert who presents facts. Similarly, EDL encourages group discussion and peer feedback, which enhances learning. It also encourages students to become self-aware and to reflect on their own thinking in ways that enable them to constantly learn, unlearn, and relearn on their own.

However, EDL differs from established methods in that it explicitly promotes prosocial behavior by encouraging students to pursue their interests and develop abilities in ways that create value for others. And it is an evidence-based process that encourages students to embrace the principles of the scientific method in a way that can be integrated into other disciplines. With EDL, students experience failure not as a punishment but as a self-directed feedback mechanism that is essential to the entrepreneurial learning process. In addition to knowledge acquisition, EDL encourages the development of creativity, critical thinking, and effective problem-solving, as well as group collaboration, effective communication, intrinsic motivation, resilience, and other entrepreneurial attitudes and skills. It also promotes autonomy and self-direction, which cultivates students' internal locus of control, through the experience of identifying and solving problems of their own choosing with minimal guidance from an instructor.

EDL increases not only student engagement but also teacher engagement and retention. Having trained thousands of teachers, I have seen firsthand how EDL can inspire, reenergize, and reengage teachers from all backgrounds and disciplines. Because it involves real-world problem-solving, it encourages teachers to explore and learn new concepts themselves. This intrinsic motivation can be highly engaging, as teachers are naturally drawn to the prospect of acquiring practical skills and knowledge that they can apply in their classrooms as well as their personal lives. Teachers who embrace this type of learning feel more prepared and adaptable to changes within the education system, thus gaining a sense of resilience and empowerment that may benefit them, as well as their schools and their communities, as much as it benefits their students. Many find that EDL resonates with their own teaching philosophies, leading to a greater sense of alignment between their professional development and their instructional practices. EDL can energize and engage teachers by providing them with relevant, practical experiences, fostering intrinsic motivation and greater alignment with the needs of their students.

To be clear, I'm not suggesting that EDL replace traditional methods of teaching. I am suggesting that entrepreneurial skills and competencies are already well aligned with existing educational goals. After all, many of the qualities associated with EDL lead to deeper learning in areas such as analytic reasoning, creative and critical thinking, complex problem-solving, self-direction, and teamwork. EDL also promotes self-awareness, self-regulation, and other social and emotional skills including empathy, self-efficacy, responsibility, communication, collaboration, global aware-ness, and cultural competence. These so-called soft skills differ from tra-ditional academic skills in that they are not primarily content based. I am also suggesting that EDL can be easily integrated into the existing cur-riculum in ways that align with established educational goals. Providing training and professional development opportunities for teachers is a great place to start, as it not only helps familiarize them with entrepreneurial discovery learning methodologies but also enables them to explore ways to connect entrepreneurial concepts with existing coursework. EDL has broad applicability across many disciplines, including social studies, his-tory, and economics, to say nothing of science, technology, engineering, and math (STEM). Professional development opportunities that famil-iarize teachers with EDL also help them create flexible learning environ-ments that support entrepreneurial activities and provide an opportunity to bridge the classroom with the community by inviting local entrepre-neurs and other community stakeholders into the learning process.

Middle school is a good place to start. As we learned in the previous chapter, adolescent children are capable of much more than we imagine. And they have both the capacity and the desire to learn on their own, with minimal instruction from adults. Middle school is where they also begin to disengage from formal learning in large numbers, which is why it is a good time to introduce EDL. Middle school students are at a stage where they are developing cognitive and abstract thinking abilities. They can grasp more complex concepts, think critically, and understand the cause-and-effect relationships involved in entrepreneurship. Adolescence is also a time when students are forming identities and exploring their interests. Introducing EDL allows them to discover their strengths, interests, and passions, helping shape their sense of self and potential career paths. Middle school is also a critical time for building self-confidence and resilience. EDL exposes students to challenges, encouraging calculated risk-taking in a supportive environment while helping them develop resilience in the face of setbacks. It also provides a foundation for students as they transition to high school and start thinking more seriously about future career paths. It sets the stage for continued exploration and skill development. Middle school is also an opportune time to begin cultivating teamwork and collaboration skills as EDL often involves group projects that foster effective communication and collaboration among students. EDL also emphasizes a growth mindset, teaching students that intelligence and abilities can be developed through deliberate effort, which is crucial for academic success and personal development. Ultimately, entrepreneurial discovery learning bridges the gap between theoretical knowledge and practical application, making learning more engaging and meaningful. By introducing entrepreneurial discovery learning in middle school, educators can increase student engagement and enhance the overall learning experience.

One such example can be found in the Erie, Pennsylvania, public school system. As a middle school social studies teacher, Dave Cross had no prior interest, much less experience, in entrepreneurship. However, after attending our Ice House Entrepreneurial Mindset facilitator training, he agreed that the entrepreneurial mindset lessons included in the Ice House Program would resonate with his students. With the support of the assistant superintendent and his principal, Dave went to work, adapting the program to meet his students' needs and ensure his classroom could still meet established performance benchmarks in social studies. He and his colleagues were astonished by the results, as students became actively engaged in entrepreneurial projects that solved real-world problems. Soon word started to spread as Dave began to facilitate workshops and present at conferences as a way to encourage other middle school teachers to embrace EDL. Even the mayor got involved, requesting a meeting with several of the students who had developed a detailed plan to address the community's lack of awareness of small startup businesses. By August 2021, the school board approved a new social studies curriculum that included the Ice House Entrepreneurial Mindset Program for all students. Since then, more than three thousand middle schoolers have been enrolled, gaining exposure to the basic principles that develop an entrepreneurial mindset. "Each year that we've offered the Ice House, we've gotten better at what we do, from teaching the materials to tailoring and streamlining the content," said assistant principal Chris Popa, who not only coordinates the program for the three middle schools in his district but also gives conference presentations on the district's success using the Ice House Entrepreneurial Mindset model. Popa is currently working with Erie's high school administrators and teachers to extend Ice House content into the freshman seminar and beyond. Although they have yet to measure the long-term impact, Popa said that based on what he has seen, "We know the entrepreneurial culture is starting to spread."[7]

Middle school is just the beginning. Imagine if all students were encouraged to participate in entrepreneurial projects of their own as they progressed from middle school to high school. How might that help them experience learning as less stressful and more rewarding? How might entrepreneurial discovery learning help them feel more optimistic and less depressed? How might this prepare them not only to adapt and thrive but to make a greater contribution to their communities?

Middle school is just the beginning.

As students progress from middle school to high school, their entrepreneurial abilities can evolve significantly, not only due to their social, cognitive, and emotional development, but also through exposure to diverse experiences and the increasing complexity of solving real-world challenges. As they progress through high school, they become more capable of abstract thinking, strategic planning, and understanding complex concepts, thus supporting the ongoing development of their entrepreneurial mindset. With more exposure to academic subjects, high school students develop a deeper understanding of the broader world and how they see themselves contributing. As one high school student told me, exposure to entrepreneurship not only helped her understand how the world works, but it also helped her understand the importance of her education. It is hard to imagine a more powerful testimony than that.

Encouraging students to embrace EDL throughout high school will enable them to develop advanced problem-solving skills as they approach challenges with more sophistication and creativity. They will also develop greater ability to analyze complex issues, identify opportunities, and develop innovative solutions with a greater depth of understanding. As they progress, they will become more adept at working collaboratively with peers, leveraging each other's strengths, and effectively contributing to team objectives. Encouraging students to undertake entrepreneurial projects of their own also provides ongoing opportunities to explore specialized subjects and learning experiences that align with their interests and potential career paths. Ongoing entrepreneurial projects contribute to the development of a more resilient attitude and a willingness to take calculated risks. EDL promotes digital and financial literacy as well as leadership skills. As they approach graduation, high school students with entrepreneurial attitudes and skills can distinguish themselves, whether they endeavor to start new businesses or pursue a more traditional career path. Simply put, ongoing exposure to entrepreneurial discovery throughout high school can be a highly effective means of developing the human capital necessary for creating societies of the future.

One example is Prepa Tec, a private preparatory high school with campuses across Mexico. What makes Prepa Tec unique is their focus on leadership, innovation, and entrepreneurship for human flourishing. This comes as no surprise, as their parent school, Monterrey Institute of Technology and Higher Education (Tec de Monterrey), is among the most entrepreneurial universities in the world. With their focus on leadership, innovation, and entrepreneurship for human flourishing, the school's motto is to encourage students to stand out in their own way, according to their own talents, to achieve their own dreams. Having personally trained more than two hundred Prepa Tec teachers, I have witnessed the impact of entrepreneurial mindset education on students and teachers alike.

Among the students I met was Julián Rios Cantú, who, at the age of sixteen, was developing a bra that would help detect breast cancer for women who are at risk. Today, he is the CEO and cofounder of Eden, the leading radiology and imaging platform in Latin America. Julián has also been awarded Mexico's Presidential Medal for Scientific and Technological Breakthroughs and the Global Student Entrepreneur Award.

Some forward-thinking policymakers have begun to incorporate entrepreneurship into their educational curricula. In South Africa, for example, the minister of education has initiated a plan to embed entrepreneurship in the entire education system as a way to increase student engagement and to better equip the next generation for the working world, be it as employees, business owners, or social entrepreneurs. As of the writing of this book we are in the process of training thousands of Technical and Vocational Education and Training (TVET) lecturers from across South Africa through a partnership with the Allan & Gill Gray Foundation.

Entrepreneurial discovery learning offers a multifaceted approach to education, equipping adolescents and young adults with attitudes and skills that enhance their academic, professional, and personal development. It can also go a long way toward engaging those who have been historically overlooked or left behind. But if entrepreneurial mindset education has so many benefits, why stop at high school? Post-secondary institutions—specifically community colleges—should encourage all students to develop entrepreneurial attitudes and skills. While many schools offer entrepreneurship classes, certificates, and even degrees, most are narrowly focused on small business creation or launching high-growth, venture-backed startups. As a result, these programs are likely to appeal to only a small number of students who are otherwise focused on more traditional careers. Moreover, such programs overlook the interdisciplinary nature of the entrepreneurial mindset advantage and its broader applicability as an essential life skill.

Community colleges can and should play a vital role in promoting entrepreneurial activity within the communities they serve. After all, the mission of community colleges is to provide accessible and affordable education to a broad segment of the population, including recent high school graduates, working adults, and those seeking career changes. They also play a vital role in workforce development by offering programs and courses that align with the needs of local industries. As such, they are likely to appeal to learners who may not thrive within a traditional learning environment yet have great potential to contribute to their organizations and communities.

Sadly, many community colleges are hamstrung by bureaucratic policies, procedures, and incentive structures that stifle rather than stimulate the development of entrepreneurial attitudes, behaviors, and skills. As a result, many are becoming increasingly irrelevant within the context of today's rapidly changing digital world. And, despite their affordability, bureaucratic barriers and a lack of support systems make it increasingly difficult to enroll. According to Davis Jenkins, a senior research scholar at the Community College Research Center, enrollment has dropped by more than a third over the previous decade. Among those who do enroll, nearly half drop out within the first year.[8] This begs the question: How might entrepreneurial mindset education reverse this trend?

What if, like Tec de Monterrey, community colleges endeavored to graduate all students with an entrepreneurial mindset? What if every student entering college was offered a freshman seminar or student success course that encouraged them to undertake entrepreneurial projects of their own? What if faculty, administrators, and staff were also encouraged to develop entrepreneurial attitudes and skills?

Cultivating entrepreneurial mindsets can be a powerful lever that can greatly enhance the community college experience for all. Infusing entrepreneurial mindset education into the curriculum can greatly enhance the student experience, empowering them with valuable skills that better enable them to contribute to the overall economic and social development of the communities they inhabit. It can also help attract, engage, and retain students. For example, one of our community college clients found that remedial students who completed the Ice House Student Success course persisted from first to second semester by a rate 28 percent higher than those who did not.

Training faculty—specifically those who may not otherwise have an interest in traditional entrepreneurship education—can go a long way to encouraging all students to develop entrepreneurial competencies. Here again, infusing entrepreneurial mindset education into the community college experience does not require faculty to abandon traditional methods of teaching. Nor does it require them to limit entrepreneurial mindset education to the creation of new businesses. Having trained thousands of community college faculty, I have found that those who may not have an interest in traditional business education are often those who become the most energized and engaged, finding creative ways to infuse entrepreneurial thinking into their classrooms.

Yet, to create a culture of entrepreneurship within an institution, it's not enough to include faculty members. In order to solve adaptive challenges, community college leaders must also learn how to think like entrepreneurs if they are to adjust and thrive in the face of decreasing enrollment and entrenched bureaucracy, not to mention the rapid increase in new technologies and easily accessible online competitors. These adaptive challenges place enormous pressure on community college leaders to seek alternate solutions. And they cannot do it alone. Unlike technical problems, which are easy to identify and solve based on experience and expertise, solving adaptive challenges requires deeper learning from all those affected by the challenges, including academic deans.

In a 2015 paper, the executive leadership professor Shannon Cleverley-Thompson writes:

> Leaders, such as academic deans—if they want their organizations to be successful and competitive—need to acquire entrepreneurial skills in order to meet the challenges of the dynamic and competitive environment of higher education today ... Academic deans are in crucial leadership roles for implementing entrepreneurial activities and programs that can impact the finances of their colleges, but these activities and programs depend on the cooperation and support of faculty members and other academic and administrative leaders.[9]

One of our clients, a community college in California, is doing just that. As the superintendent and president of Victor Valley College, Dr. Dan Walden recognized that, in order to adapt to the ever-changing nature of learning and work, he would need to empower his leadership team to think like entrepreneurs. He began by recruiting volunteers who would be willing to undertake entrepreneurial projects of their own. Initially only a handful were willing to step forward. Among them was Dr. McKenzie Tarango, who was then the dean of instruction, public safety & industrial technology. While initially reluctant, Tarango quickly grasped the value of entrepreneurial thinking as an effective means of solving adaptive challenges. She immediately got to work, reaching out to colleagues to work together to streamline bureaucratic processes that resulted in saving the college hundreds of thousands of dollars each year. As a result of her early success, others soon began to get involved, working to improve the college experience by reducing barriers to enrollment, providing easy access to tutoring and support services, streamlining communication, encouraging interdepartmental collaboration, and improving community outreach. Tarango has since been promoted to associate vice president of instruction.

"I am more excited now than I've ever been because I see it growing," Walden said. "I have my managers meeting every week and talking about entrepreneurial mindset. This is too good to be true!" Over the long term, Walden would like to see faculty apply an entrepreneurial mindset to curriculum and pedagogy. The college also recently opened a new entrepreneurship and innovation center to encourage students to nurture their own entrepreneurial mindsets. His vision is to get more faculty and students involved so as to permeate the whole campus with an entrepreneurial mindset.[10] Walden's vision is to shift entrepreneurship from the perimeter to the core of Victor Valley College. By doing so, he is paving the way for other academic leaders to do the same.

In his landmark book *Experience and Education,* the educational theorist John Dewey asks: "How many students, for example, were rendered callous to ideas, and how many lost the impetus to learn because of the way in which learning was experienced by them?"[11] Now, nearly a century later, the question remains: Why do we continue to educate our children in ways that stifle rather than stimulate their desire to learn?

We seem to be caught in a self-fulfilling prophecy whereby our assumptions about the capabilities of our students lead us to administer systems that cause them to behave in ways that reinforce our assumptions. Clearly, young people are capable of more. Not only are they capable of more; they are desirous of more, yet we continue to perpetuate learning environments that alienate rather than engage them in the learning process. The lack of engagement then seems to reinforce the need for more oversight, more testing, longer school days, and more homework, all of which lead to less engagement and more anxiety, more boredom, and more stress. Without realizing it, we've created a self-perpetuating system that stifles rather than stimulates the hidden entrepreneurial potential that lies dormant in our youth. As a result, we are failing to produce the human capital necessary for creating the societies of the future.

If we are to create vibrant and sustainable communities, we must recognize entrepreneurial mindset education as essential for all students to adapt and thrive amid complexity and change. If we are to cultivate the human capital necessary for creating the societies of the future, we must also recognize the latent entrepreneurial potential that lies dormant in those whom our systems of education might otherwise overlook. Indeed, if we are to face the most daunting challenges of our time, we must unlock the entrepreneurial potential that remains hidden in our youth.

As I have said, doing so does not require massive restructuring of our systems of education. It simply requires us to recognize the value of entrepreneurial mindset education as essential for all students to adapt and thrive. It requires us to acknowledge that, while not every student may want to start a business, all students have within them a desire to learn and to grow, to pursue their interests and develop their abilities in ways that contribute to the greater good. It also requires us to create learning environments that are conducive to curiosity and creativity, exploration and experimentation. Unlocking the untapped potential in our schools requires us, as Jaime Casap suggests, to stop asking students what they want to *be* when they grow up and start asking them what problems they want to solve, and what they need to learn in order to solve those problems. It requires us to prepare our students for *their* future rather than our past.

Instead of doubling down on prior beliefs by adding more testing, longer school hours, and more oversight, we must recognize that, as the world continues to change, we, too, must change. Rather than trying harder or blaming others, we must recognize the ways in which today's problems arise from yesterday's solutions. We must examine the ways in which the deeply held values and assumptions that once enabled us to succeed may now be holding us back. Rather than drawing from the past, like entrepreneurs, we must use our imagination to envision a future that looks different from the past.

Imagine if, as a society, we were to value entrepreneurial mindset education with the same fervor and reverence that we do baseball, football, or soccer. Imagine if, like physical education, we had national standards for entrepreneurial mindset education to ensure that all students graduate with basic entrepreneurial competencies. Imagine what would happen if we were to enlist entrepreneurial directors who, like athletic directors, were tasked with overseeing entrepreneurial activity within every school district. Where might we be in ten or twenty years if all middle schoolers were encouraged to undertake entrepreneurial projects of their own? Imagine where we might be if our high schools, colleges, and universities endeavored to graduate all students with an entrepreneurial mindset with an emphasis on human flourishing. Imagine if we were to engage local entrepreneurs, business leaders, and other community stakeholders to sponsor student projects and provide ongoing mentorship and support. Where might we be if parents, relatives, and neighbors regularly filled gymnasiums and stadiums to cheer on students as they showcased their entrepreneurial projects and the problems they endeavored to solve? Imagine if, like talent scouts, investors were to frequent such events, looking for kids like Julián, who have promising ideas that have the potential to change the world. Now let's imagine where we will be in ten or twenty years if we don't.

The American theologian Richard Shaull once said: "Education either functions as an instrument which is used to facilitate integration of the younger generation into the logic of the present system and bring about conformity, or it becomes the practice of freedom, the means by which men and women deal critically and creatively with reality and discover how to participate in the transformation of their world."[12]

While Shaull's assertion may resonate with some, I argue that he presents a false dilemma by framing the options as mutually exclusive. Yes, we must bring the younger generation into the logic of the present. After all, we must teach them what we know about how the world works. Yet, we must do so in a way that acknowledges that the logic of the present is clearly flawed, evidenced by the mounting social, environmental, and political challenges we currently face. We must acknowledge that the world is flawed in ways that we cannot see, flawed in ways that may be obscured by our own entrenched perspectives. We must bring the younger generation into the logic of the present with a sense of humility, in a way that acknowledges the value and the purpose of the beginner's mind and the unbridled exuberance of youth. We must bring the younger generation into the logic of the present in a way that acknowledges the fact that, because they are young and naïve and not yet steeped in our way of thinking, they may have the ability to see things, and a willingness to try things, that those of us who are older, wiser, and more experienced may not. If we are to adapt and thrive in the face of change, we must educate the next generation in a way that stimulates rather than stifles creativity, critical thinking, exploration, and experimentation. Indeed, we must bring the younger generation into the logic of the present while also empowering them to participate in the transformation of their world. By doing so, we can unlock the vast reservoir of untapped potential that lies dormant in our schools.

Chapter Twelve

Creating Entrepreneurial Organizations

If you want to teach men how to build ships, don't just assign
them tasks, but instill in them a longing for the vast and endless sea.

—Antoine de Saint-Exupéry[1]

Several years ago, while giving a lecture to a group of business and community leaders, a CEO asked, "What happens if I train my people how to think like entrepreneurs? Won't they all leave?" My answer: What if you don't and they all stay?

The long-term sustainability of an organization relies upon its ability to harness the untapped entrepreneurial potential that lies dormant within its people. As the rate of change continues to increase, top-down bureaucratic leadership models of the past are becoming increasingly obsolete. While managerial systems and the mindsets they produce are necessary for the efficient replication and distribution of useful things, they are no longer sufficient in the face of dynamism and complexity. After all, the most daunting problems your organization faces are likely to have less to do with efficiency and replication but instead require entrepreneurial thinking. Yet, because the managerial systems we rely on are focused on replication and efficiency, and because they tend to be hierarchical, they are not conducive to exploration and experimentation, creativity, and critical thinking. As organizational leaders, we are increasingly likely to be confronted with complex challenges that cannot be solved through traditional top-down managerial methods of the past. In order to keep pace, leaders must increase the organization's ability to adapt by tapping into the entrepreneurial potential of its people. The problem is that managerial values and assumptions have become so deeply ingrained that we cannot see how they may now be preventing us from adapting in the face of change. Here again, today's problems arise as a result of yesterday's solutions.

The factory system gave rise to an industrialized way of thinking that lifted huge swaths of humanity from poverty. Now, some 250 years later, the underlying values and assumptions inherent in these industrialized systems have become so deeply ingrained in our individual and collective mindsets that we are no longer aware of them, much less the ways in which they may be preventing us from adapting in the face of change. While we may adopt the latest technologies to streamline our business functions, in all likelihood we are still operating on antiquated management theories and outdated incentive structures of the past. By overemphasizing efficiency and short-term profitability, leaders unwittingly overlook the untapped entrepreneurial potential that lies dormant within their organizations. It's not that managerial systems have become obsolete, it's that they are no longer sufficient in a world that is constantly changing. Here again, the most obvious, important realities are often the hardest to see. In order to navigate the future, leaders must recognize the need for both managerial and entrepreneurial thinking. Doing so requires Entrepreneurial leadership (EL).

Entrepreneurial leadership is focused on enabling the adaptive capacity of an organization by unlocking the entrepreneurial potential of its people. Entrepreneurial leadership draws from a variety of human-centered leadership principles, yet its core underlying distinction lies in the belief in the untapped entrepreneurial potential of ordinary people. Unlocking the entrepreneurial potential of an organization requires leaders to create conditions that are conducive to exploration and experimentation while also preserving the core functions of the organization.

Entrepreneurial leadership is focused on enabling the adaptive capacity of an organization by unlocking the entrepreneurial potential of its people.

Entrepreneurial leaders can create the conditions in which others—*especially those who are affected by the problems*—are empowered to solve them. Ultimately, entrepreneurial leaders can create the conditions that enable their organizations not only to adapt to change but also to thrive in the midst of it. Doing so requires leaders to recognize the distinction between entrepreneurial and managerial values and assumptions. It also requires us to create organizational culture that is conducive to both.

As we discussed in chapter 5, managerial values and assumptions tend to focus on the efficient reproduction and delivery of useful things (see figure 12.1). This is a phase two, growth-oriented paradigm that focuses on the efficient replication and distribution of known products and services. Broadly speaking, the underlying values of managerial paradigms prioritize efficiency, profitability, and error reduction. Within such paradigms, it is generally assumed that the useful things the organization produces, as well as the processes and procedures for producing them, are the correct way to perceive, think, and act. Therefore, those who work in the organization are incentivized to follow established processes and procedures in order to maximize productivity.

Such paradigms tend to be rooted in hierarchical assumptions: those at the top make all the decisions while those who work in the organization are expected to follow the rules.

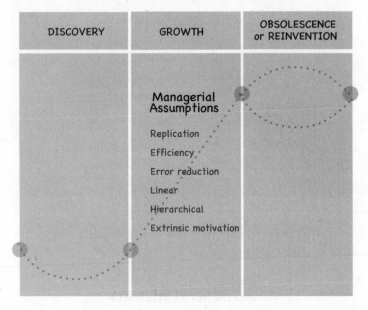

Figure 12.1 | Managerial Assumptions

In contrast, entrepreneurial values and assumptions are focused on the discovery of useful things (see figure 12.2). Broadly speaking, the underlying values of entrepreneurial paradigms are rooted in exploration, experimentation, and adaptation. Such discovery-oriented paradigms tend to be nonlinear and error *inducing*, the underlying assumption of which is that we may *not* have the correct way to perceive, think, and act in relation to a particular problem or the pursuit of a particular goal. This way of thinking tends to be much more divergent and much less hierarchical, encouraging workers to collaborate, to challenge convention, to question assumptions, and to search for ways to not only improve existing products and services but also to invent new ones.

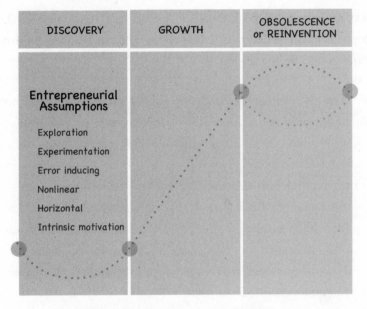

Figure 12.2 | Entrepreneurial Assumptions

A Conflict of Interests

Both managerial and entrepreneurial functions are valuable, but we can see the conflict of interests that might arise between the two. On one hand, managerial systems are essential for the efficient replication and distribution of useful things, yet they tend to discourage or even punish exploration and experimentation. After all, many successful businesses were created by former employees who left their jobs because their employers were not receptive to new ideas or because they offered no incentives to those who were inclined to be innovative and entrepreneurial. One entrepreneur I interviewed was fired from his job after inventing a new process that ultimately revolutionized an industry and created a multibillion-dollar company. By discouraging entrepreneurial activity, organizations often overlook the diamonds in their own backyard.

As leaders, if we are to adapt and thrive in the face of change, we must create work environments that are conducive to exploration and experimentation while also preserving the core of the organization's current functions. We must recognize that the attitudes and skills that are required to discover useful things are almost entirely distinct from those required to exploit them. Indeed, if we are to create entrepreneurial organizations, we must create the conditions that are conducive to both entrepreneurial and managerial functions.

History is replete with examples of individuals, organizations, and communities, even entire societies, that have perished or become obsolete due to an inability to adapt in the face of change. The inability to adapt lies not in a lack of knowledge, talent, or skill, but in underlying assumptions of which we are not aware. It's a glitch in our mindset that causes us to respond inappropriately to change.

Recall that a mindset works to our advantage within stable environments, yet it often prevents us from adapting in the face of change. Rather than responding and adapting, we react to change by doubling down on prior beliefs, adopting what George Land refers to as a "siege mentality," cutting costs, initiating layoffs, and shuttering all nonessential projects while simultaneously asking everyone to do more with less.[2] While such measures may be effective for temporary economic downturns, they are likely to be maladaptive in the face of change. As we have seen, when faced with such adaptive challenges (the second break point in transformation theory), doing more of what we have always done is rarely the answer.

If we are to create entrepreneurial organizations, we must distinguish between technical problems and adaptive challenges, as we discussed in chapter 2. As author Ronald Heifetz observed: "The most common leadership failure stems from trying to apply technical solutions to adaptive challenges." In other words, the key to survival is to know which type of problem we are trying to solve so that we know which mindset to apply.

In his book *The Practice of Adaptive Leadership: Tools and Tactics for*

Changing Your Organization and the World, Heifetz describes technical problems as easy to identify and relatively easy to solve, often lending themselves to quick, cut-and-dry solutions that are produced by experts or outside consultants. He also points out that people are generally receptive to technical solutions, which can be implemented quickly, often by authority or decree. The point is that technical problems can usually be solved with managerial thinking.

In contrast, Heifetz describes adaptive challenges as difficult to identify and, more importantly, easy to deny.[3] Solving adaptive challenges requires leaders to think systemically in order to understand the needs of everyone involved. In other words, they need to understand the root causes, which will require commitment of time and energy. Solving adaptive challenges also requires leaders to look within, to challenge their own deeply held values and assumptions, and to be willing to change beliefs and to adopt new approaches to the organization's goals. More importantly, the solutions to adaptive challenges are not yet known and therefore cannot be solved by experts or authority figures. Instead, those who are affected by the problems need to do the work of solving them, which often requires changes across organizational boundaries. What makes adaptive challenges particularly difficult is that people in the organization often resist any possible solutions while at the same time acknowledging the existence of the challenge. As a result, solving adaptive challenges requires exploration, experimentation, and new discoveries. Like any new idea, solutions to adaptive problems can take a long time to implement and cannot be done so by decree. Instead, they require leaders to achieve buy-in by winning the hearts and minds of early adopters who, over time, will communicate their value to their more reluctant peers. In simple terms, adaptive challenges cannot be solved with the same mindset that we use to solve technical problems.

Clearly, the mindset and the methods required for solving adaptive challenges are similar to those of an everyday entrepreneur. After all, the opportunity discovery process requires entrepreneurs to understand the problems they are solving from an empathic perspective, that is, from the perspective of those who have the problem. And it requires the entrepreneur to look beyond the functional dimensions to address the deeper social and emotional dimensions of their customers' needs. Because the entrepreneur is less likely to be wedded to a particular orthodoxy, they are more likely to be willing to challenge conventional wisdom, to experiment, to try things on a small scale and learn from the results. Simply put, the process of solving adaptive challenges is the same process entrepreneurs use to discover new opportunities. Solving adaptive challenges requires the cultivation of entrepreneurial attitudes and skills. This requires us to create spaces that are conducive to entrepreneurial activity while also preserving the core of the organization's goals.

The fundamental principles for creating an entrepreneurial organization aren't much different from creating entrepreneurial learning environments. The underlying assumptions are the same: The individual employee is not only capable of more but also desirous of more, and although they may not have the same credentials as those at the top of the organizational chart, they are likely to have both the capacity and the desire to identify and solve problems through the use of their own initiative and intellect. They also have an innate desire to contribute to the organization's goals and to be recognized and appreciated for their contribution. It is our job as leaders to create the conditions that encourage such behavior while also preserving the core of the organization's goals. Doing so may require us to challenge some of our own deeply held assumptions about the ability of ordinary people—specifically those we might otherwise overlook or ignore.

The first step in accessing the untapped entrepreneurial potential in an organization is to identify early adopters. These are the champions of new ideas, the people most willing to try something new. While we should assume that the capacity and desire to be innovative and entrepreneurial are innate, in the beginning, this is likely to be a small percentage of the broader group. As entrepreneurial leaders, we should refrain from mandating entrepreneurial behavior. Instead, we must cultivate intrinsic motivation by winning hearts and minds while also creating conditions that support the innate need for autonomy, competency, and relatedness. Like any new venture, this requires us to identify the early adopters who, like early customers, are eager to jump in before all the details have been worked out. Like early customers, early adopters play multiple important roles, not only providing vital feedback that enables us to refine our entrepreneurial processes, but also convincing their more cautious colleagues to buy in. Many of the organizations we work with begin by exposing a broad range of their workforce to the basic principles of entrepreneurial leadership and the opportunity discovery process as a way to identify early adopters. Then, once the cohort of early adopters has been identified, the next step is to encourage them to undertake entrepreneurial projects of their own as described in part 2, "The Entrepreneurial Process." Here again, such projects are encouraged in the margins, in ways that enable participants to maintain the core of their day-to-day responsibilities. Many forward-thinking organizations do this by encouraging their workers to carve out time to undertake entrepreneurial "side" projects of their own, not only as an innovation strategy but also as a way to attract and retain talent. Doing so requires leaders to create physical spaces where people are free to identify problems and exchange ideas, and also, more importantly, the psychological spaces where opportunity discovery can happen. As author Steven Johnson observed, good ideas need creative spaces to emerge. Like the coffeehouses of the Enlightenment, such spaces encourage free thinking and the open exchange of ideas. After all, good ideas seldom manifest as sudden epiphanies but rather as gradual intuitions nurtured through interaction with others.[4] The creativity to cultivate early inklings into full-fledged concepts is facilitated by creating creative spaces in which workers feel free to ask hard questions, to exchange ideas, and to take small, calculated risks without fear of punishment, ridicule, or jeopardizing their careers.

Such spaces also require bandwidth: the mental capacity for deeper thinking and creativity, both of which are necessary for new ideas to emerge. This kind of higher mental functioning is much less likely to occur when those who are asked to engage in the process are constantly interrupted by meetings or overwhelmed by constant pressure to perform. Entrepreneurial leadership requires a dynamic relationship between the bureaucratic, managerial functions that an organization depends on and the organization's adaptive capacity. In order to create this kind of balance, we must carve out some amount of time and space for people to undertake entrepreneurial projects of their own. By doing so, we can enable the entrepreneurial capacity of the organization to emerge.

Innovation and Entrepreneurship

Much has been written about innovation in leadership literature, but despite their similarities, there is far less discussion of entrepreneurship. In many cases, this omission overlooks an essential component of the opportunity discovery process because innovation and entrepreneurship are inextricably linked. Broadly speaking, the term *innovation* refers to the process of finding and solving problems, whereas the term *entrepreneurship* refers to the process of bringing ideas to life in a way that creates value for others while also creating value for those who undertake such endeavors. As we discussed earlier in this book, the process of finding and solving problems can be relatively easy compared to the difficulties of bringing new ideas to life. Doing so requires passion, dedication, and long-term commitment. By separating innovation from entrepreneurship, we may be overlooking a powerful synergy that can occur by combining the two.

Thus far, I have avoided making a distinction between breakthrough innovations and incremental innovations. After all, as we discussed in previous chapters, the vast majority of entrepreneurs do not invent anything new. Instead, they are more likely to improve upon an existing product or service in some way. Breakthrough innovations are exceptionally rare and therefore should not be used as exemplars. When they do occur, they are much more likely to come from independent inventors and inexperienced, cash-strapped entrepreneurs rather than well-funded R&D labs that have access to top talent with advanced knowledge and years of experience. In fact, a disproportionate number of celebrated innovators had little technical training and, in many cases, not much formal education at all.[5]

However, those who produce breakthrough innovations are not always adept at bringing their ideas to life in a way that enables them to reach their full potential. As it turns out, large, established organizations (that have access to top talent, resources, marketing, and technical expertise) are much more adept at incremental innovations, which are essential for breakthrough innovations to reach their full potential. For example, the Wright brothers were independent bicycle mechanics, neither of whom graduated from high school, and yet they pioneered human flight. But it was the incremental improvements contributed by large, established corporations such as Boeing, Lockheed Martin, and others that made the modern jet airplane what it is today. The same is true for countless other innovations that would not be nearly as meaningful without both the groundbreaking idea and its successful development and deployment. In short, innovation without entrepreneurship may not get us where we want to go. However, by combining the two, we can create a powerful synergy that can transform an organization's culture.

Ideas, like people, often have great potential, yet they are unable to reach that potential because they do not have champions to fend for them while they are in their adolescent state. As entrepreneurial leaders, we must recognize that ideas are fragile and need advocates to nurture, support, and protect them against the status quo, against incumbents, against competing ideas and priorities, to say nothing of the managerial nature of the organization itself. We must also recognize that breakthrough ideas are often counterintuitive and are therefore not obvious at their inception. History is replete with examples of breakthrough innovations that were initially rejected or dismissed as a passing fad. Bicycles, automobiles, telephones, and laptop computers come easily to mind. In many cases, new ideas can take years, if not decades, to reach their full potential. As entrepreneurial leaders, we must also recognize that opportunity discovery is an error-inducing process whereby lots of bad ideas often lead to good ideas. It can be difficult, if not impossible, to predict which people or which ideas will emerge. Above all, we must recognize that breakthrough ideas are exceptionally rare and that the jockey is likely to be much more important than the horse.

> Ideas, like people, often have great potential, yet they are unable to reach that potential because they do not have champions to fend for them while they are in their adolescent state.

The point is that those who pursue new ideas will require ongoing mentorship and support, both from within the organization as well as from outside entrepreneurs. Internal sponsors can play a crucial role in fostering the emergence of new ideas, not only by providing encouragement and support but also by advocating for the most promising ideas by allocating resources and breaking down silos to facilitate cross-functional collaboration. In many ways, internal sponsors help protect the initiator of new ideas against the prevailing managerial paradigm while also helping to shift the organizational culture. Because they have credibility, these advocates can also act as bridges between the entrepreneurial and managerial functions of the organization. Yet, internal sponsors may not be enough.

Forward-thinking leaders have begun to recognize that a powerful synergy can occur by combining internal sponsorship with the guidance and perspective of experienced entrepreneurs from outside the organization. These "entrepreneurs in residence" have entrepreneurial experience, yet they are unencumbered by organizational culture. As such, they can help stimulate new insights in ways that those who are immersed in a particular cultural paradigm may not, thus creating an adaptive advantage over those who remain bound by entrenched beliefs. Having functioned in such a capacity for corporate, academic, nonprofit, and government clients alike, I have seen firsthand the synergistic energy that occurs by combining the two.

Keep in mind that entrepreneurial leadership is similar to systems leadership in that it requires those who are engaged in the entrepreneurial process to understand the broader system. Just as aspiring entrepreneurs blind themselves to opportunities by focusing on their own needs, managers can limit an organization's ability to adapt by focusing only on the parts of the system over which they have control. As author Lynn Shostack observed: "Leaving services to individual talent and managing the pieces rather than the whole makes a company more vulnerable and creates a service that reacts slowly to market needs and opportunities."[6] Shostack's work led to the development of what is now known as service design, a method of designing optimal services that accommodate the needs of customers as well as the competencies and capabilities of those who serve them.

Similarly, when describing systems leadership, Peter Senge observed:

> In any complex setting, people typically focus their attention on the parts of the system most visible from their own vantage point. This usually results in arguments about who has the right perspective on the problem. Helping people see the larger system is essential to building a shared understanding of complex problems. This understanding enables collaborating organizations to jointly develop solutions not evident to any of them individually and to work together for the health of the whole system rather than just pursue symptomatic fixes to individual pieces.[7]

In order to create entrepreneurial organizations, leaders must help those who are asked to undertake entrepreneurial projects to understand how the whole system works. After all, solving adaptive challenges requires collaboration; it requires us to work in small teams, to venture outside the scope of our individual perspectives, and to break down silos so as to understand the needs of our colleagues as well as our customers.

Ultimately, entrepreneurial leadership is human-centered leadership. When we think of an ideal worker, we think of those who are passionate and dedicated, those who are constantly searching for new and better solutions to challenging problems. We think of those who take it upon themselves to identify and solve problems and take manageable risks. We think of those who are well connected, those who work across silos to deliver results. When we think of an ideal worker, we think of those who are optimally engaged. Of course, we are thinking of those workers who think—*and act*—like entrepreneurs.

Ultimately, entrepreneurial leadership is human-centered leadership.

At the same time, we also know that such workers are the exception rather than the norm. The truth is that the vast majority of workers are not engaged. Here I am referring to those who are languishing in our organizations, those who live for weekends and holidays, those who avoid challenges and do the least to get by. Here I am referring to those whose untapped entrepreneurial potential is being overlooked or ignored. In order to reverse this trend, we must stop blaming our workers for their lack of engagement and look within to examine the ways in which the underlying industrial-era assumptions of the past may be contributing to the lack of engagement we deplore. As entrepreneurial leaders, we must abandon the carrot-and-stick behaviorist ideals of the past.

When a small percentage of workers are not engaged, we tend to blame the individual, attributing their lack of engagement to laziness or poor character. However, when a substantial number of workers are not engaged, we must step back and examine the culture so as to understand the root causes that lead to the widespread lack of engagement. We must recognize, as W. Edwards Deming suggests, the ways in which a bad system will beat a good person every time.[8]

Harness the wind. We know that workers are capable of more and that they are desirous of more. In many cases, they are capable of more than they themselves are aware. We also know that entrepreneurial behavior is largely the result of cognitive, motivational, and situational factors rather than dispositional traits. Many of these factors are within our control. Just as entrepreneurs must understand their customers' needs, harnessing the entrepreneurial potential of an organization requires us to consider the deeper social and emotional dimensions of our employees' needs. It requires us to recognize that workers *want* to be engaged in work that matters, they *want* to contribute, and they *want* to be heard. More importantly, they want to work for organizations that are making a difference in the world. They also want their employers to care about their well-being. While such needs are often unarticulated, creating the conditions that encourage and support them is the key to optimizing engagement and unleashing the untapped entrepreneurial potential in your organization.

Entrepreneurial leadership is an emerging idea, one that arose from my observations and analysis of hundreds of everyday entrepreneurs combined with the latest research in the science of motivation. It is an idea that is rooted in the awareness that ordinary people are indeed capable of being innovative and entrepreneurial.

Entrepreneurial leadership is the antithesis of Taylorism and the carrot-and-stick management theories of the past. Certainly there is no one-size-fits-all approach. Like any entrepreneurial endeavor, creating an entrepreneurial organization will require you to learn by doing, through a process of experimentation and adaptation. While you may lose an occasional employee who will leave to start a business of their own, the benefits of creating an entrepreneurial organization far outweigh the costs of leading an organization that relies on workers who will simply do as they are told. By creating the conditions that encourage and support entrepreneurial behavior, we also create the conditions that support lifelong learning and growth. Isn't that what leadership is all about?

Chapter Thirteen

Creating Entrepreneurial Communities

Our greatest natural resource is the untapped potential of people.
> —Thom Ruhe, president and CEO, NC IDEA[1]

We know that entrepreneurial activity is essential for creating vibrant, equitable, and sustainable communities. So why do entrepreneurs coalesce and thrive in some communities more than others? Thus far we have discussed the importance of cultivating entrepreneurial mindsets in our children, our students, and our organizations, all of which are vital to creating vibrant entrepreneurial communities. Yet, we must also encourage and support entrepreneurial mindsets within our communities, not only for those who start and grow businesses but also for those whose jobs have been displaced and who must now reinvent themselves.

With the right support systems, entrepreneurial communities can thrive. Economic developers and other community stakeholders have begun to recognize the importance of creating entrepreneurial support systems to stimulate entrepreneurial activity in a particular region. Just as an acorn requires the right balance of soil, sunlight, and water to reach its full potential, unlocking the untapped entrepreneurial potential of a community requires environmental conditions that nurture and sustain entrepreneurial activity. In this chapter, we'll explore the idea of creating entrepreneurial communities—from small, grassroots initiatives to large, statewide economic development efforts. We will also provide examples of ordinary people who are cultivating entrepreneurial activity in their communities and show how they leverage existing resources to make a difference. In addition, we'll explore simple, easy-to-implement strategies that anyone can put into action.

Starting a business, or being entrepreneurial for that matter, has taken on a new meaning in recent years. As we discussed in earlier chapters, entrepreneurship is the self-directed pursuit of opportunities to create value for others. In that sense, I make no distinction between a small business owner and an entrepreneur. When creating entrepreneurial communities, we must look beyond brick-and-mortar startups to include side hustlers, freelancers, and even those who are self-employed. We must also include those whose jobs have been disrupted and must now reinvent themselves.

As such, workforce development initiatives should also be included in our efforts to create entrepreneurial communities. As the changing nature of the economic landscape is likely to disrupt huge swaths of the existing workforce, millions of midcareer adults will not only need to learn new technical skills, but they will also need new perspectives and new ways of thinking about learning and work. After all, entrepreneurial attitudes and skills such as creative and critical thinking, problem-solving, effective communication, collaboration, and teamwork are the skills employers now demand. When creating entrepreneurial communities, we must include anyone who is pursuing opportunities to create value for others, be they small business owners, traditional entrepreneurs, or employees.

The idea of deliberately creating entrepreneurial support systems is relatively new. In the past, economic development efforts focused exclusively on attracting and retaining large, established businesses. This approach was based on the belief that these large businesses would bring significant job opportunities and economic stability to a community or region. These approaches were often predicated on the assumption that entrepreneurs were outliers and that small businesses played an insignificant role in the economic well-being of a particular community or region. When entrepreneurial communities did emerge, they were likely to do so organically rather than by design.

More recently, however, there has been a shift in economic development strategies, with more emphasis on supporting entrepreneurship and small businesses, as policymakers and community stakeholders have come to understand the vital role that startups and small businesses play in job creation, innovation, and fostering economic resilience. Yet our understanding of entrepreneurship—the person, the process, and the underlying causes of the behavior—remains shrouded in popular myths and common misperceptions that have thus far limited our ability to create effective entrepreneurial support systems. To be fair, many in the economic development world are under enormous pressure to meet short-term performance metrics, like the number of jobs created or the number of investment dollars leveraged, whereas creating entrepreneurial ecosystems may seem abstract and perhaps less expedient. As a result, many economic development initiatives continue to focus exclusively on attracting and retaining large, established businesses while ignoring the need to encourage and support entrepreneurs.

In recent decades, however, the idea of creating "entrepreneurial ecosystems" began to emerge as a new economic development strategy. In many cases, these ecosystems, which are typically located in major metropolitan hubs, are designed to organize regional stakeholders such as government institutions, universities, private and institutional investors, and large corporations in a way that supports high-potential startups. The problem is that much of these efforts are focused exclusively on the creation of venture-backed, high-growth firms and do not address the needs of everyday entrepreneurs. Nor are such efforts likely to be effective in rural areas or smaller communities that do not have the population density to warrant such initiatives. Moreover, they fail to recognize that large, established firms are often created by everyday entrepreneurs who initially pursue small niche opportunities that take decades to unfold.

While there are clearly benefits to supporting startups with obvious high-growth potential, it is crucial to recognize the diverse nature of both the entrepreneurial process and the entrepreneurs themselves. To focus only on high-potential startups while ignoring the needs of the everyday entrepreneur may indeed be a shortsighted approach.

Small business development centers (SBDCs) and other government-sponsored entrepreneurial support organizations (ESOs) can play a vital role in creating entrepreneurial communities. Such organizations provide valuable technical training and support to help aspiring entrepreneurs navigate the very real and necessary legal, financial, accounting, and marketing pieces of starting and running a business, yet when it comes to providing initial guidance for validating ideas, many fall short. These shortcomings are not for a lack of effort but a failure to recognize the distinction between entrepreneurial and managerial mindsets.

Rather than encouraging first-time entrepreneurs to prove their concept by embracing an iterative, experimental, evidence-based approach, many continue to prescribe a build-it-and-they-will-come strategy that includes formal planning and the pursuit of outside funding. Others focus primarily on the need to understand managerial functions such as accounting, payroll, filing taxes, legal structures, and other aspects that are essential for managing an established business, yet they neglect to promote the skills needed to validate their ideas through experimentation and adaptation. They fall short because they fail to distinguish between the attitudes and skills required to discover opportunities and those required to exploit them. By doing so, the guidance they provide can be misleading if not downright discouraging for the typical entrepreneur. As a result, many of these government-sponsored initiatives are underutilized and often seen as an option of last resort. Yet here again, many of these challenges can be addressed by training those who are tasked with supporting aspiring entrepreneurs to embrace the mindset and the methods described in part 2, "The Entrepreneurial Process."

There is vast untapped entrepreneurial potential lying dormant in people and places we might otherwise overlook. Unlocking this untapped entrepreneurial potential requires new models and new frameworks for understanding the entrepreneurial person as well as the mindset and methods that enable them to succeed. The idea of creating entrepreneurial support systems at the community level is an emerging idea, one that requires us to look beyond the Silicon Valley narrative or the industrial-era assumptions of the past. After all, entrepreneurial support systems are complex and multidimensional, and there is no one-size-fits-all approach. What works in one community may not work in others. Those that are the most effective tend to be hyperlocalized and tailored to the needs of their communities. Building effective entrepreneurial support systems requires us to understand the cultural contexts and the deeper social and emotional dimensions of those we seek to serve. It also requires us to start where we are and use whatever resources we have to make it work. In other words, accessing the entrepreneurial potential in our communities requires us to think and act like entrepreneurs.

Over nearly two decades, I have worked with a wide range of individuals and organizations dedicated to supporting everyday entrepreneurs, from small rural and urban communities to regional and statewide initiatives. Here I will highlight a few examples of those who are creating effective entrepreneurial support systems in their communities.

At the age of fifty, Jim Correll was looking for his next job. Thus far, his career path had wandered from professional photographer to bank auditor to managing a receiving crew at his local Amazon fulfillment center in Coffeyville, a small, rural community in southeast Kansas where

Correll now lives. When Amazon asked him to work the night shift, he quit and started a tool-sharpening business. He preferred the freedom of working for himself, but his fledgling business wasn't generating enough income to pay the bills. As it happened, the community college in a neighboring town was looking for a staff instructor to run their new "Successful Entrepreneur Program." And because they wanted someone who would take a hands-on approach, he decided to apply. "I guess I was just the kind of misfit they were looking for," Jim said. Little did he know, he was about to embark on a journey that would help shift the economic landscape of an entire community.

At first, Jim wasn't sure where to begin to help teach others to become successful entrepreneurs. Like many others in such a position, he insisted that his students begin their entrepreneurial journeys by writing a business plan. "I did it the way that I thought you were supposed to do it," Jim told me. "At the time, I thought you needed a business plan and lots of money to start a business." Despite the fact that he was attempting to do everything "right" to help students become entrepreneurs, each semester he struggled to find people who were interested in taking his classes. Not only did he struggle to attract students, but the faculty also ignored him because he didn't have a four-year degree. "In the beginning, nobody listened to me," he said. For his first few years, the Successful Entrepreneur Program at Independence Community College was struggling to stay afloat.

Things began to change after he attended our facilitator training, which helped shift his focus from business planning to encouraging his students to embrace the opportunity discovery process. Soon word began to spread and people began to notice, including nontraditional students, some who wanted to start businesses and others who were interested in revitalizing their careers. With the approval of his boss, Jim then set out to create a fabrication lab (Fab Lab) that would combine entrepreneurial mindset training with tools that would enable students to actually make things. With no budget, he was forced to look to the community for financial support, which turned out to be a blessing in disguise. Slowly but surely, Jim's vision began to grow as he gained the attention of nonprofit organizations and local business owners who began to add their support. He also connected with local entrepreneurs who became regular guest speakers and mentors to new entrepreneurs who were starting businesses of their own. Within a few years, Jim had not only created a hive of entrepreneurial activity, both on and off campus, but he had also garnered the attention of other community colleges throughout the region that were interested in replicating his success.

"I've always believed that supporting entrepreneurs was a better economic development strategy than chasing big employers," Jim told me. "Later, I somehow came to see the Fab Lab as a way to increase self-efficacy by helping people make things. I knew increasing self-efficacy would have a positive impact on the community." Jim's story is one example of how a dedicated individual can become an entrepreneurial catalyst in a community.

Similar examples can also be found in urban communities where everyday entrepreneurs like Myron Pierce are working to catalyze grassroots entrepreneurial support systems. "The American Dream, the envisioning of a land where economic opportunities are available to everyone, is a powerful idea," Myron told me. "Yet in urban communities, the echoes of that dream often go unheard." Reflecting on his own life as a formerly incarcerated man now in his early forties who grew up amid poverty, crime, and violence, he added, "The possibility of a better, richer, and more fulfilling existence once seemed unimaginable to me."

Now, after two decades in the penal system, Myron discovered that, by embracing an entrepreneurial mindset, that dream may indeed be within his reach. This realization prompted him to encourage others from similar situations to reach for the same dream. "In communities like mine, human potential lies dormant, awaiting exploration, yet too often it remains untapped, diverting energies toward destructive paths." After helping kick-start grassroots entrepreneurial support systems in urban communities in Colorado Springs and Kansas City, Myron is now doing the same in Omaha and beyond. Inspired by his early success, he recently created Own the Pond, an organization dedicated to creating entrepreneurial "blue zones" that can be replicated in urban communities across America. His vision is to help build a future where the American Dream is a reality for all.

While Jim Correll and Myron Pierce provide powerful examples of ordinary people who are working to help create vibrant grassroots entrepreneurial support systems in their own communities, Thom Ruhe of the NC IDEA Foundation is doing something similar in North Carolina on a much larger scale.

Raleigh-Durham is an area considered to be among the nation's most vibrant high-tech entrepreneurial ecosystems in the United States. Yet, as an experienced entrepreneur himself, Thom recognized that the untapped potential of everyday entrepreneurs was being overlooked. He also saw an opportunity to strengthen the economy of North Carolina by helping those everyday entrepreneurs—specifically those who have historically been overlooked or underserved.

As part of his strategy, Thom and his team began by offering our Ice House Entrepreneurial Mindset program statewide by establishing partnerships with K–12 education, community colleges, universities, and other nonprofit organizations to increase public awareness while also providing meaningful training and support for aspiring everyday entrepreneurs. They also provided financial support to hundreds of educators and community stakeholders to complete our entrepreneurial mindset facilitator training to cultivate entrepreneurial thinking in classrooms and communities throughout the state. By doing so, they have now created a statewide network of small, hyperlocalized entrepreneurial support systems that not only provide training but also mentoring and grants for those who emerge with promising new businesses that have the potential to create new jobs. And his strategy is paying off. Thus far, NC IDEA has supported hundreds of startups that have created thousands of new jobs and attracted millions in investment, thus proving that supporting every-day entrepreneurs is indeed a viable, cost-effective strategy for equitable economic development. Beyond training and grant programs, NC IDEA now functions as the state's lead entrepreneurial ecosystem advocate by ar-ticulating a shared vision for the state, one in which many localized efforts are working to support the specific needs of their unique communities. "People need to understand that creating a vibrant and equitable entre-preneurial ecosystem benefits everyone, but it requires effort, and it must be sustained," Thom told me. "By nurturing the entrepreneurial potential of everyone, we can create an economic impact that will benefit genera-tions that follow." By addressing the many nuances of a state as diverse as North Carolina, NC IDEA is redefining best practices in entrepreneurial economic development and, in so doing, creating a road map to help other states do the same.

Think big, start small, and act fast. Creating entrepreneurial commu-nities can be a powerful means of social impact and economic growth. And unlocking the entrepreneurial potential in your community may be easier than you think. As we have seen, doing so does not necessarily re-quire large-scale initiatives or the coordinated efforts of large institutions. It can be accomplished by ordinary people who understand the power of entrepreneurship and are committed to the cause. Ultimately, the process of creating an entrepreneurial community is similar to the opportunity dis-covery process: start where you are and use what you have to make it work.

Think big, start small, and act fast.

The fundamental principles for creating entrepreneurial communities are the same as those required for creating entrepreneurial organizations: provide effective guidance for aspiring entrepreneurs, create spaces where entrepreneurs can regularly convene, and connect with local entrepreneurs who can provide inspiration, guidance, and support. While these concepts are similar to those required for creating entrepreneurial organizations, here we'll explore each of them in more detail as they pertain to supporting traditional entrepreneurs.

Provide Effective Guidance for Aspiring Entrepreneurs

Providing effective guidance for everyday entrepreneurs is the cornerstone for creating vibrant entrepreneurial communities. This requires those who are tasked with doing so to have a clearheaded understanding of the mindset, motivation, and methods that enable inexperienced unfunded entrepreneurs to succeed. Providing such guidance does not require subject-matter expertise or years of experience as an entrepreneur. It does, however, require those trusted with providing such guidance to understand the distinction between entrepreneurial and managerial attitudes, behaviors, and skills.

As we all know, the failure rate for small business startups is extremely high. However, much of this failure can be easily avoided by encouraging aspiring entrepreneurs to abandon the plan-and-pitch method in favor of the opportunity discovery process described in part 2, "The Entrepreneurial Process." As discussed in previous chapters, entrepreneurship is an evidence-based process that, like the scientific method, requires experimentation and adaptation rather than careful planning and in-depth research. More than anything, it requires the aspiring entrepreneur to balance their enthusiasm with a healthy dose of skepticism to prevent them from making predictable yet easily avoidable (and potentially catastrophic) mistakes. As we know, first-time entrepreneurs are likely to be enthusiastic yet inexperienced and therefore highly vulnerable to a host of cognitive biases that can easily lead them astray. Many are enamored of their ideas yet have little understanding of the underlying logic or the processes that will ultimately enable them to succeed. Instead, they are convinced that all they need is the money to "open" their business and that their success is all but guaranteed. Encouraging them to write business plans, conduct formal market research, and pursue outside investment or bank loans may be leading them down the wrong path.

When supporting entrepreneurs, it is important to recognize that the need for autonomy and the desire to fulfill human needs and to create meaning and prosperity are powerful motivational forces. And, when properly harnessed, they can empower ordinary people to accomplish extraordinary things. However, these formidable motivational forces can also work against the aspiring entrepreneur, exposing them to a range of predictable errors in judgment that can easily lead to failure. The key to providing effective guidance is to harness the enthusiasm of the aspiring entrepreneur while also helping them understand the latent, unpredictable, and multidimensional nature of human needs and to therefore balance their enthusiasm with a healthy dose of skepticism to prevent them from fooling themselves. Rather than encouraging them to write business plans and pursue outside funding, we should encourage them to embrace an iterative, experimental approach by starting where they are and using what they have to prove the feasibility of their ideas on a small scale while also developing their capabilities as fledgling entrepreneurs. We must also recognize that our role is that of a facilitator rather than of a subject-matter expert. As we discussed in earlier chapters, entrepreneurship is the *self*-directed pursuit of opportunities to create value for others. The more prescriptive we are, the more likely we are to undermine the ability of the individual to develop entrepreneurial attitudes and skills. As we also discussed, our role as facilitators is to provide initial guidance while also encouraging the aspiring entrepreneur to develop their own network of experienced entrepreneurs who are more qualified to provide ongoing guidance and support. We should also avoid judging the feasibility of an idea, instead encouraging the entrepreneurs to discover for themselves through experimentation and adaptation. After all, as we know, the opportunity discovery process relies on evidence of usefulness rather than the opinions of others, including our own.

Create Entrepreneurial Spaces

Throughout history, creativity and innovation have been catalyzed—and have flourished—by creating physical spaces where everyday innovators and entrepreneurs can share ideas, collaborate, and learn from their fellow entrepreneurs. As we learned in previous chapters, good ideas seldom manifest as sudden epiphanies but rather as gradual intuitions nurtured through interaction with others. For some communities, like Southeast Kansas, where Jim Correll works, maker spaces or Fab Labs can become creative spaces where innovators and entrepreneurs regularly convene. However, creating such spaces doesn't necessarily require the physical tools of creativity as much as it does the need to establish a meeting space where people can share ideas and learn from each other. Here, too, establishing entrepreneurial hubs can be accomplished by leveraging underutilized spaces that already exist through partnerships with local libraries, church groups, maker spaces, community colleges, and local nonprofit organizations. You can also leverage existing programs such as the Kauffman Foundation's 1 Million Cups[2] initiative as a way to encourage entrepreneurs in your community to convene. Like any entrepreneurial endeavor, start where you are using what you have to prove the concept on a small scale. In many cases, as you gain traction, you will also garner the attention of business leaders and other community stakeholders who have access to resources that can help you expand.

Connect with Local Entrepreneurs

Experienced entrepreneurs are essential to catalyzing entrepreneurial communities. While they may not be highly visible, they are often ready and willing to help. Inviting them to share their knowledge and experience not only increases the motivation for aspiring entrepreneurs but also drastically increases the likelihood that they will succeed.

This approach to social and behavioral change is nothing new. In the 1970s, researchers began to notice that, among malnourished communities in the developing world, they would occasionally encounter families whose children were healthy. They also discovered that information gathered from these families could benefit those families whose children were suffering from malnourishment. This discovery led to a highly effective approach to behavioral and social change that is based on a simple idea: within any given community, some individuals engage in unusual behaviors that allow them to solve problems better than others who face similar challenges. These individuals are referred to as "positive deviants." These positive deviants exist in every community in the form of everyday entrepreneurs. While they have no advantage over others, they manage to recognize opportunities that others overlook. In many cases, engaging with them holds the key to catalyzing effective grassroots entrepreneurial communities. After all, when encouraging people to adopt new behavior, exposure to those who have come from similar backgrounds who are succeeding by embracing that behavior can significantly increase the likelihood that others will follow suit. Without them, our best efforts are likely to yield disappointing results.

When creating entrepreneurial communities, our job is not necessarily to provide answers but to identify and interact with local entrepreneurs who come from backgrounds and circumstances similar to those we endeavor to help. Include them in the learning process as guest speakers and mentors so as to glean from them the underlying beliefs, assumptions, and behaviors that enabled them to succeed. This approach to creating grassroots entrepreneurial communities can be highly effective, not only because it leverages the community's existing assets but also because it acknowledges the cultural values of those it seeks to help. This approach differs from other entrepreneurial support initiatives that are more prescriptive and therefore difficult to sustain.

Creating entrepreneurial communities requires us to widen the aperture and take a longer-term view. If we are to harness the untapped entrepreneurial potential that lies dormant in our communities, we must look beyond the high-growth entrepreneurs to recognize the value of supporting everyday entrepreneurs. This can be done by elevating the stories of those who start with little or nothing yet manage to succeed.

Desmond Tutu said, "There comes a point where we need to stop just pulling people out of the river. We need to go upstream and find out why they're falling in."

When creating entrepreneurial communities, there comes a point when we need to stop investing solely in those who have already jumped into the entrepreneurial river and go upstream to address the systemic issues that discourage others from jumping in. In many ways, the extent to which a community supports entrepreneurial activity reflects its deeper cultural values and assumptions, some of which may be obsolete. We must also recognize the ways in which managerial paradigms may stifle rather than stimulate the development of entrepreneurial attitudes and skills. After all, we don't expect professional athletes to miraculously appear; we know they must begin training at an early age and that they must be encouraged and supported throughout their formative years. We also know that they are likely to fail many times before they make it to the major leagues. Moreover, we encourage our children to participate in sports from a very early age, not with the hope that they will become professional athletes but for the developmental benefits such activities provide. Why, then, do we expect high-growth entrepreneurs to magically emerge from the shadows, with no prior experience, yet ready to play in the major leagues? Why would we expect a novice ballplayer to hit a grand slam their first time at bat?

The concept of deliberately creating effective support systems for everyday entrepreneurs holds great promise for unlocking the entrepreneurial potential that lies dormant in our communities. While we are just beginning to understand the underlying causes of entrepreneurial behavior, people like Jim Correll, Myron Pierce, Thom Ruhe, and others continue to show us how to unlock the untapped entrepreneurial potential in people and places we have historically overlooked or ignored. They also demonstrate that creating entrepreneurial communities is something anyone can do. As Margaret Mead once observed, "Never underestimate the power of a small group of committed people to change the world. In fact, it is the only thing that ever has."[3]

Chapter Fourteen

The Hidden Logic That Unleashes Human Potential

I slept and dreamt that life was joy. I awoke and saw that life
was service. I acted and behold, service was joy.
—Rabindranath Tagore

It has been more than thirty years since I stumbled across the story of a
man who had lost his job and was struggling to adapt. It was the story
that provoked a simple question in my mind: If I could see opportunities
everywhere, why couldn't he? What was it that was blinding him to the
opportunities that were within his reach? What was it that was holding him back? Little did I know that I would discover something much
bigger than I could have ever imagined. Little did I know that the answers to these questions would ultimately reveal a framework for thinking
that could empower ordinary people to accomplish extraordinary things.
Through my journey, I came to understand that the essence of an entrepreneurial mindset is an underlying assumption that it is our individual
responsibility to figure out how to make ourselves useful to others, in

whatever circumstances we may find ourselves, and that by doing so, we can empower ourselves. I came to realize that each of us has within us interests and abilities—*gifts that we have been given*—and it is our duty to figure out how to use those gifts to create value for others. By doing so, we become intrinsically motivated and therefore optimally engaged. When that happens, learning and work become a source of meaning and purpose that energize us rather than drudgery and toil that drain us. By pursuing our interests and developing our abilities in ways that create value for others, we connect with the core and defining characteristics that are considered essential to human flourishing. This is the entrepreneurial mindset advantage, the hidden logic that unleashes human potential. This is the answer to the questions that I asked more than thirty years ago.

My journey to deconstruct the entrepreneurial mindset has had a profound impact on my life. After all, I have not just studied everyday entrepreneurs; I *am* an everyday entrepreneur. Like many of those I have interviewed, I started with very little yet somehow I managed to succeed. Hearing the stories of everyday entrepreneurs inspired me to reach beyond my grasp, to forge ahead in spite of my fears, in spite of my self-imposed limitations and self-doubt. They inspired me to learn and to grow, to pursue my interests and develop my abilities in ways that were helpful to others. I also realized that it was the goal itself that was energizing me, engaging my faculties in ways that enabled me to move forward in spite of my trepidation and self-doubt. Through my entrepreneurial journey I also discovered the inherent joy of learning and meaningful work. Through the ups and downs, the successes and failures, I realized that it was the compelling nature of the goal itself that enabled me to persevere, thus enabling me to achieve things that once seemed unimaginable to me. Through my journey, I came to realize that the vision that had landed in my brain more than thirty years ago was acting upon me, pulling me into a future that looked very different from my past. Now, as I reflect on my life, I, too, have discovered the untapped potential that was hidden within myself.

In his book *Transcend: The New Science of Self-Actualization,* psychologist Scott Barry Kaufman defines the need for purpose as "the need for an overarching, self-organizing, future-oriented aspiration that energizes one's efforts and provides a central source of meaning and significance in one's life."[1]

There is an impulse toward growth within us all. Yet this self-actualizing tendency can easily be thwarted by a constellation of subtle, underlying situational forces of which we may not be aware. Many of these forces are within our control; however, control is contingent upon awareness. In many ways, our mindset holds the key to unlocking our full potential.

"The need for purpose [is] the need for an overarching, self-organizing, future-oriented aspiration that energizes one's efforts and provides a central source of meaning and significance in one's life."

In the same way that other-directed, routinized work can stifle our innate curiosity and diminish our sense of agency and capacity for solving problems, self-directed, purposeful work can have the opposite effect. To paraphrase Adam Smith, those who engage in entrepreneurial endeavors have every occasion to exert their understanding and to exercise their invention for removing difficulties that occur with great regularity. They naturally gain, therefore, the habit of such exertion, and generally become as curious and creative, resilient and resourceful as is possible for a human creature to become.

The ability to make ourselves useful to others is a source of power—it is a source of power that is freely available to *anyone* in virtually any set of circumstances. As we have seen, accessing this power does not require big ideas, venture capital, or an advanced degree. Nor does it require us to quit our jobs, drop out of school, or undertake significant financial risks. It simply requires us to reappropriate some modicum of our discretionary thought, time, and effort to pursue our interests and develop our abilities in ways that create value for others. By doing so, we can empower ourselves to create more meaningful and prosperous lives.

> In the same way that other-directed, routinized work can stifle our innate curiosity and diminish our sense of agency and capacity for solving problems, self-directed, purposeful work can have the opposite effect.

Once we are aware of the ways in which subtle situational factors can influence our behavior, we become much less vulnerable to those that undermine our ability to realize our full potential. Now that we understand the ways in which our deeply held, taken-for-granted assumptions can also hold us back, we can no longer blame others for the outcome in our lives. Instead, we must recognize that our mindset is a belief system that is perfectly designed to create the outcomes it creates. Rather than allowing our circumstances to dictate our lives, we can now consciously and deliberately create the conditions and curate the beliefs that are conducive to self-actualization.

I often wonder if the man I read about in the newspaper so many years ago was struggling to adapt because he was waiting for someone else to tell him what to do. Without realizing it, the top-down hierarchical systems to which we have all become accustomed are such that we come to assume that someone else will tell us what to learn and do in order to be successful. In other words, we unwittingly develop an external locus of control. When that happens, we stop looking for answers, we stop learning, and we stop trying. As a result, we stop growing. Instead, we turn our attention to coping strategies, spending whatever discretionary time and energy we have on recreation, entertainment, and leisure rather than investing in exploration, experimentation, and growth. And in many cases the coping strategies we pursue further undermine our ability to learn and grow, thus creating a vacuous cycle that can be difficult to escape. Yet, now that we understand the entrepreneurial process, we must find a way to be more innovative and entrepreneurial in spite of our circumstances. Rather than looking outside of ourselves, we must look within to explore the ways in which the deeply held values and taken-for-granted assumptions that once enabled us to survive might now be holding us back. Rather than spending all our discretionary time and effort on entertainment and leisure, we must find a way to undertake an entrepreneurial project of our own. By doing so we will discover that we are indeed capable of more than we currently believe. Perhaps the questions we should all be asking ourselves are: *What is the "useful thing" that we exchange, and with whom do we exchange it? And what are the means by which we learn how to become useful? More importantly, what is preventing us from becoming more useful to more people?* The answers to these questions may reveal underlying assumptions that may be holding us back.

At the same time, as parents, educators, and organizational leaders we must also recognize that behavior is a function of the person and the situation. As such, we can no longer blame our children, our students, or our employees for their lack of engagement. Instead, we must recognize the ways in which the top-down hierarchical assumptions of the past may actually be an underlying cause. We must recognize, as many systems thinkers have, that every system is perfectly designed to get the results that it gets. As leaders, we must recognize that people are not only capable of more, but they are also desirous of more, yet the routinized hierarchical paradigms of the past may be undermining their ability to actualize their full potential. If we are to unlock the entrepreneurial potential in others, we must consider the ways in which carrot-and-stick incentive structures may be holding us back. As those who are responsible for the well-being of others, we must also recognize that the development of entrepreneurial attitudes, behaviors, and skills is largely dependent upon social, environmental, and situational factors rather than dispositional traits.

From a systems perspective, policymakers, economic developers, and ecosystem builders must recognize the entrepreneurial mindset as a teachable framework for thinking that has become essential for cultivating the human capital necessary for creating the societies of the future. If we are to compete in today's rapidly changing, hyperglobalized world, we must ensure that all students are encouraged to develop basic entrepreneurial attitudes and skills. We must train teachers, workforces, and small business development professionals to encourage entrepreneurial behavior in their classrooms and communities. If we are to lead organizations that can adapt and thrive amidst complexity and change, we must recognize the distinction between managerial and entrepreneurial attitudes, behaviors, and skills so that we can create learning and work environments that are conducive to both. If we are to create vibrant, sustainable, and equitable communities, we must develop entrepreneurial ecosystems that nurture entrepreneurial mindsets in all sectors, at all levels of society. Rather than creating innovators and entrepreneurs by accident, we must now create them by design. To do otherwise is to become increasingly irrelevant on the world stage.

The future belongs to those who can think like entrepreneurs. Clearly, the rules for survival have changed and the mindset that once enabled us to succeed is rapidly becoming maladaptive. Yet while the future may seem daunting, at the same time we are also entering an era of extraordinary opportunity for those who can think like entrepreneurs. In many ways we're at the dawn of a new workforce revolution whereby the need to distinguish between an entrepreneur and an employee is rapidly becoming obsolete. The study of everyday entrepreneurs reveals a powerful framework for thinking that exposes a new dimension of untapped human potential. As we have seen, accessing this potential does not require us to make monumental changes in our lives. Nor does it require massive restructuring of our organizations and institutions. It simply requires us to recognize the untapped potential in people and places we have historically overlooked or ignored. After all, the great advances in human history (as well as in our own lives) rarely come about as a result of doing more of what we're already doing. Instead, they come about as a result of a shift in our perspective that leads to a change in our behavior. The ideas in this book are such that anyone can embrace them, regardless of their circumstances, stature, or chosen path. As Seneca suggests, it is incumbent upon each of us to embrace these ideas, in whatever way we can so as to advance the welfare of mankind.

Acknowledgments

This book would not have been possible without the encouragement and support of family, friends, and colleagues. First and foremost, I owe an enormous debt of gratitude to my wife, Karen, who not only believed in my ideas from the beginning, but has tolerated my incessant ramblings over the years. I am also grateful to my dear friends and colleagues at ELI, Rob Herndon, Nic Houle, Alex Fuller, and Joanie Weber, for their unwavering commitment to the entrepreneurial mindset mission.

I owe an enormous debt of gratitude to my writing coach, Anne Dewvall, whose patience and clearheaded thinking were essential to bringing this book to life. And to my dear friend Maureen McHugh who was instrumental in the creation of my book proposal. Also to my agent, Steven Harris, for believing in my crazy ideas and to my publisher, Matt Holt, and the team at BenBella who worked tirelessly to bring this book to life.

To my brother John Schoeniger, my cousin Bob Houle, and my friends Stephen Post, Clifton Taulbert, Lorenzo Angeli, Michael Crawford, Frank Hamilton, Thom Ruhe, Craig Zamary, Paul Corson, and others who spent countless hours helping me plumb the depths of these ideas.

Acknowledgments

And to my dear friend Donny Knific who listened patiently to my ideas as they began to unfold.

I am also grateful to Ted Moore, Dawn Halfaker, Brian Scudamore, Diana Bezanski, Steve Orlando, Yiannis Nikolopoulos, Rob Vigil, John Kendale, Elias Ruiz, Jim Correll, Thom Ruhe, and Myron Pierce, who willingly lent their stories to this book.

Notes

Introduction

1. Lucius Annaeus Seneca, *Dialogues*.
2. Gary Schoeniger, "Ice House Entrepreneurship Program," 2011.
3. Gary G. Schoeniger and Clifton L. Taulbert, *Who Owns the Ice House?: Eight Life Lessons from an Unlikely Entrepreneur* (Mentor, OH: Eli Press, 2011).

Chapter One

1. George Land and Beth Jarman, *Breakpoint and Beyond: Mastering the Future Today* (New York: Harper, 1992).
2. "2020 Edelman Trust Barometer Reveals Growing Sense of Inequality Is Undermining Trust in Institutions," Edelman, accessed December 19, 2023, https://www.edelman.com/news-awards/2020-edelman-trust-barometer.
3. Jared M. Diamond, *Collapse: How Societies Choose to Fail or Succeed* (New York: Penguin Books, 2011).
4. Edward Lazear, "Entrepreneurship," *Journal of Labor Economics*, 2002, https://doi.org/10.3386/w9109.
5. Karen E. Wilson et al., "Educating the Next Wave of Entrepreneurs: Unlocking Entrepreneurial Capabilities to Meet the Global Challenges of the 21st Century," *Social Science Research Network*, January 1, 2009, https://doi.org/10.2139/ssrn.1396704.
6. Martin Lackeus, "BGP Entrepreneurship-in-Education" (Organisation for Economic Co-Operation and Development, 2015).

7. Peter F. Drucker, *Innovation and Entrepreneurship: Practice and Principles* (London: Routledge, 2015).

8. Amar V. Bhidé, *The Origin and Evolution of New Business* (Oxford, UK: Oxford University Press, 2000).

9. Valerie J. Calderon, "How to Keep Kids Excited About School," Gallup.com, July 3, 2023, https://news.gallup.com/opinion/gallup/211886/keep-kids-excited-school.aspx.

10. Allie Grasgreen, "Provosts, Business Leaders Disagree on Graduates' Career Readiness," *Inside Higher Ed* | Higher Education News, Events and Jobs, accessed December 19, 2023, https://www.insidehighered.com/news/2014/02/26/provosts -business-leaders-disagree-graduates-career-readiness.

11. Dan Witters, "U.S. Depression Rates Reach New Highs," Gallup.com, September 14, 2023, https://news.gallup.com/poll/505745/depression-rates-reach-new-highs.aspx.

12. Kayla N. Anderson et al., "Emergency Department Visits Involving Mental Health Conditions, Suicide-Related Behaviors, and Drug Overdoses Among Adolescents—United States, January 2019–February 2023," *Morbidity and Mortality Weekly Report* 72, no. 19 (May 12, 2023): 502–12. https://doi.org/10.15585/mmwr .mm7219a1.

13. Bill Breen and Gary Hamel, *The Future of Management* (Boston: Harvard Business School Press, n.d.).

14. Gallup Inc., "State of the Global Workplace Report," Gallup.com, November 18, 2023, https://www.gallup.com/workplace/349484/state-of-the-global-workplace -2022-report.aspx#ite-506891.

15. Mihaly Csikszentmihalyi, *Flow: The Psychology of Optimal Experience* (New York: Harper and Row, 2009).

Chapter Two

1. Adam Smith, *An Inquiry into the Nature and Causes of the Wealth of Nations* (Charleston, SC: Bibiobazaar, 2010).

2. Ashok Bhanudas Navale, "Developing Entrepreneur Skills for Corporate Work," October 2013, https://web.archive.org/web/20170329060112/http://research direction.org/UploadArticle/48.pdf.

3. Amar V. Bhidé, *The Origin and Evolution of New Business* (Oxford, UK: Oxford University Press, 2000).

4. George Land and Beth Jarman, *Breakpoint and Beyond: Mastering the Future Today* (New York: Harper, 1992).

5. Smith, *An Inquiry into the Nature and Causes of the Wealth of Nations.*

6. Land and Jarman, *Breakpoint and Beyond: Mastering the Future Today.*

7. Jared M. Diamond, *Collapse: How Societies Choose to Fail or Succeed* (New York: Penguin Books, 2011).

8. Land and Jarman, *Breakpoint and Beyond: Mastering the Future Today.*

9. Ronald Heifetz, *Leadership Without Easy Answers* (Cambridge, MA: Harvard University Press, 1998).

10. Shunryū Suzuki, *Zen Mind, Beginner's Mind: Informal Talks on Zen Meditation and Practice* (S.I.: PublishDrive, 2018).

Chapter Three

1. Gary Schoeniger, "Ice House Entrepreneurship Program," 2011.

2. Annie Murphy Paul, *The Cult of Personality: How Personality Tests Are Leading Us to Miseducate Our Children, Mismanage Our Companies, and Misunderstand Ourselves* (New York: Free Press, 2004).

3. John M. Darley and C. Daniel Batson, "'From Jerusalem to Jericho': A Study of Situational and Dispositional Variables in Helping Behavior," *Journal of Personality and Social Psychology* 27, no. 1 (July 1, 1973): 100–108, https://doi.org/10.1037/h0034449.

4. Peter F. Drucker, *Innovation and Entrepreneurship: Practice and Principles* (London: Routledge, 2015).

5. "Learning as Meaningful and Holistic Process," University of Illinois, accessed December 19, 2023, https://psychology.illinoisstate.edu/aehouse/233_Personality/233_units/humanistic_Rogers.html.

6. Carl R. Rogers, *On Becoming a Person: A Therapist's View of Psychotherapy* (London: Robinson, 2020).

7. Abraham H. Maslow and Robert Frager, *Motivation and Personality* (New Delhi: Pearson Education, 1987).

8. Saul Mcleod, "Operant Conditioning in Psychology: B.F. Skinner Theory," Simply Psychology, February 2, 2024, https://www.simplypsychology.org/operant-conditioning.html.

9. Robert W. White, "Motivation Reconsidered: The Concept of Competence," *Psychological Review* 66, no. 5 (1959): 297–333, https://doi.org/10.1037/h0040934.

10. Richard M. Ryan and Edward L. Deci, "Self-Determination Theory and the Facilitation of Intrinsic Motivation, Social Development, and Well-Being," *American Psychologist* 55, no. 1 (2000): 68–78, https://doi.org/10.1037/0003-066x.55.1.68.

11. Edward L. Deci, Richard Koestner, and Richard M. Ryan, "A Meta-Analytic Review of Experiments Examining the Effects of Extrinsic Rewards on Intrinsic Motivation," *Psychological Bulletin* 125, no. 6 (1999): 627–68, https://doi.org/10.1037/0033-2909.125.6.627.

12. Ryan and Deci, "Self-Determination Theory and the Facilitation of Intrinsic Motivation, Social Development, and Well-Being."

13. Henry David Thoreau, *Walden* (Borders Press, 1996).

14. Albert Bandura (1994), "Self-Efficacy." In V. S. Ramachaudran (ed.), *Encyclopedia of Human Behavior*, New York: Academic Press, vol. 4: 71–81. (Reprinted in H. Friedman [ed.], *Encyclopedia of Mental Health* San Diego: Academic Press, 1998.)

15. Jack Mearns, "The Social Learning Theory of Julian B. Rotter," accessed December 19, 2023, http://psych.fullerton.edu/jmearns/rotter.htm.

16. Mihaly Csikszentmihalyi, *Flow: The Psychology of Optimal Experience* (New York: Harper and Row, 2009).

17. Viktor E. Frankl, Harold S. Kushner, and William J. Winslade, *Man's Search for Meaning* (Boston: Beacon Press, 2006).

18. "Steve Jobs Secrets of Life," YouTube Video, posted by Santa Clara Valley Historical Association, 2011, https://www.youtube.com/watch?v=kYfNvmF0Bqw.

19. Albert Bandura, "Exercise of Human Agency Through Collective Efficacy," *Current Directions in Psychological Science* 9, no. 3 (2000): 75–78, https://doi.org/10.1111/1467-8721.00064.

20. Peter Senge, *The Fifth Discipline: The Art & Practice of the Learning Organization* (New York: Doubleday, 2006).

Chapter Four

1. Edgar H. Schein and Peter A. Schein, *Organizational Culture and Leadership* (Hoboken, NJ: Wiley, 2017).

2. Daniel Kahneman, *Thinking, Fast and Slow* (London: Penguin Books, 2011).

Chapter Five

1. Farnam Street, "This Is Water by David Foster Wallace (Full Transcript and Audio)," Farnam Street, November 22, 2023, https://fs.blog/david-foster-wallace-this-is-water/.

2. This is a phrase made popular by Emmanuel Kant.

3. Adam Smith, *An Inquiry into the Nature and Causes of the Wealth of Nations* (Charleston, SC: Bibiobazaar, 2010).

4. Smith, *An Inquiry into the Nature and Causes of the Wealth of Nations.*

5. Kalpesh Arvind Shah, "5 Functions of Management by Henri Fayol," LinkedIn, February 7, 2021, https://www.linkedin.com/pulse/5-functions-management -henri-fayol-kalpesh-shah/.

6. Frederick Winslow Taylor, *The Principles of Scientific Management* (New York: Norton, 1967).

7. Karl Marx, *Economic and Philosophic Manuscripts of 1844* (Moscow: Progress Publishers, 1982).

8. Marx, *Economic and Philosophic Manuscripts of 1844.*

9. Peter Gray, *Free to Learn: Why Unleashing the Instinct to Play Will Make Our Children Happier, More Self-Reliant, and Better Students for Life* (New York: Basic Books, 2015).

10. Gray, *Free to Learn.*

11. William H. Whyte, *The Organization Man* (Philadelphia: University of Pennsylvania Press, 2002).

12. Gary Klein, *Seeing What Others Don't—the Remarkable Ways We Gain Insights* (New York: PublicAffairs, 2013).

13. Richard W. Hamming, *The Art of Doing Science and Engineering: Learning to Learn* (San Francisco: Stripe Press, 2020).

14. Bill Breen and Gary Hamel, *The Future of Management* (Boston: Harvard Business School Press, n.d.).

Chapter Six

1. *Selective Attention Test, YouTube* (YouTube, 2010), https://www.youtube.com/watch ?v=vJG698U2Mvo.

2. Peter F. Drucker, *Innovation and Entrepreneurship: Practice and Principles* (London: Routledge, 2015).

3. Saras D. Sarasvathy, "Causation and Effectuation: Toward a Theoretical Shift from Economic Inevitability to Entrepreneurial Contingency," *Academy of Management Review* 26, no. 2 (2001): 243–63, https://doi.org/10.5465/amr.2001.4378020.

4. Paul Graham, "Startup = Growth," accessed December 21, 2023, http://www .paulgraham.com/growth.html.

5. George Land and Beth Jarman, *Breakpoint and Beyond: Mastering the Future Today* (New York: Harper, 1992).

6. Sarasvathy, "Causation and Effectuation: Toward a Theoretical Shift from Economic Inevitability to Entrepreneurial Contingency."

7. Adam Smith, *An Inquiry into the Nature and Causes of the Wealth of Nations* (Charleston, SC: Bibiobazaar, 2010).

Chapter Seven

1. Peter F. Drucker, *Innovation and Entrepreneurship: Practice and Principles* (London: Routledge, 2015).
2. Shaunta Grimes, "Science, My Boy, Is Made up of Mistakes," Medium, May 10, 2019, https://medium.com/the-1000-day-mfa/science-my-boy-is-made-up-of-mistakes-11f09709e241#.
3. Everett M. Rogers, *Diffusion of Innovations* (New York: Free Press, 2005).

Chapter Eight

1. Daily Reflections, "'I Have Not Failed. I've Just Found 10,000 Ways That Won't Work.'—Thomas Edison," Medium, March 6, 2023, https://medium.com/@officialprpatel002/i-have-not-failed-ive-just-found-10-000-ways-that-won't-work-thomas-edison-6d12b1650d4b.
2. Gary Schoeniger, "Ice House Entrepreneurship Program," 2011.
3. Martin E. P. Seligman, *Learned Optimism: How to Change Your Mind and Your Life* (London: Nicholas Brealey, 2018).

Chapter Nine

1. Laura A. King, "The Health Benefits of Writing About Life Goals," *Personality and Social Psychology Bulletin* 27, no. 7 (2001): 798–807, https://doi.org/10.1177/0146167201277003.
2. Robert A. Culp and Christina R. Mannion, "Person-Centered Principles in Graduate Education," *Person Centered Journal*, 2011.
3. Irving B. Weiner and W. Edward Craighead, *The Corsini Encyclopedia of Psychology* (Hoboken, NJ: Wiley, 2010).
4. Shane J. Lopez, *Positive Psychology: Exploring the Best in People* (Westport, CT: Praeger, 2008).
5. Albert Bandura, *Self-Efficacy in Changing Societies* (Cambridge, UK: Cambridge University Press, 1997).
6. Martin E. P. Seligman, *Learned Optimism: How to Change Your Mind and Your Life* (London: Nicholas Brealey, 2018).
7. L. P. Jacks, *Education Through Recreation* (Washington, DC: McGrath Pub. Co., 1972).

Chapter Ten

1. Lenore Skenazy, *Free-Range Kids: Giving Our Children the Freedom We Had Without Going Nuts with Worry* (San Francisco: Jossey-Bass, 2010).

2. Sheina Lew-Levy et al., "How Do Hunter-Gatherer Children Learn Subsistence Skills?" *Human Nature* 28, no. 4 (2017): 367–94, https://doi.org/10.1007/s12110-017-9302-2.

3. Susan Engel, "Children's Need to Know: Curiosity in Schools," *Harvard Educational Review* 81, no. 4 (2011): 625–45, https://doi.org/10.17763/haer.81.4.h054131316473115.

4. Brandon Busteed, "The School Cliff: Student Engagement Drops with Each School Year," Gallup.com, March 13, 2020, https://news.gallup.com/opinion/gallup/170525/school-cliff-student-engagement-drops-school-year.aspx.

5. Jon Haidt and Peter Gray, "Play Deprivation Is a Major Cause of the Teen Mental Health Crisis," After Babel, July 27, 2023, https://www.afterbabel.com/p/the-play-deficit.

6. Haidt and Gray, "Play Deprivation Is a Major Cause of the Teen Mental Health Crisis."

7. Paul Graham, "A Project of One's Own," accessed December 21, 2023, http://www.paulgraham.com/own.html.

Chapter Eleven

1. Gary Schoeniger, "Shifting Entrepreneurship from the Perimeter to the Core," ELI Mindset, December 12, 2023, https://elimindset.com/shifting-entrepreneurship-from-the-perimeter-to-the-core/.

2. Karen E. Wilson et al., "Educating the Next Wave of Entrepreneurs: Unlocking Entrepreneurial Capabilities to Meet the Global Challenges of the 21st Century," *Social Science Research Network*, January 1, 2009, https://doi.org/10.2139/ssrn.1396704.

3. "PISA 2022 Results Factsheets: United States," OECD, https://www.oecd.org/publication/pisa-2022-results/country-notes/united-states-a78ba65a/.

4. Peter Senge, *The Fifth Discipline: The Art & Practice of the Learning Organization* (New York: Doubleday, 2006).

5. Jonathan Wolff and David Leopold, "Karl Marx," Stanford Encyclopedia of Philosophy, December 21, 2020, https://plato.stanford.edu/entries/marx/.

6. Tim Walker, "Survey: Alarming Number of Educators May Soon Leave the

Profession," NEA, accessed December 21, 2023, https://www.nea.org/nea-today/all-news-articles/survey-alarming-number-educators-may-soon-leave-profession.

7. "Erie Public Schools Case Study," ELI Mindset, October 14, 2022, https://elimindset.com/resource/eries-public-schools-case-study/.

8. Jon Marcus, "'The Reckoning Is Here': More Than a Third of Community College Students Have Vanished," Hechinger Report, May 8, 2023, https://hechingerreport.org/the-reckoning-is-here-more-than-a-third-of-community-college-students-have-vanished/.

9. Shannon Cleverley-Thompson, "Entrepreneurial Leadership and Activities of Academic Deans in Independent Colleges and Universities," accessed December 21, 2023, https://www.researchgate.net/publication/275643617_Entrepreneurial_Leadership_and_Activities_of_Academic_Deans_in_Independent_Colleges_and_Universities.

10. "Victor Valley College Case Study," ELI Mindset, March 4, 2023, https://elimindset.com/resource/victor-valley-college-case-study/.

11. John Dewey, *Experience and Education* (New York: Free Press, 2015).

12. Brenda J. Allen, "Optimizing Technology's Promise," EDUCAUSE Review, accessed December 21, 2023, https://er.educause.edu/articles/2016/10/optimizing-technologys-promise.

Chapter Twelve

1. Antoine de Saint-Exupéry, *Citadelle* (Paris: Gallimard, 1988).

2. George Land and Beth Jarman, *Breakpoint and Beyond: Mastering the Future Today* (New York: Harper, 1992).

3. Ronald A. Heifetz, Alexander Grashow, and Marty Linsky, *The Practice of Adaptive Leadership: Tools and Tactics for Changing Your Organization and the World*, Harvard Business Press, 2009.

4. Steven Johnson, *Where Good Ideas Come From* (New York: Riverhead Books, 2011).

5. William J. Baumöl, *The Free-Market Innovation Machine* (Princeton, NJ: Princeton University Press, 2002), https://doi.org/10.1515/9781400851638.

6. G. Lynn Shostack, "Designing Services That Deliver," *Harvard Business Review* 62, no. 1 (January 1, 1984): 133–39, https://strategicdesignthinking.files.wordpress.com/2012/11/hbr-shostackpdf.pdf.

7. Peter Senge, Hal Hamilton, and John Kania, "The Dawn of System Leadership," *Stanford Social Innovation Review*, Winter 2015, https://ssir.org/articles/entry/the_dawn_of_system_leadership#.

8. "A Bad System Will Beat a Good Person Every Time—the W. Edwards Deming Institute," The W. Edwards Deming Institute, n.d., https://deming.org/quotes/.

Chapter Thirteen

1. Erica Sweeney, "How One Durham-Based Foundation Is Investing in North Carolina's Entrepreneurs and Growing the State's Innovation Footprint," Business Insider, accessed December 21, 2023, https://www.businessinsider.com/how-nc-idea-investing-north-carolina-durham-entrepreneurs-innovation-2021-6.

2. "1 Million Cups," accessed April 26, 2024, https://www.1millioncups.com/s/.

3. Donald Keys, *Earth at Omega: Passage to Planetization* (Boston: Branden Publishing Co., 1985).

Chapter Fourteen

1. Scott Barry Kaufman, *Transcend: The New Science of Self-Actualization* (London: Penguin, 2020).

Index

experimentation
business planning and, 86–88
creating conditions conducive to, 142–143
for entrepreneurial discovery, 27
in managerial systems, 195
micro-, 90, 93–95, 132, 133, 140
in opportunity discovery process, 103–107
explanatory style, 41, 154
exploration
by adolescents, 168–169
creating conditions conducive to, 142–143
in managerial systems, 195
in opportunity discovery process, 101–103
external locus of control, 40, 83–84, 226
extrinsic motivation, 35, 36, 42, 72, 75, 144, 167

F
fabrication labs (Fab Labs), 212, 218
face-to-face interactions, 125, 153
factory system, 66–68, 192
faculty training, college, 185–187
failure, 132–134, 149, 178
false positives, 109, 133
fast thinking, 54–55
Fayol, Henri, 66
feasibility, 85, 89–91, 147, 217
"five whys" technique, 125
Frankl, Viktor, 42–43, 156
fundamental attribution error, 32–33
funding, pursuing, 87–89, 93, 210, 216–217

G
GarySchoeniger.com, 119
Gen Z, 8
globalization, 70, 228
goal-directed behavior, 54
goal setting, 41–43, 112, 167
go-in-order-to-know strategy, 93–95, 119
Goldstein, Kurt, 35
Good Samaritan study, 32–33
government-sponsored entrepreneurial
support organizations, 210–211
Graham, Paul, 166
grassroots entrepreneurial communities,
211–214, 219
Gray, Peter, 69

great man theory, 31, 47, 66
growth phase, 18, 19, 91–92, 108, 193

H
Haidt, Jonathan, 163, 164
Halfaker, Dawn, 29–31, 41, 102
Hamel, Gary, 9, 75
Hamming, Richard, 75
Heifetz, Ronald, 21, 196–197
high-potential startups, 209–210
high schools, EDL in, 181–183
human-centered leadership, 204
hypothesis, defined, 100
hypothesis formation, 128–129
hypothesis testing, 100, 129–131

I
iceberg metaphor for mindset, 52–56
Ice House Entrepreneurial Mindset
Facilitator Training, 180, 212
Ice House Entrepreneurial Mindset Program,
139–140, 181, 214
Ice House Entrepreneurship Programs, xxiv
Ice House Student Success course, 185
ideal worker, 204
ill-structured problems, 23–24, 145–146, 177
imagination, 144, 188–189
inattentional blindness, 82, 88, 89
incidental learning, 168–169
incremental innovations, 200, 201
Independence Community College, 212–213
individualized learning, 177
Industrial Revolution, 6, 13, 62–72
innovation(s), 109–110, 200–203
intelligence, mindset vs., 50
internal locus of control, 40, 164, 178
internal sponsorship, 202
intrinsic motivation, 36, 42, 111, 113, 144,
157, 167, 167–168, 168, 178, 199, 224
invasive parenting style, 74, 164
"invisible gorilla" experiment, 82

J
Jacks, L. P., 158
James, William, 57
Jenkins, Davis, 184

About the Author

Gary G. Schoeniger is an internationally recognized thought leader in the field of entrepreneurial mindset development. His work has influenced a broad audience from higher education and economic development organizations to government, corporate, and nonprofit clients worldwide including the Ewing Marion Kauffman Foundation, the Allan Gray Orbis Foundation, the South African Department of Education, the Cisco Entrepreneur Institute, and the US State Department. His first book, *Who Owns the Ice House?*, which he coauthored with Pulitzer nominee Clifton Taulbert, has become an international bestseller. Schoeniger also led the development of the Ice House Entrepreneurship Programs, which have been recognized by the Kauffman Foundation as "redefining entrepreneurship education in classrooms and communities around the world."

To learn more about how you can unleash the entrepreneurial potential in your classroom, organization, or community, visit GarySchoeniger.com.